THE CALL
TO
Radical Discipleship
A Study of Matthew 5-7

Reuven & Yanit Ross

The Call to Radical Discipleship

Cover Photograph – Overlooking the Sea of Galilee with the Mount of Beatitudes, Israel
Photograph and layout by Reuven Ross
Cover layout and design by Kudzai Musumhi

ISBN-13: 978-1517355562, Copyright © 2015

Printed in the United States of America
Printed by CreateSpace, an Amazon.com Company

Website: www.making-disciples.net
Email: reuven@making-disciples.net
          yanit@making-disciples.net

First printing, 2001, 2002 – Malaysia
Second printing, 2004, 2006 – USA
Third printing, 2006, 2009 – South Africa
Revision, 2014 – USA
First printing of combined Sermon on the Mount, 2015 – USA

CONTENTS

FOREWORD

The Call to Radical Discipleship is a study of Matthew 5-7, Jesus' teaching commonly known as the Sermon on the Mount. This Sermon, in essence, is an explanation of Matthew 5:17, the scripture in which Jesus Christ spoke of fulfilling (explaining) the law. In these three chapters, we see God's heart and intentions behind the laws He gave to His people in the old covenant.

The Sermon on the Mount is about God's righteousness manifested through human lives. It is an explanation of what God expects of His new covenant people. We who have embraced Jesus' salvation and are called by His name need to know what He requires of us! It is important that we learn this material in our training as the Lord's disciples. In order to share in the benefits of our Father's family and kingdom, we also need to share in His nature. We must learn to conduct ourselves in ways that please Him.

In Hebrews 12:10, we are told that God, as a loving Father, disciplines us for our good so that we may share His holiness. What a wonderful promise! As we yield to God's training and discipline, we will eventually look just like Him. We will love what He loves and hate what He hates. His values will become our values, and His priorities, our priorities. We will not only belong to Him, we will also *look and act like* we belong to Him! **1 John 3:1-2** says, *"Behold, what manner of love the Father has bestowed on us, that we should be called children of God! Therefore, the world does not know us, because it did not know Him. Beloved, now we are the sons of God; and it has not yet been revealed what we shall be, but we know that when He is revealed, we shall be like Him, for we shall see Him as He is."*

The Call to Radical Discipleship is most beneficial when used as study material in a small group. Meeting weekly to go over the exercises, quote the memory verses, and share in corporate prayer is as important as receiving the teaching. In addition to the increase of biblical knowledge, spiritual insights, and growing to know the Lord better, the group gathering yields an opportunity for personal growth in trusted relationships and accountability. It provides a supportive prayer group and a safe place where victories and struggles can be shared.

This study on the Sermon on the Mount can be used together with the *Go and Make Disciples* manual. Together, the materials comprise a one-year curriculum for growth into the character and conduct of the Lord Jesus Christ. The manual, *Go and Make Disciples*, contains motivational material for making disciples as well as essential discipleship teaching. We recommend that you go to our website and download *for free* our book entitled *Introducing Discipleship* that will offer further explanation of these discipleship books. It is available in both A4 (European) and US Letter (North American) formats.

We pray that the Lord will lead you into all truth and transform you into His image as you ingest and apply His Word through these sessions. As you hear and read the Scriptures, be careful to be a doer of the Word, not merely a hearer. May God's Word accomplish that which He pleases in each of you!

Yanit and Reuven Ross

ACKNOWLEDGEMENTS

The Call to Radical Discipleship has been a long project for us. This discipleship material was initially developed for use in our congregation in Haifa, Israel, Carmel Assembly. In 1995, while we were teaching *Go and Make Disciples* (Vision for Discipleship) and praying for a suitable sequel, the idea came to me (Yanit), *"Why not teach the same material that Jesus taught His first disciples—the Sermon on the Mount?"* Upon receiving strong encouragement and confirmation from our congregational leadership, I began developing this material. Although I did the bulk of the study and preparation of the material, I received invaluable help from others. This was definitely a team effort.

Reuven played a major role in producing this manual. He added his spiritual insights, knowledge, and wisdom to many of the sessions. Reuven also did the photography for the cover and the layout of the material. By working together on this manual, we have grown closer to the Lord and to one another. Beverly Schneider and Gwen Whatley spent numerous hours (months!) meticulously editing and proofreading this book. Beverly had the wisdom and experience of years of Bible teaching to offer as she examined the theological content and layout of each lesson for easy presentation. Gwen carefully edited each chapter, enabled by her expertise in written English and her knowledge of God's Word. She was masterful at finding and correcting our grammatical errors, incongruent phrases, and colloquialisms. Both women cheerfully gave up a great deal of their time and energy to help Reuven and me complete this project. Later, Joan Painter re-edited the material as we combined the two volumes into one book.

While writing and teaching this discipleship material, we served the Lord for over ten years in Haifa alongside godly and gifted spiritual leaders. Their prayer support and encouragement kept us working on this material until it reached completion. Now, many years later, that congregation, its daughter congregations, and numerous other groups in Israel continue to use this material in making disciples and training spiritual leaders.

At the time of combining the two volumes of the Sermon on the Mount studies in 2015, there are over 30 translations of this material into other languages. We are awed and humbled at how the Lord is using this for the growth and maturation of His Body and for His glory around the world. We are so blessed and honored to be a small part of His work!

Most importantly, we want to express our thanks to the Lord Jesus for teaching the Sermon on the Mount in the first place! Where would we be without His guidelines on how to live a life worthy of Him?!

Jesus, our hearts' desire is to glorify You!

Yanit Ross

GOD'S CALL TO KINGDOM LIVING

The first discipleship material Jesus taught His disciples is what we call the Sermon on the Mount. How appropriate it is for each of us to use this same material in our training as the Lord's disciples! We will not approach this study with the western thinking of "What do I *think about* this verse?" Instead, we will approach it with Hebraic thinking: "How do I *live* this verse?" In this session, we will look at how Jesus' public ministry began and some general information on discipleship. We will conclude with an overview of this classic sermon.

Matthew 4:13-16 *"And leaving Nazareth, He [Jesus] came and dwelt in Capernaum, which is by the sea, in the regions of Zebulun and Naphtali, that it might be fulfilled which was spoken by Isaiah the prophet, saying: The land of Zebulun and the land of Naphtali, by the way of the sea, beyond the Jordan, Galilee of the Gentiles: the people who sat in darkness have seen a great light, and upon those who sat in the region and shadow of death light has dawned."*

At the age of 30, Jesus left Nazareth where He had lived and worked as a carpenter (in the first century, he would have worked with stone more than with wood) for years, and He moved His residence to Capernaum. He left His family, friends, and hometown to enter into public ministry. Jesus had recently been baptized in water and had endured an extended fast and a severe time of temptation in the wilderness. All of this was part of His consecration to God, and necessary in order for Jesus to fulfill His Father's call upon His life. In His release into public ministry, Jesus modeled important lessons to us about answering the call of God upon our own lives.

The Call of God

1. God has perfect timing in releasing us into the call He has placed upon us. He may spend years preparing us for His service, and that preparation may be quite uncomfortable at times. His timing does not always fit into our planned or preferred schedule; in fact, His Word to us may come at a time when we are very settled in our current lifestyle.

2. We are to be faithful in what we know to do—what is our natural responsibility—until He says something new and different to us (such as releasing us into a new area of service).

3. God's call upon us, just as it was upon Jesus, will often require major life changes. These changes move us out of our comfort zones into places of total reliance upon Him. This is not something to be feared, but to be anticipated with excitement!

"From that time Jesus began to preach and to say, "Repent, for the kingdom of heaven is at hand" (**Matt. 4:17**). Repentance means to turn from going our own way to going God's way. It is a willful decision that results in a change of mind, which then leads to a change of purpose and action. Repentance means to let go of those things that hinder God's rule over us. There is nothing worth clinging to that is more precious or important than God's will.

In Luke 9:57-62, Jesus emphasized the seriousness of a commitment to follow Him. He says that after we begin to follow Him, we are not to look back and long for what the world offers. If we look back, we are not ready to be His disciples. We must count the cost, and when we decide to give our lives fully to God, we move forward with Him, very possibly leaving everything else behind.

Discipleship was not a new idea, originating with Jesus. Moses had a disciple: Joshua. Elijah had Elisha. Look at what Elisha did in 1 Kings 19:19-21. When the prophet Elijah called Elisha to serve him, Elisha not only left his family and vocation behind, he also destroyed the instruments of his former work. He slaughtered and boiled the oxen, using the tools of his trade (his plowing equipment) as the wood for the fire. He left all of his former life, literally "burning his bridges behind him," and followed his new master, Elijah.

Follow Me!

Read Matthew 4:18-22. We see the call to "come and follow" that Jesus gave to the fishermen. Each man immediately left his net, family, and vocation to follow Him. They left their security, comforts, conveniences, and familiar surroundings. They walked away from their possessions and the futures they had envisioned for themselves. It cost them everything to follow Jesus, yet we see no hesitation in them. They recognized Jesus' invitation as too wonderful and valuable to refuse!

Just as Jesus called those men to leave everything to be His disciples, so He is calling us today. We cannot belong to the Lord and live however we please. Being His disciple means we are willing to leave everything to follow the Master wherever He leads. It is choosing to do whatever He says. True discipleship is a full commitment to His lordship. Jesus always has a better plan for us than we can come up with for ourselves! As we yield to Him, He fits us into specialized areas of service that are custom-made for us, and while doing that, He molds us into His own image and likeness.

Followers Are Not Always Disciples

Many believers today call themselves Jesus' *disciples* when actually they are only His *followers*. They still live as they please. St. Gregory the Great said, *"God never intended a distinction between being a Christian and being a disciple."* Being a disciple of Jesus is defined biblically in terms of its *maximum expression*, not its minimum requirements. We are to be *fully transformed* into His image, not only to part of that image.

In Matthew 4:23-25, we see that Jesus walked throughout the Galilee, teaching, preaching, and healing the sick. His fame traveled even to Syria, and many who were sick and demonized were brought to Him for healing and deliverance. Some Bible scholars say that as many as 10,000 people at once followed Jesus. They heard His teachings and partook of His blessings, but they never became His disciples. There are people like that today, following Jesus for what He can do for them. Self-serving, they recognize that following Jesus is a blessing to them, yet they hesitate to commit themselves to Him in order to bless *Him*. The heart of a true disciple asks, "What can I offer Jesus?" not only, "What can Jesus do for me?"

"And seeing the multitudes, He went up on a mountain, and when He was seated His disciples came to Him" (**Matt. 5:1**). The other place in Scripture containing the Sermon on the Mount is Luke 6:17-20. The traditional Galilean site where Jesus preached this Sermon contains a natural amphitheater, which allowed Him to be easily heard as He taught.

In Luke 6:12-16, Jesus called his many disciples to Himself so that He could name 12 of them to be His trainees for future apostleship. Many scholars believe that those who received the teaching of the Sermon on the Mount were only the 12 chosen disciples. Notice the distinction in Luke 6:17 between the 'multitude' and the 'crowd of His disciples.' True disciples are *always* only a remnant of those who proclaim to follow our Lord. In verse 20, we see that Jesus *"lifted up His eyes toward His disciples"* and began teaching them the principles of His kingdom.

Background of Jesus' Teaching

We who have always had the written Word of God accept the Sermon on the Mount without question or hesitation. We have been taught that the Holy Spirit indwells the believer, and that the kingdom of God is spiritual and not of the natural realm. The men that Jesus addressed that day, however, believed that God's kingdom would only come *after* the Messiah recruited an army that would free them from the Roman Empire. They believed the Messiah would annihilate the Romans with a Jewish liberation force, and then would rule over a physical Jewish kingdom like King David's kingdom centuries earlier. They looked for a Messiah who would restore their personal liberties and fortunes in freeing them from Rome. They believed his kingdom would actually surpass King David's in wealth and power, and would never be overthrown or even weakened.

Jesus preached a hard sermon to the men that day. He dashed their hopes by teaching them that the kingdom of God is *internal,* not external, and that it is built for God's glory, not the glory of man. Through His sermon, Jesus was inviting His listeners to surrender their selfish dreams of an earthly kingdom that would bring them personal and national honor. He taught them that to gain their lives, they would have to lose them.

God's Kingdom Contrasts with Earthly Kingdoms

In many ways, the sermon Jesus preached that day is a commentary on John 18:36. In this verse, Jesus said, *"My kingdom is not of this world..."* The Sermon on the Mount is a practical teaching on how the kingdom of God is different from this world.

To live in the kingdom of God is to be in contrast to the world, for His kingdom is the *opposite* of the world. This sermon challenges us to count the cost of being a believer in Jesus and eliminates the possibility of an "uncommitted" walk with the Lord.

Overview of Jesus' Sermon

In Matthew 5, Jesus uses the word "blessed" nine times, the first seven defining godly character traits, and the last two describing what will happen to us as we live out His character in our lives. In Matthew 6, we see how these traits of God become ours through the spiritual disciplines we are to embrace. In Matthew 7 are some of the obstacles and hindrances that block the implementation of these attitudes. The seven beatitudes that Jesus began his teaching with reflect seven chief qualities of God. Each beatitude is an *attitude* that we are to *be* (have) as believers in Jesus.

The beatitudes challenge us to live out God's kingdom through dying to self. As we surrender to the Lord, He establishes His life in us. Looking at being *poor in spirit*, we see how life begins in the kingdom of God. It is only those who are know their desperate need of God who can live in the kingdom because only they can allow the King entrance. The poor in spirit die to self-reliance. To *mourn* is to have godly sorrow for sin. We must hate sin so much that we are uncomfortable with it in us and in the world. In godly mourning, we die to self by refusing self-gratification.

To be *meek* is to be gentle through exercising self-control. We show true strength when we release the drive to prove our value to others. In giving up self-assertion, we inherit the earth from God. We trust Him to give us our worth. In *hungering and thirsting for righteousness*, we forfeit finding our identity elsewhere and realize we are satisfied only in God. We die to attempting to find satisfaction outside of the Lord. In being *merciful*, we die to self by repenting of judging others. Knowing how much we have been forgiven, we give mercy freely. We receive more mercy as a result of giving it away.

To be *pure in heart* includes an inner moral purity and an outward holiness. We accept that we are not our own. We die to self by giving up the freedom to do whatever we want. To be a *peacemaker* is to avoid strife by relinquishing our rights. We lay down our rights in order to promote peace and harmony. In doing that we resemble our Father, and are given the rights of a son. To be *persecuted for the sake of righteousness* is to be accused falsely. It is sharing in the sufferings of Jesus, losing our reputation for His sake. In laying down our glory, we are entitled to share in His glory.

The seven attributes of God mentioned in Matthew 5 also correspond with the seven qualities lacking in the churches written to in Revelation 2-3. While many believe these churches relate to specific periods in church history, others claim that they refer to attitudes that influence the entire Body of Christ at any point in history. We will consider the beatitudes as qualities of God missing in the churches, appropriate throughout history. For instance, the first beatitude, poverty of spirit, is what was missing in the first church of Asia, Ephesus. The second beatitude, mourning, matches the second church, which faced suffering. The third church was lacking in meekness, the submissive willingness to obey. The church of Pergamos was disobedient and compromising. And so on. Seeing the qualities that these churches needed to develop, we realize that *we* are in need of developing these same qualities. If we live out these beatitudes, we can potentially walk in the fullness of the Spirit of God and exhibit the character and conduct of His kingdom.

EXERCISE #1 – Matthew 5:1-3 ~ POOR IN SPIRIT

> **Memory verses:** *Matthew 5:1-3*

1. Read Matthew 4:12–7:29 without stopping and without distraction. Ask the Lord to speak to you as you read. Write down your first impressions of these chapters. What caught your attention? What did you feel as you read?

2. After reading these chapters, do you see anything that you can apply to your life *now*?

3. Define the "kingdom of God."

4. Look again at Matthew 4:17-22. Is there anything you are clinging to that is keeping you from fully grasping the kingdom of God? If so, what is it?

5. Referring to Matthew 5:3, who are the *poor in spirit*?

6. What did Jesus mean by His promise to the poor in spirit: " *...theirs is the kingdom of heaven?* "

7. Take time to read the following evidences of having left one's first love (see Revelation 2:4), and evaluate yourself before the Lord in prayer on each point.

I have left my first love when…

… my delight in the Lord is not as great as my delight in someone else (Mark 12:30).

… I do not long for times of fellowship with Him in prayer or in His Word (Psalm 42:1).

… my thoughts during leisure moments do not reflect upon the Lord (Psalm 10:4).

… I easily give in to those things that do not please the Lord.

… I do not cheerfully give to God's work or to the needs of others (Matt. 25:40).

… I am unable to forgive another for offending me (1 John 4:20).

… I become complacent to sinful conditions around me (Matt. 24:12).

… I strive for the acclaim of this world or for the recognition of others, rather than for the approval of God (John 15:19, 1 John 2:15).

#1 – POOR IN SPIRIT

Matthew 5:3 *"Blessed are the poor in spirit, for theirs is the kingdom of heaven."*

The term translated "poor in spirit" in the Greek language is the word **ptochos**. It speaks of a person who crouches or cowers like a beggar. The word translated "kingdom" is the Greek word, **basileia**, which means sovereignty or royal power.

This verse says those who realize their humble, beggarly position before the Lord and their total dependence on Him are blessed; they will inherit the royal power and sovereignty of heaven. God delights to care for those who depend fully on Him. *"Fear not, little flock, for it is the Father's good pleasure to give you the kingdom"* (**Luke 12:32**). In **Mark 10:14** Jesus said, *"Let the little children come to Me, and do not forbid them, for of such is the kingdom of heaven."*

The Poor Know Their Need

The poor in spirit admit their need of God and of others. They are aware of the probable destruction and ruin they will experience if they rule their lives independently of God. So they embrace Jesus' lordship. Because the King is living in them, they carry His life into their homes and businesses, and as a result, His kingdom is expressed through them. They are not self-sufficient; they realize they need others and are not ashamed to ask for and receive their help.

Commentator William Barclay explained how this beatitude in Hebrew underwent a four-stage development of meaning:

(1) The 'poor in spirit' simply meant being poor.

(2) Because they were poor, they had no influence, help, or prestige.

(3) Having no influence, they were downtrodden and oppressed by men.

(4) Finally, the term came to describe the man who put his whole trust in God because he had no earthly resources whatsoever.

So, the word 'poor' was used to describe the humble and the helpless man who put his whole trust in God. Being poor in spirit is an attitude of absolute humility. It is the portrait of one who sees himself as spiritually bankrupt and deserving of nothing. Because of that position, he turns in trust to the Almighty God. Peter showed he was poor in spirit in **Luke 5:8** when he said to Jesus, *"Depart from me, for I am a sinful man, O Lord."* Peter understood his need and spiritual poverty, and when he saw the Lord, he felt unworthy. The poor are those who know they are destitute of genuine righteousness. Everyone needs the Lord, but only those who admit their need receive His attention!

A Humble and Contrite Spirit

The phrase "poor in spirit" is linked with other Biblical phrases such as "broken spirit" and "humble and contrite spirit." Psalm 51:17 speaks of the sacrifice of a broken spirit, referring to a person who is broken of pride and self-indulgence. To be contrite is to be remorseful, sorry, and repentant. Contrition implies total surrender to the Lord—to be as non-resistant as fine powder, where any former hard places of rebellion and stubbornness have been crushed.

Isaiah 57:15 could be reworded to say: *"I choose to be around those who need Me. They are not rebellious; they are gentle and submissive. Fellowship with them is easy because there is no power struggle. They believe My words and trust in Me."*

Isaiah 66:1-2 reworded has a similar tone: *"The tenderhearted person is the one I'm looking for. He knows he needs Me. He has the utmost respect for My Word, honoring and adhering to it. He takes My Word seriously, and lives by every word that proceeds out of My mouth."*

Jesus calls us to be poor in spirit where we are completely dependent on God with no resistance to His rule. Knowing we need the Lord places us in the humble position of continually asking. Based on that childlike attitude of trust, the kingdom of heaven is promised.

God is Generous

The omnipotent God, Creator of all that exists, holds nothing back. He continuously gives Himself away. God does not hoard His treasures for Himself. He does not lust or covet anything because that would be contrary to His generous nature. The ultimate expression of God's generosity is when He gave His own Son to die for the sins of humankind. Just as parents gladly give generously to their children, not even considering it a sacrifice, so God gives to us. In the same way, we are to freely and lovingly empty ourselves for others. We are to be generous givers, not lusting after or coveting anything. We must understand that *all* blessings come from God and are given to us so that we can bless others. We should seek opportunities to give, not just desire to receive. This is being poor in spirit.

Our First Love

In His message to the church of Ephesus in Revelation 2:1-7, Jesus challenged the believers to be poor in spirit by returning to their first love. Being poor in spirit is an intense desire to give oneself away, to empty oneself for the sake of others. "First love" qualities are the same. The person who is fresh or deeply in love wants to empty himself for the one he loves. He will do almost anything for his beloved, regardless of the price. Serving becomes an honor for him, not a sacrifice.

The Ephesian believers had once been like that, joyfully and lovingly serving the Lord. They had worked hard, and had matured in areas of ministry and service. They probably had endured persecution because they lived in the city where the emperor and the goddess Diana were worshiped (Acts 19:23-41). These believers went against the accepted idolatry and had endured hardships. They maintained pure doctrines and theology, and did not tolerate false apostles and those who taught heresy.

So, what was the problem? They were doing good works, showed maturity, endured persecution faithfully, and had correct theology. It sounds like a perfect congregation. However, Jesus knew that beneath their impressive exterior they had lost their first love. They were working for God's kingdom as they had for many years, but they were laboring out of habit rather than out of passionate love for Jesus. They were focusing on what they were accomplishing rather than focusing on Jesus Himself.

Jesus' complaint against the Ephesians was not that they were failing in their work for God, but that they had abandoned their first love qualities of serving Him with cheerful, generous hearts. When we want men to recognize our ministry or good works, we have left our first love for Jesus and have assumed Pharisaic qualities of wanting to be seen. We must beware of seeking personal glory, rather than being content to empty ourselves for God's glory. The desire to be known for the work we do rather than for the work He has done in us tempts all of us at times. We resist this temptation by seeking God's glory rather than our own.

Repent!

Verse 5 says, *"...repent and do the first works..."* Jesus was not referring to their many religious deeds. He was calling them to that first love quality of doing everything just for Him. We may be busy with the work of God, and yet have abandoned the God of the work. If Jesus needed a regular prayer life to sustain Him in ministry (Mark 1:35, Luke 5:16), *how much more do we?!*

We show our self-sufficiency when we do not depend on God, when we neglect the secret place of prayer. Admitting our need of Him goes against our human nature of independence. In our pride, we do not want to be reduced to a position of asking, *and* we refuse to empty ourselves for the sake of others. However, there is hope for us if we repent. We can die to this world and turn away from all that distracts us from our devotion to Jesus, and return to serving Him and living only for Him, for no other reason except out of sheer love for Him. God's kingdom is within the hearts of those who are poor of spirit.

For Consideration and Prayer

Are you guilty of leaving your first love? Of desiring to receive rather than to give? Of being unwilling to empty yourself for the sake of others?

Are you guilty of neglecting prayer? Of being self-sufficient rather than dependent on God?

Are you generous? Are you willing to give, serve, and sacrifice for others? Are you aware of your great need of God? If not, ask Him to give you that awareness.

Take some time to do business with God in prayer. Confess your sins, receive His forgiveness, and thank Him for His mercy. Then with the Holy Spirit's help, determine to change.

"Blessed are the poor in spirit, for theirs is the kingdom of heaven."

EXERCISE #2 – Matthew 5:4 ~ MOURN

Memory verses: *Matthew 5:1-3 & 1 John 1:9*

1. What kind of mourning is Jesus speaking of in Matthew 5:4?

2. Referring to 2 Corinthians 7:8-11, what is the difference between godly and worldly sorrow?

   What is the fruit of godly sorrow?

3. Considering Isaiah 59:2 and Jeremiah 5:25, why should God's people mourn over sin?

4. Read 1 John 1:7-9 and 1 Peter 1:17-19. Have you known God's forgiveness and cleansing of your sin? Do you walk free of guilt? Explain.

5. What are some hindrances to holy mourning?

Eph. 4:19 _____

Acts 7:51 _____

Prov. 1:22-25, 9:1-6 _____

Name others you can think of:

6. After a season of mourning and comfort, what can we expect to experience? (Ps. 16:7-11)

7. Have you ever agonized in intercession for someone? Share briefly.

8. Meditate on Psalm 30 and write down anything the Lord shows you from this chapter.

#2 – BLESSED ARE THOSE WHO MOURN

Matthew 5:4 *"Blessed are they that mourn, for they shall be comforted."*

Those who mourn their sin and their desperate condition of being destitute of righteousness will be forgiven. The primary function of the law is to produce godly sorrow. It shows us how we have come short of God's glory by breaking His laws; we deserve His judgment. If in true repentance we turn from and confess our lawless deeds, God will forgive us and comfort us with His mercy. The person who realizes the depth of his sin and the greatness of God's mercy will love Him extravagantly. We see this illustrated in Luke 7:36-48 where Jesus forgave the woman who was broken over her sin.

Read John 16:20-22. Just as there must be physical travail for a child to be born, there must also be mourning and sorrow for fullness of joy to follow. Only the heart that weeps knows the true meaning of joy. When we grieve our sin, we can expect to experience the joy of God's forgiveness. **Luke 6:21b** says, *"Blessed are you who weep now, for you shall laugh."*

God Suffers

We read of Jesus weeping in John 11:35 and Luke 19:41. He did not mourn His sin, because He never sinned. But the Lord does mourn *our* sin and losses. He is well acquainted with suffering, as Isaiah 53:3-8, 11-12 tells us. He was rejected for *us*, bore *our* sicknesses and pain, and was wounded and bruised for *us*. Jesus poured out His soul to death, bearing the sin of many.

We tend to struggle with the idea of God suffering for two main reasons:

1. We do not like to suffer, so we do not like to contemplate anything related to suffering. However, if we reject any one of the attributes of God, then we reject the totality of Jesus and His Person. In rejecting part of Who He is, we will see only a fuzzy image of Him, and we will pass on that distorted image to those we disciple. We can make the Lord known only to the extent that we know Him.

2. We wrongly conclude that if God could experience suffering, then He would cease to be God. That thinking naturally brings us to the conclusion that we, His children, should never have to suffer because our all-powerful, loving Father will shield us from it.

Our Sufferings Can Reveal Jesus as Messiah

This mentality reveals our tunnel vision. We do not see beyond our desire for God to use His infinite resources to make us comfortable; we forget that Jesus came to save the world from perishing, not merely to make us happy. God's plan for us is that we will be a revelation of Jesus to a lost world, blessing many around us (not just ourselves). So He calls us at times to willfully subject ourselves to unpleasantness for the sake of the salvation of others.

The early believers are a good example of this. They suffered torture rather than renounce the Lord, not only for Jesus' sake, but also for the sake of those who would see Jesus in them if they endured (and for those who would not see Jesus if they renounced Him).

Certainly, God takes no pleasure in seeing His children suffer, but He has *great* desire to draw all men to Himself. We should be willing to undergo whatever it takes to bring God's salvation to others. Jesus suffered crucifixion, Paul spent years in prison, John was exiled, and other apostles were martyred, all for the sake of the gospel. *"For you have been called for this purpose, since Christ also suffered for you, leaving you an example for you to follow in His steps"* (**1 Peter 2:21**).

Psalm 4:1b says, *"You have relieved me in my distress."* The Hebrew word **rachav** is translated *relieved* in the NKJV, but literally it means to enlarge, broaden or make room. The Hebrew word **tzar** is translated *distressed* in the NKJV, but it literally means narrow, a tight place, trouble, anguish, and tribulation. So this phrase literally says, *"You have enlarged me when I was in trouble and anguish."* Our sorrows and sufferings are used by God to enlarge and broaden us, teaching us empathy for others, and setting us free from our shackles to comfort, control, and self-centeredness.

The Spirit of Suffering

Read Revelation 2:8-11. The church in Smyrna was lacking in the spirit of suffering. Jesus told them not to be afraid to suffer, and to be faithful unto death. He reminded them that He had conquered death, and promised that life would follow death for them, also. They did not want to embrace the suffering and tribulation that were awaiting them.

We can relate to their apprehension because we don't like to suffer either! When we are in pain, we are unable to function and live as we want. One of the things God wants to deal with regarding our inherited human nature is the desire for control. Our thirst for control makes us want to rebel against God's rule and do what we want. This drive for control is incompatible with suffering.

Our control issues can be frequently seen in two areas: (1) The desire to control health, and (2) the desire to control finances. Health and wealth are often linked together in the popular prosperity teaching. Where this teaching prevails, the spirit of suffering is virtually nonexistent. This does not mean that we are not to seek healing or to have our needs met; it just means that we should give God complete control over these areas of our lives, and be willing to accept suffering in them if He wants to use it to touch others. When believers are wrapped up in a message of health and wealth, they may lack the true spiritual wealth and enlargement possible through intimacy with Jesus.

Suffering Can Lead to Intimacy with Jesus

Some people *must* suffer in order to come into the sort of relationship that God wants to have with them. The Apostle Paul wrote, *"I have lost all things. I count them but rubbish, that I may win Christ"* (**Phil. 3:8**). King David said, *"Before I was afflicted I went astray, but now I obey Your Word"* (**Ps. 119:67**). Affliction can be positive and beneficial if it brings us into greater obedience to and richer fellowship with Jesus.

Any time we experience loss as believers, we can take heart and rejoice for God comforts us by His Spirit. The blessing and comfort we receive through mourning is greater intimacy with the Lord. The late author Richard Wurmbrand spent years in a Communist prison. He said the intimacy with Jesus was so rich inside the prison that he felt sorry for those on the outside.

13

Read 2 Corinthians 1:3-7. These verses speak of strong comfort, implying *"strength intensive as steel to the backbone."* The Lord braces us against our sufferings with His comfort and presence. Many of the promises in Scripture have to do with the Lord going through our trials and tribulations *with* us. He does not always protect us *from* difficulty, but He is always with us *in* it.

A back brace illustrates this truth well. The brace gives comfortable room to the damaged nerves and soft tissue, which reduces the pain. It does not remove the damage; rather, it supports the sufferer, allowing him to walk straight and with less discomfort even though the cause of the pain is still there.

Through the Holy Spirit, Jesus gets alongside us and supports us in our pain. He does not always remove our suffering, but He *always* strengthens us in the midst of it so that we can overcome. Jesus said, *"In the world you shall have tribulation* (stress, pressure, adversity, oppression)*: but be encouraged, I have overcome the world"* (**John 16:33**). There is a rich depth of fellowship that is available with Jesus while we suffer that we do not have in the "mountain-top" experiences. Weeping together brings deeper unity than laughing together does. There is great intimacy in sharing sorrow.

"Though I walk through the valley of the shadow of death, I will fear no evil, for You are with me..." (**Ps. 23:4a**). *"You, Who have shown me great and severe troubles shall revive me again, and bring me up again from the depths of the earth. You shall increase my greatness, and comfort me on every side"* (**Ps. 71:20-21**).

When the daughter of William Booth was held captive in a dark chamber in Switzerland's Neufchatel Prison, God inspired her to write a hymn that said, *"Best-beloved of my soul, I am here alone with Thee; and my prison is a heaven since Thou sharest it with me."*

Those in the church in Smyrna in Revelation 2 had suffered and would suffer some more, but they would also experience the presence of God like never before in the midst of their affliction. They would learn that the presence of God is the greatest gain of all.

Suffering In Intercession

Suffering *for* Jesus is involuntary, but there is a suffering *with* Jesus that we can choose to enter into, which is intercession. Intercession is where we perceive the heart of God for the lost, the hurting and the needy, and our hearts break as we pray fervently for them. Interceding for others is standing in the gap for them; the 'gap' is the place between the need and God's provision (*see* Ezekiel 22:30).

Intercession is love on its knees. It is a way we can comfort our Master and bear His burdens with Him. It is dying to comfort and giving up time spent on ourselves to wrestle in prayer for someone else. If we do not join in Jesus' sufferings through intercession, we leave Him to suffer alone. Jesus is *our* intercessor, according to Hebrews 7:25. For whom are *you* interceding?

At Calvary, Jesus demonstrated how suffering is essential to giving life. We would have no life if it were not for the death of our Lord. Just as Jesus' intercession required Him to suffer for us, so our intercession for others involves our suffering for them.

When we see people and dire circumstances as God does, our hearts will begin to break; then out of our brokenness will emerge intercession that will move the heart and hand of God.

The Heart of Intercession

There is a story about an intercessory prayer meeting in a church. The prayer room was divided with a sheet, with the men on one side of the room and the women on the other. As a man knelt in prayer near the sheet, he could hear a woman on the other side praying passionately for a lost loved one. She was praying, *"God, don't let him sleep until he makes You his Lord. Don't let him eat until he surrenders to You. Make him miserable until he turns his life over to You."* As the man listened, God began to stir his heart to pray for the same man. The Lord challenged him to pray this way: *"God don't let* me *sleep until he makes You his Lord. Don't let* me *eat until he makes You his Lord. Make* me *miserable until he gives his life to You."*

That is the heart of intercession. The intercessor will go to the cross on behalf of the one for whom he is praying. As we bear the cross in prayer, we find that through our death, the one for whom we pray gains life. In carrying God's burdens with Him and to Him in prayer, we suffer alongside Him. We receive God's comfort as He lifts the burdens we pray for, and as He answers those prayers. We may not always suffer *for* Jesus, but we all have the obligation to suffer *with* Him, which is expressed through intercession.

"Blessed are they that mourn..." Yes, blessed are they that mourn their sin (believers and unbelievers), being truly repentant, for they will receive the comfort of personal reconciliation and peace with God along with everlasting life.

Also, *"blessed are they that mourn,"* suffering voluntarily or involuntarily, for God Himself comforts them. He understands their suffering, having suffered Himself. He enters into their sufferings with them, enlarging their prisons by sharing them. His eternal comfort is available in His intimate presence. Those who suffer are comforted, and even able to rejoice in their afflictions because of His precious presence.

And, *"blessed are they that mourn,"* carrying a burden of prayer for someone else and interceding until God answers. Their suffering for others in intercession will result in the comfort of God's presence and in the comfort and provision of the ones for whom they pray.

"Blessed are they that mourn, for they shall be comforted."

EXERCISE #3 – Matthew 5:5 ~ MEEK, NOT WEAK

> **Memory verses:** *Matthew 5:5 & Galatians 5:22-23*

1. Using dictionaries or Bible helps, define meekness.

2. Read Numbers 12. Keeping in mind the definition of meekness, explain how Moses acted meekly in this story.

3. How are we to live out meekness according to the following Scriptures?

   Ephesians 4:1-3 –

   Colossians 3:12-17 –

   James 1:19-22 –

   James 3:13-18 –

4. After reading these passages, what do you see regarding meekness in your own life?

5. What specific steps are you going to take to increase the fruit of meekness in your attitudes and behaviors?

6. It is easier to walk in meekness when we know God loves us and is ruling over our lives. Look up the following verses to see those things over which God reigns.

Daniel 4:34-35 –

Deut. 32:39 –

Isaiah 45:6-7 –

Rev. 19:15-16 –

7. What do Romans 8:28-29 and 1 Cor. 10:13 say about the sovereignty of God over our lives?

#3 – BLESSED ARE THE MEEK

Matthew 5:5 *"Blessed are the meek, for they shall inherit the earth."*

In Matthew 5:5, Jesus was quoting Psalm 37:11. "Meek" is also often translated "poor" which shows how closely allied these two features are. To be meek is to be patient, humble, gentle, easily imposed upon, and submissive. The Greek word translated 'meek' in Matthew 5 is **praus**, which means, "gentle." Those who are gentle and humbly wait, who do not demand their own way or fret with worry will receive an inheritance from God.

The poor in spirit (who know their need and depravity before God) and those who mourn (emotionally expressing that knowledge) are also meek; they are lowly and gentle. They know they have nothing to be proud of. Every good gift they have – mercy, grace, land, eternal life – is from a good and kind God. We see that expressed well in Titus 3:1-7.

Meekness, a fruit of the Holy Spirit, enables us to choose God's will instead of insisting on our rights. It is the opposite of a "clutching" or "grabbing" spirit, a vengeful or angry spirit. *"You are blessed when you are content with just who you are—no more, no less. That is the moment you find yourselves proud owners of everything that cannot be bought"* (**Matt. 5:5**, TM). By giving up our rights to serve others, we will one day receive everything God has in store for us.

Read 1 Thess. 2:7-8. The Greek word translated as *"gentle"* in verse 7 is **epios**, which means gentle or mild. In 1 Timothy 6:11, the word translated "gentle" is the Greek word, **praotes**. It refers to an even-tempered and tranquil disposition. The person who possesses this quality pardons injuries, controls his passions, and rules his spirit well. *The Discovery Bible* defines meekness as "strength under control."

Trusting God Is The Key To Gentleness

"And they that know Your name will put their trust in You..." (**Ps. 9:10**). A paraphrase of this verse could be, *"Those who know Your nature and have a personal relationship with You will trust You. They find it reasonable to do so because they know You and have experienced Your faithfulness."* When we know the Lord—not just know about Him, but really know Him—we will trust Him. We will know that everything He does is motivated by love. When we trust Him, we quickly and easily submit to Him.

One of the primary downfalls of many of us who serve the Lord is that we are too busy doing the work of the kingdom, and we do not spend enough time with the King. The Lord wants to have rich communion with us. Through times fellowship with Him, we gain gentleness, strength, and wisdom; we take on His likeness. If we are intimately acquainted with Jesus Who is meekness personified, we will reflect His nature of humility. He said, *"I am gentle and humble"* (**Matt. 11:29**).

Spirit of Obedience

Meekness is the willingness to obey, regardless of what ridicule or persecution we may have to endure. It requires strength; it is the opposite of being spineless.

Those who will rule and reign with Jesus are the meek. *Blessed are the meek for they will inherit the earth.* Why? They are the only people with enough strength of character to allow Jesus full rein without their egos getting in the way.

Obedience Leads to Victory

An American newspaper prints an article regularly about the horse that wins the weekly race at the local racetrack. Below the photo of the horse, the caption reads, "The Meekest Horse." The horse that is completely submitted to his master always wins the race. We can learn a great lesson from this: if we will submit to our Master, we will finish our race on earth victoriously. We will overcome! But those who feel they know more than God and have a better way of doing things never win.

Pergamos, the Compromising Church

We see a deficit of obedience in the church written to in Revelation 2:12-17. The church in Pergamos was guilty of compromise and disobedience. In verse 13, Jesus commends them for their faithfulness, but in verse 14, He reproves them for idolatry and immorality, the doctrine of Balaam.

The story of Balaam is found in Numbers 22-25. When Balaam saw that God would not let him curse the Israelites, he knew the only way for Israel to come under a curse of failure was for them to choose disobedience over obedience. Once they yielded to self-serving attitudes, pride, and immorality, they would become susceptible to failure in battle.

The Israelites lusted after the Moabite women, and before long, they worshiped their gods. As a direct result, they came under God's judgment. This was Balaam's scheme; he knew God's people could be drawn away and enticed by their lustful desires, and that their compromise would cause them to lose their God-given might.

Israel's strength was dependent upon her obedience to God. When the Israelites were meek and obedient, they had victory in battle. It is the same with us. Because of the Lord's love for us, He confronts the sin and worldliness in us so that we can have victory in battle. In 1 Timothy 6:7-11, 17-19, we see some of the gods of this world: wealth, possessions, money, and prestige. We overcome worldliness, self-seeking, and fleshly lusts by resisting them and by trusting God.

Repent of Worldliness

Read 1 John 2:15-17. If we choose friendship with this world, we forfeit having God's love in us. What can we do to remedy the worldliness in ourselves and in the Body of Christ? We can repent and confess our personal and collective sin to God (Rev. 2:16, 21-22; 3:19). The Holy Spirit is willing to convict us if we will allow Him to as we pray. Prayer keeps the ministry of the Holy Spirit alive in us. We overcome the world by submitting to the Lord and by allowing Him to make us increasingly more like Himself (*see* James 4:4-10).

We cannot build meekness into our lives at will; what we *can* do is submit to Jesus, placing our will and desires beneath His. We can surrender to Him. We can reach a point where we are consumed with wanting His purposes for us.

As we identify with His interests, we are able to let go of our personal ambitions (even godly ambitions), and our claims to fame in His kingdom. We submit to Him to the point of saying, *"Lord, I belong to You. Do with me as You wish, and whatever that means, I trust you."*

Seek God's Honor and Glory

Jesus said in **John 5:44**, *"How can you believe, you who receive honor one from another, and you do not seek the honor that comes from God only?"* In other words, how can you have faith in God and depend on Him when you are looking for recognition and honor from men? Pride inspires you to seek your own glory; humility inspires you to seek God's honor and glory. As we seek His honor, humility matures within us.

When we fail to pray, we reveal our independent attitudes toward God. Eventually, we take the throne of our hearts away from Jesus, and we sit in His place. Our desires and pleasures become increasingly important to us until they mean more to us than God does, and we lose the desire to obey Him in everything. At that point, we worship self more than we worship God.

The lack of a deep, personal prayer life reveals independence and selfishness. This does not mean that those who pray consistently have conquered self, but that they are on the path toward victory.

The way of the Lord is filled with what seems to be paradoxes to our minds, two of which are these: in order to gain life, you must die, and in order to inherit this earth, you must give it up.

For Consideration and Prayer

• How meek are you?

• Are you obedient to God? Do you want His will more than you want your own?

• Ask the Holy Spirit to reveal to you any areas of worldliness or compromise in your life (i.e., your words and thoughts, what you buy, how you dress, how you treat people...). Confess any areas of sin to Him and repent.

• How is your prayer life? Are you meeting regularly with the meek Messiah?

Remember to keep the ministry of the Holy Spirit alive in you by praying regularly!

"Blessed are the meek, for they shall inherit the earth."

EXERCISE #4 – Matthew 5:6 ~ HUNGER FOR RIGHTEOUSNESS

1. Do a word study on righteousness. Define it and record what you learn.

2. According to Micah 6:8, what does the Lord require of us?

3. In Isaiah 59:17 and Ephesians 6:14, we see righteousness referred to as a breastplate. Why is that particular piece of armor is linked with righteousness?

4. Read John 6:35 and 7:37-39. The verbs *come* and *drink* are in the continuous present tense in Greek, implying habitual action. What are we to be eating and drinking of, and what is to be flowing out from us?

5. Will merely reading God's Word make you righteous? Read Psalm 119:1-16, 97-112. What else do you see that is necessary for attaining righteousness, according to these verses?

6. Read Matthew 25:31-46. List the acts of righteousness that are mentioned in these verses.

Which of these are you doing? Explain.

7. Acts of righteousness make up the wedding garment of the Bride of Jesus, referred to in Rev. 19:8. This garment is different from the garment of salvation given to each of us when we were born again. We need the garment of salvation to enter the presence of God. After we receive that, we make our own wedding garments for the Marriage Supper of the Lamb through the righteous acts that we do.

Take time to pray and ask the Lord what acts of righteousness He wants you to add to your life in quantity or quality. Write down what He says to you.

#4 – HUNGER FOR RIGHTEOUSNESS

Matthew 5:6 *"Blessed are those who hunger and thirst for righteousness, for they shall be filled."*

Our hunger for God motivates us to walk uprightly with Him. We *want* to be holy. We hate evil and want to separate ourselves from it. We love the Lord with all of our hearts, and are willing to part with anything and everything that distracts us from Him. We eagerly read and study God's Word because we are obsessed with knowing the Lord.

David Wilkerson, in his book *Hungry for Jesus*, wrote,

> *The mark of one who walks in the Spirit is that he has an insatiable appetite for Jesus. It is not just because he is sick of the sin and garbage he sees in the world. No, he is simply anxious to be with the Lord. He is moved upon by the Spirit to pursue Jesus with such passion and emotion that he is overwhelmed. His heart so longs for Jesus that no words can express his hunger and love.*

Read Psalm 63:1-2 and 42:1-2. When we are hungry for God, we are desperate for Him (not for what He can do for us, but for HIM!). If we lose our hunger for the Lord, we will find our hunger for righteousness waning as well. Author Smith Wigglesworth wrote, *"Whet our appetites, Lord. Save us from ever decreasing in desire for You."*

What Is Righteousness?

Righteousness is the rightness of God in your spirit, soul, and body, as well as in your home, relationships, and business. It is laying down your rights and comforts so that others will be drawn to the Father. It is a walk of holiness—being set apart from this world and its ways of doing things and treating people. Jesus gave us good examples of observable righteousness in Matthew 5:38-48.

We are not to be like the world—avenging and defending ourselves, loving only those who love us, and being indifferent to the hurting. We are supposed to be like our Father! We are God's children and are to reflect Him by being kind, loving, and generous to all.

People are always searching for God whether they realize it or not. They need His forgiveness, love, and sovereignty in their lives. Some men were searching for Jesus in John 12:20-25. When Andrew and Philip told Jesus, His response was, *"It's time for Me to be glorified."* And then He began to teach them the principle that there must first be death before life can come.

We Want To See Jesus!

Why did Jesus talk about death and life when they said, *"There are some men who wish to see You"*? Jesus often gave spiritual principles, rather than direct answers. To paraphrase His words, Jesus said, *"My death and glorification are at hand. This is the only way life can come to others. The same is true for all—those who cling to their own lives will lose true life, and those who give up their lives for the sake of others will gain abundant life."*

In His next words He seemed to say, *"Philip and Andrew, not only is it My time to die, it is also your time to die to yourselves so that you can transmit My life to others. When people come to you in the future wanting to see Me, let them see Me in you."*

He says the same thing to us today! People all around us are saying, "We wish to see Jesus," and it is our responsibility to show Him to them. If we will die to ourselves for the sake of others, then they will see Him in us. *"For we who live are always delivered to death for Jesus' sake, that the life of Jesus also maybe manifested in our mortal flesh. So then death is working in us, but life in you"* (**2 Cor. 4:11-12**).

"Except a grain of wheat falls into the ground and dies, it remains alone; but if it dies, it produces much grain" (**John 12:24**). A simple definition of death to self is 'embracing that which is not comfortable to me so that Jesus may be seen and glorified in me, and that His life may be released through mine to a greater extent.'

In the midst of the deception of false religions and cults today, there is a world crying out, "We want to see Jesus! What does He look like?" We, as His representatives, are to reveal Jesus to those who desperately need to see Him.

"The nations will know, understand, and realize that I am the Lord, <u>when I shall be set apart by you and My holiness vindicated in you</u> before their eyes." (**Ezek. 36:23b**, Amplified Bible). We must live lives that are so godly that when people look at us they see Jesus. Let's not be like Philip who went to another and said, *"They want to see Jesus. (Now what do we do?)"* We should have the same attitude as the Apostle Paul who said, *"If you want to see the Lord, look at me. Follow me as I follow Christ."*

Immorality and Idolatry Cannot Co-exist With Righteousness

Read Rev. 2:18-21. In verse 19, Jesus commends the church in Thyatira, but He begins to rebuke them in verse 20. Sexual immorality and idolatry were overcoming the spirit of righteousness in Thyatira. The believers were losing their good testimony to the community by their compromise.

Righteousness and immorality cannot co-exist because of their contradictions. Righteousness sees others as God sees them, blessing them selflessly as Jesus would. Immorality looks at a person made in God's image and regards him or her as something to be used and exploited for personal gratification. To think righteously of someone is to think of them the way God does; to have immoral thoughts about a person is to think of him the way Satan does. We need to think of every person the way we would want people to think of our own children.

Called To Be Holy

God *calls* us to be righteous, enduring any suffering that comes to us as a result, so that others may see Him in us and be drawn to the Father. We say 'yes' to self-death and 'no' to self-will; 'yes' to forgiveness, and 'no' to revenge and bitterness; 'yes' to holiness and righteousness and 'no' to sin and compromise. Through disciplining ourselves, we defer our *immediate* gratification in the hope of nurturing another's *eternal* gratification (knowing the Lord).

"Make every effort to live in peace with all men and to be holy; without holiness no one will see the Lord" (**Heb. 12:14**). In context, this verse says if God's people are not holy, no one will see God. We are to be lamps that reveal the Lord to the world. As we reflect His image, many will see Him. Our friends, family, and neighbors can be won to Jesus through our righteousness.

Read Hebrews 12:10-11. Holiness is the fruit of righteousness referred to in verse 11. Returning good for evil is the spirit of righteousness in action. It is being kind to those who are unkind to us. It is showing mercy to the hurting, the hungry, and the poor. It is interceding for the abortionist and the alcoholic, weeping for the addict and the sex abuser. We cannot be indifferent to these people. We must remember that we were sinners in great need when God found us! He chose us although we were undeserving. Our calling is to share Jesus with others so that they might know Him as we do.

The Apostle Paul was hungry for God and His righteousness, as we read in Philippians 3:8-14. Walking in righteousness and doing good to others crucify our old nature, especially when we are rejected for our kindness. The power to love others in the face of rejection is only possible through the resurrection power of the Holy Spirit. Like the Apostle Paul, we must press on to be found righteous in Jesus, and to reach the goal of expressing His holiness, His nature of righteousness.

Show Jesus To Others

Beware of the attitude of not taking responsibility for showing Jesus to others. Resist thoughts such as: "The pastor should do the work of the ministry!" "Let others share Jesus with my neighbors, not me!" "I have served long enough; I deserve to be served now!" The Apostle Paul said, *"I'll do whatever I have to do to minister the gospel! I have become all things to all men so that I might win some!"* (*see* 1 Cor. 9:22). We need to have that same attitude. We should be praying, "Lord, let ME show Jesus to others!" "I'll visit the sick! I'll feed the hungry." "Let ME go the second mile!"

These attitudes are birthed in us in the prayer closet. That is where we mature in the character of God. A daily prayer life is vital to developing righteousness. We manifest Jesus' righteousness as we yield to the Lord. We have to die to self in order to return good for evil. If someone is mistreating us, we must spend time in God's presence so that we can gain the strength we need to die to our natural human reactions. When our hearts are full of the Spirit of God, we will hunger and thirst to see others treated like Jesus has treated us.

While we are praying, God births in us His heart for the lost. We begin to hunger and thirst to see people come to faith and to see righteousness in our nation. We become one with the Lord as we travail in prayer. Our hearts break with the things that break God's heart and we say, *"Lord, use me. Here am I, send me."* We so fervently desire to see others come to the Lord that we offer ourselves to be the ones to reveal Him to them, no matter what it costs us.

Each generation is responsible for evangelizing their generation. So, *we* are responsible for reaching *this* generation for Jesus. Our neighborhoods and cities are obvious places of potential ministry for us. We are called to walk in Jesus' righteousness in such a way that others are drawn to Him.

Blessed are those who hunger and thirst for righteousness, for they shall be filled.

EXERCISE #5 – Matthew 5:7 ~ BE MERCIFUL!

Memory verses: *Matthew 5:7 & Psalm 103:11*

1. Define mercy.

2. Carefully read Eph. 2:1-7. What did God's mercy cause Him to do? To whom was He merciful? What kind of people were they?

3. What should be our attitude in showing mercy to others? (Romans 12:8; Micah 6:8)

4. Read Matt.18:21-35. What relationship does mercy have with forgiveness? Explain what principle(s) Jesus was teaching in this passage.

5. Is there anyone you need to forgive? Make a note to yourself here about it and with God's help, forgive that person and pray about the situation.

26

6. What does James 2:13 mean?

7. Describe the difference between the wicked and the righteous from Psalm 37:21.

8. Read Psalm 103 and list all the areas where God is merciful towards us.

#5 – BLESSED ARE THE MERCIFUL

Matthew 5:7 *"Blessed are the merciful, for they shall obtain mercy."*

There is a convent in southern California with a sign that says, "Absolutely No Trespassing – Violators will be Prosecuted to the Full Extent of the Law." It was signed, "The Sisters of Mercy."

Mercy is defined as the kind, forgiving, and compassionate treatment of others. It enables us to be sympathetic with people who feel pain or sorrow. Mercy includes not only the ability to forgive, but also the ability to receive forgiveness for oneself. Read what these Scriptures say about God's mercy: Ps. 36:5; 89:1-2; 90:14; Lam. 3:22-23.

Jonathan and David Cut Covenant

Mercy is giving to others when there is nothing to gain for oneself. Consider David and Jonathan as examples in 1 Samuel 18:1-4. Jonathan (approximately age 29) was the heir to the throne, and David (age 17) was a shepherd. Jonathan saw God's anointing on David; he knew David was the one God had chosen to be the next king. He acknowledged God's choice by giving David his robe, denoting his identity and authority as the king's son. He also gave him his armor, signifying his protection and his ability to defend himself. His gifts communicated, *"I give you my identity and authority, and I am willing to lay down my life for you. I recognize that you are the successor to the throne."*

David did not give anything to Jonathan in return except a commitment. In a similar way, Jesus offered us His identity and authority, and in exchange, we committed our lives to Him.

Read 1 Samuel 20:42. The descendants of both David and Jonathan were to be affected by their covenant. We see that covenant demonstrated in 2 Samuel 9:1-13. Notice King David's question, *"Is there not still some one of the house of Saul to whom I may show the unfailing, unlimited mercy and kindness of God"* (**2 Sam. 9:3**, Amplified Bible)?

Our Blood Covenant With God

When we cut covenant with God through the blood sacrifice of Jesus, we automatically enter into a special relationship with His children. We are in covenant with each other by virtue of our covenant with God; we have a 'family loyalty.' Our desire to show kindness should be like David's; we should ask, *"Is there anyone of the house of God to whom I can show mercy?"* Being in covenant with God, we should want an opportunity to show mercy and kindness to His family members. The more we love the Lord, the more we love what He loves, and those who are precious to Him become precious to us.

Mercy to the Wounded

David showed mercy to Jonathan's son, Mephibosheth. In those days, the new king usually had all the descendants of the previous king killed so that none of them could claim the throne. King David did not do the expected, acceptable thing. Instead, he showed mercy to the descendant of the former king.

2 Samuel 9:3b says, *"There is still a son of Jonathan who is lame in his feet."* To paraphrase this statement we could say, "There is a family member of Jonathan still alive, but he was wounded and is now crippled. He can receive, but he cannot give."

Have you ever met anyone like that, even in the Body of Christ? There are some individuals who are so hurt that they have very little to give; they are so needy and tired that they require tremendous amounts of energy and love from others.

Mephibosheth was wounded as a child, and he carried the effects of that hurt as an adult. He was unable to function normally. There are those in the Body of Christ who are in the same predicament. They have suffered hurt and have not been fully healed. Some are physically impaired; others are psychologically disturbed or emotionally handicapped. Many people are broken somewhere in their *soul*, and they carry inner, crippling pain. As a result, they have established defenses and built walls of self-protection to keep others at a safe distance. They have learned to react out of their anger, mistrust, and insecurities.

Our Covenant With Members of God's Family

Being in God's family as His covenant people, we have a responsibility toward one another. Our individual commitments to the Lord automatically imply our covenant loyalty to each other. We have cut covenant with *Him*, so we are to walk in covenantal kindness with others. Our expressed love is often part of bringing others to wholeness: His love in you heals me; His love in and through me heals you. It can sometimes be that simple. We transfer grace and healing as we interact with others in love and mercy.

Covenant relationships mean that we care enough about people to get involved. We slow down to listen to their hurts and struggles. We take time to pray for and with them. It means we reach out to the unlovely and unlovable. We help the handicapped. We try to understand each other, and we always believe the best of one another.

Covenant love means we allow the Mephibosheths in our lives to sit at our table. We treat them as our own sons and family members even though they are crippled. We do not mock, ignore, or accuse them. We give them mercy.

Mercy allows others to make a mistake and continues to love them unconditionally. It feels pain at another's shame, and takes no part in harsh criticism and condemnation.

Mercy loves and treats others as individuals of worth even when they do unworthy things. It does not judge, ridicule, or criticize. It always loves, protects, and covers.

Mercy chooses to look for good when there is little good to see. It turns its head with embarrassment when confronted with the faults of others. It takes no pleasure in the failure of any of God's children, and chooses to cover sin quickly with forgiveness.

"He has shown you, O man, what is good; and what does the Lord require of you but to do justly, and to love mercy and to walk humbly with your God" (**Mic. 6:8**)? We are to *love* giving mercy to others.

29

"Let not mercy and truth forsake you; bind them about your neck, write them upon the table of your heart. So shall you find favor and high esteem in the sight of God and man" (**Prov. 3:3-4**). Do not let mercy and truth get away from you! Write them on your emotions, thoughts, and values. Inscribe across your heart: mercy and truth!

Approximately 20 Scriptures speak of mercy and truth, with mercy always preceding truth. God's character and acts are expressions of His mercy and truth; our behavior and actions toward others must be the same. *"All the paths of the Lord are mercy and truth..."* (**Ps. 25:10**). *"You, O Lord, are a God... abundant in mercy and truth"* (**Ps. 86:15**).

The Spirit of Mercy

Read Revelation 3:1-6. The church in Sardis was lacking in the spirit of mercy, although they may have had an appearance of godliness. Perhaps they met in a nice building and had vigorous praise and worship. Maybe they even had a sense of God's presence. Yet, Jesus denounced them as dead. In His compassion, Jesus tried to wake them up from spiritual slumber (verse 2). He wanted them to remember what they had received, which is what we have received, also—*unqualified, undeserved mercy.* He wanted them to not only remember His mercy towards them, but also to extend mercy freely to others.

Like those in Sardis, we too can get comfortable in our spiritual settings and focus only on our spiritual appearance, while forgetting the importance of the *first* things—like mercy. Proudly, we can treasure our reputations more than we treasure the Lord. Are we in love with Him or with our accomplishments? Are we able to love the person who is different from us—dirtier, smellier, or less attractive? Or, do we look on those people with distance and even disdain?

Truth—A Demonstration of Mercy

When God reveals our sin to us, it is always an act of His mercy. Truth is a demonstration of mercy. It would be cruel for Him to let us destroy ourselves by living in unrepentant sin and hypocrisy without trying to stop us. Because God is merciful, He wants to set us free from iniquity and selfishness. He will do whatever is necessary to pry us loose from sin so that we can enjoy intimate joyful communion with Him. Therefore, His judgments are always acts of mercy. *"In mercy and truth atonement is provided for iniquity..."* (**Prov. 16:6**).

To reveal someone's sin to him without offering him forgiveness is tragic. Truth without mercy will kill us. The only reason the weight of our sin does not crush us is because mercy is available. Truth with mercy brings life. All of God's deeds and judgments are merciful and designed to draw men closer to Him. The heart of mercy *wants* to forgive. It willingly cancels debts. It resembles the heart of Jesus who said while on the cross, *"Father, forgive them..."* (**Luke 23:34**).

The message to the church in Sardis was that they had forgotten the mercy *they* had received, and as a result, they had become proud and deficient in mercy towards others. This church had a good name before men, but in verse 5, Jesus said it was better for *Him* to know their name than for the world to recognize them.

Our reputation can easily become what we cherish the most. It is what exalts us in the eyes of men. When someone offends us, we usually perceive it as an attack upon our reputation. That is what hurts! Not until we want God more than we love ourselves will we be able to really have mercy on those who hurt us.

Jesus' reputation was the last thing on His mind as He hung on the cross. He did not draw the praises and respect of men at that time. He did not consider equality with God something to be grasped. He laid it all down, and in that setting, He said, *"Father, forgive them."* That is overcoming the world. He forgave before they (and we) asked Him to. Because He gave up His reputation, Jesus looked as if He was dead. Yet He lives! Those who cherish their reputation look as though they are alive, yet they are dead.

Jesus said in **Matt. 16:25**, *"...whoever desires to save his life will lose it, and whoever loses his life for My sake will find it."* Part of our losing and finding life happens as we extend mercy to others. We are dependent on mercy ourselves, and the Lord God is pleased when we freely give undeserved mercy to others.

"Blessed are the merciful, for they shall obtain mercy."

EXERCISE #6 – Matthew 5:8 ~ PURE IN HEART

1. Look up the word 'pure' in a dictionary or concordance and write out a definition.

2. What does having a pure heart mean? Consider Ezek. 36:26, Heb. 10:19-22, and 2 Cor. 5:17.

3. To maintain a clean heart, we must guard our thoughts, beliefs and values, making sure they are pleasing to God. Read Phil. 4:8 and write down a description what should be in our minds.

4. Read 2 Cor. 6:11-7:1. What promises is the Apostle Paul referring to in 2 Cor. 7:1?

How would you suggest we *"cleanse ourselves from filthiness of the flesh and spirit?"*

5. Considering that 2 Cor. 6:11-7:1 is a call to holiness, evaluate yourself in light of these verses:

Verse 12 – *"...they were restricted by their own affections..."* What do you love? What attracts your attention and affection?

Verse 14 – Are you unequally yoked in some way with unrighteousness? Do you commune with darkness? (With whom are you in close relationship? Are your business dealings upright?)

Verse 16 – Are there any idols in your "temple?" Is there anything you love more than you love God? Do any of the following things demand your time or attention more than He does: material possessions, money, position or status?

Verse 17 – Are you touching or embracing anything that is unclean? What attracts your eyes and ears?

Read 2 Cor. 7:1 again. Having the promise of God's Fatherhood, acceptance and presence, and the joy of belonging to Him, let us determine to rid ourselves of anything that could contaminate us in the flesh, soul or spirit. Take time to pray about these things, repenting where necessary.

#6 – BLESSED ARE THE PURE IN HEART

Matthew 5:8 *"Blessed are the pure in heart, for they shall see God."*

Purity of heart means purity at the center of one's life. The heart represents the inner person. It is what distinguishes us from others and sets us apart as unique. It is the combination of all of our past experiences and of what has entered through our senses. It is a collection of our values, affections, desires, and dreams. *"A man's heart reveals the man"* (**Prov. 27:19**).

The heart is who we are, and it is here where we see God. The phrase 'to see' in Greek means "to perceive, see, or attend to." This seeing is not of the physical realm; it is the perceiving of God's presence. *To the degree that we are pure in our inner man, we will perceive God.*

God Has A Pure Heart

There is nothing unclean or prejudiced about God. All that He does is motivated by love; He has no impure or selfish motives. He is light and truth. **1 John 1:5** says, *"In Him is no darkness at all."* Because God is love, He sees through a heart of love. He is righteous, so He sees righteously. Being merciful, He sees through eyes of mercy. We, likewise, "see" according to what we are within. People who criticize and complain see negatives and faults because their hearts contain bitterness and strife. Others see hatred and adultery because that is what fills their hearts.

Author Herb Cohen wrote, *"You and I do not see things as they are; we see things as we are."* **Proverbs 23:7** says, *"As a man thinks in his heart, so is he."* When our hearts are pure, not only do we see God clearly, we also see the same way He sees. We view circumstances and people as He does.

Read Titus 1:15. Those who are pure see through the eyes of the Spirit, so they naturally perceive the purity of all things. However, those who are defiled and unbelieving see things through the impure eyes of the flesh; therefore, they perceive things as impure.

Purity of Heart or Hypocrisy?

Read Revelation 3:7-13. **Rev. 3:7** says, *"...these are the words of Him who is holy* (pure) *and true who holds the key of David* (which refers to authority)..." Jesus addressed two groups. The first group He praised because they kept His word and did not deny His name. The other group He called *"those of the synagogue of Satan, who claim to be Jews though they are not"* (**Rev. 3:9**). He associated the second group with Satan because of the condition of their hearts. What was in their hearts was inconsistent with what they portrayed to others. They lacked purity of heart. They were hypocrites.

The quest of our lives should be to have clean, pure hearts before God. How we perceive the Lord, how we see and interact with others, and everything we are has its roots in that place of purity or impurity. Above all other endeavors in life, we should keep our hearts pure. *"Guard your heart with all diligence, for out of it flow the issues of life"* (**Prov. 4:23**).

A Circumcised Heart

"And the Lord your God will circumcise your heart and the heart of your descendants, to love the Lord your God with all your heart and with all your soul, that you may live" (**Deut. 30:6**). The circumcised heart loves God totally. Such a heart contains no lust, because lust is of the flesh; it demands gratification. Love desires to give itself away for the sake of another.

According to Phil. 3:3, a person with a circumcised heart will worship God in the spirit (loving Him with all of his heart, mind, soul, and strength). He will rejoice in Jesus (be joyful in Him and put his full confidence in Him). And he will put no confidence in the flesh (have no mixture of trusting both God and self).

When an eight-day-old Jewish boy is circumcised, there is a cutting away of excess flesh that could cause problems later in life. The great significance of circumcision is the identity with God's covenant. God's ancient covenant with Abraham was demonstrated in the physical removal of the foreskin surrounding the male reproductive organ. God's new covenant with the house of Israel (*see* Jer. 31:31) through Jesus is in the willful removal of areas of flesh surrounding the heart. Both circumcisions are significant; both involve identity with God's covenants.

If our heart's condition is right, we will embrace repentance, submission, and commitment. We gladly welcome the conviction of the Holy Spirit, and are willing to repent toward God when we've sinned.

King David prayed, *"Create in me a clean heart..."* (**Ps. 51:10a**). David was a Jew inwardly as well as outwardly. He wanted a pure heart, one that was free of carnality and sin. He had reached a place of repentance following his terrible sins. Look at his testimony in Acts 13:22. The man with a heart after God will do whatever He asks. He recognizes that the flesh is an enemy of God, and that the removal of flesh is for his own benefit. But the person with an impure, uncircumcised heart chooses his flesh and sin over God's will.

Contaminants of The Heart

Jeremiah 17:9 says, *"The heart is deceitful above all things, and desperately wicked. Who can know it?"* We all have blind spots, weaknesses, and areas of deception that we cannot or will not see. Even when we are oblivious to our shortcomings, they exist, preventing Jesus' rule over us. Sin carries a death sentence with it, so God lovingly and mercifully reveals our sin to us so that we can turn from it.

Not only does sin contaminate our hearts; hurts do, too. Disappointments may cause feelings of resentment, mistrust, and fear. Inner pain affects our relationship with God and others. *"The spirit of a man can endure his sickness, but a wounded spirit who can bear"* (**Prov. 18:14**)?

A wound is a place in one's soul where deep hurt has penetrated. Disappointment or grief can crush the spirit of a person. *"By sorrow of the heart, the spirit is broken"* (**Prov. 15:13**). Unhealed wounds lodged within the soul manifest in behaviors and emotions. Wounded people tend to act in the present in response to old pain whether or not they are aware of it.

A lake may look clean on the surface, but if there are bottles, tin cans, and tires beneath the surface of the water, the lake is polluted. In the same way, the pollutants we carry deep within us contaminate our souls. What flows out from us is often not the fruit of the Spirit but the fruit of woundedness.

"How can you, being evil, speak good things? For out of the abundance of the heart the mouth speaks. A good man out of the good treasure of his heart brings forth good things, and an evil man out of the evil treasure brings forth evil things" (**Matt. 12:34-35**).

The Fruit of Woundedness

Wounds in the spirit/soul show up in a person's attitudes and behaviors. Some of the more common manifestations of wounds are these:

- *a deep sense of unworthiness* revealed by feelings of inferiority, inadequacy, and anxiety. The hurt has gone deep enough to drain one's self-esteem.

- *perfectionism, insecurity, jealousy, being easily offended*

- *depression, sexual problems* (perversion, fear of intimacy, distorted views of sexuality)

- *fears* of rejection or betrayal, of relationships, of intimacy, and other fears

- *addictions* (e.g. drugs, food, sex, crime, entertainment, internet, pornography, gambling)

We cannot give God's peace to others when we are not at peace ourselves! As long as we carry unhealed hurts in our souls, we will have some degree of turmoil within. Deep wounds in the heart restrict the life of God. We need to allow Him access to *all* wounded areas so that He can heal them. And we need to confess our carnal character traits to Him (many of which are reactions to inner pain) that do not reflect His nature. *"Lord, be merciful to me; heal my soul, for I have sinned against You"* (**Ps. 41:4**).

God Heals Inner Wounds

Psalm 147:3 says that God *"...heals the broken-hearted and binds up their wounds."* And **Isaiah 53:5** says, *"...by His (Jesus') stripes we are healed."* In Isaiah 61:1-3 and Luke 4:18 we see a description of Jesus' anointing, which includes healing the brokenhearted and granting freedom to the oppressed. Jesus is *"the same yesterday, today, and forever"* (**Heb. 13:8**). He can heal today what was wounded yesterday, last year, even 20 years ago!

To Receive Healing

1. *Bring your pain into the light.* Admit the hurt to yourself and the Lord, and when necessary, to others. Face the past; refuse to live in denial anymore. It is not bad or wrong to have been wounded; we have all been wounded. It is wrong when we cling to those wounds and find our identity there, and refuse to ask God to cleanse and heal them. We are wrong when we stubbornly hold onto our guilt or anger toward others rather than letting Jesus' blood be sufficient for it.

Sometimes healing can take place between you and the Lord alone, but usually you need the involvement of another person. Talking out the problem can expedite healing. *"Confess your faults one to another. Pray for one another that you may be healed. The effective fervent prayer of a righteous man accomplishes much"* (**James 5:16**).

2. *Forgive all who have hurt you.* This step may also include forgiving yourself. As long as you refuse to forgive, you will be bound to the past and unable to live fully in the present. You must want freedom from the past more than you want to feel like a victim or martyr. Refuse to enjoy self-pity. Don't use the past as an excuse for not moving on. Once you forgive, the wounds lose their power to enslave you. *Forgiveness is the key to all inner healing and transformation.*

3. *Pray over individual hurts or disappointments.* Name each painful incident before God, asking for healing. Grieve as you need to, and then bring the grieving to an end! (We must bring closure to hurts in order to live emotionally mature as adults.) As you bring your pain to God, ask Him to comfort you. In spite of any remaining pain you may feel, begin to praise and worship the Lord. Shift your focus from yourself onto Him. Stay in His presence as long as you can, soaking in His love, healing, and peace.

4. *Change!* Turn from your old behaviors. Repent of self-pity, bitterness, and a desire for revenge. Forsake old habits of anger, repent of being easily offended and of being self-centered. You are not responsible for the wounds inflicted on you, but you *are* responsible for your reactions to them. You cannot justify *your* sin because of what you have suffered. Repenting will require you to make changes in your behavior, thoughts, and relationships.

5. *Deal with anything that defiles your heart*—all sin, ulterior motives, lusts, and self-seeking desires. Forgive anyone you have been offended by and seek the Lord's healing for all inner turmoil. Then ask God to seal your time of prayer, solidifying the cleansing and sanctifying work of His Holy Spirit in your heart.

When our hearts are cleansed, reconstructed, and made pure, we will be those who are envied, for we will perceive God as He really is.

"Blessed are the pure in heart, for they shall see God."

EXERCISE #7 – Matthew 5:9 ~ PEACEMAKERS

Memory verses: *Matthew 5:9-10*

1. Peacemakers must first be at peace with God and with themselves before they can help others find peace. Concerning our reconciliation with God, read Col. 1:20-22 and answer these questions:

   a. Who did the reconciling?

   b. What was the state of man when he was being reconciled?

   c. How were reconciliation and peace made possible?

2. Now that you have been reconciled to God, what are you to do (2 Cor. 5:18-21)?

3. Compare Jesus as identified in Isaiah 9:6 with His own words in Luke 12:51-53. How do these verses relate to one another?

4. Read John 14:27 and Phil. 4:6-7. What do these verses mean?

5. Eph. 4:1-3 tells us to be *"diligent to preserve the unity of the Spirit in the bond of peace."* How do we do that?

6. Read Romans 8:12-17, and answer these questions:

   a. What does it mean to live *"according to the flesh?"*

   b. How do we know that we are sons of God?

   c. What is the connection between being a peacemaker and being led by God's Spirit?

7. Ask the Lord in which of your relationships you can or should be more of a peacemaker.

#7 – BLESSED ARE THE PEACEMAKERS

Matthew 5:9 *"Blessed are the peacemakers for they shall be called sons of God."*

In the beatitudes, Jesus was talking about character qualities, not individual acts. He was describing the process of our becoming like Himself—complete in the fullness of the qualities of God. Peacemaking is the result of that process. When our will is completely surrendered to God's will and we are living out the other beatitudes, then we are considered peacemakers and sons of God. Blessed are those who are instruments of peace.

Peacemaker Or Peace-keeper?

There is a great difference between the term "peacemaker" and the term "peace-keeper." The use of the word "peace-keeper" has significantly increased since the United Nations was formed. However, there is a kingdom difference between these two terms. A *peace-keeper* is settles differences between two opposing forces through compromise. He works it out so that each side makes concessions, establishing "give and take" for both. A *peacemaker* reconciles two opposing forces not through compromise, but through his death! A peacemaker has made peace with God through the cross of Jesus, and in turn, he lays down his life for others to find peace. Compromise is not an option for a peacemaker. Since he fears God more than he fears man, he yields to God's process of *making* peace rather than man's process of *keeping* the peace.

James 3:17 gives us a good description of a peacemaker. This verse supports the sequence of Matthew 5:9 following verse 8; our hearts must be pure before we can be peacemakers. We must first have peace with God before we can have peace with ourselves. If we are not at peace with ourselves, we cannot be at peace with others. When we feel estranged from God, we experience turmoil within. This turmoil manifests itself outwardly in irritation, anger, envy, and jealousy. If you are easily offended and angered, ask yourself, *"Where am I not at peace?"*

A Guilty Conscience

A lack of peace can also indicate a sense of guilt. Anytime we reject God's standards, our consciences are defiled and a residue of guilt is produced. If we cover over that guilt without dealing with it directly with the blood of Jesus, it will affect us emotionally. This is especially true for moral transgressions. Moral sins often must be confessed and forgiven specifically for the feelings of guilt to be removed. Residues of guilt and shame reveal a defiled conscience. Remember the verse of the well-known hymn, "He breaks the power of cancelled sin?" That refers to sin that is cancelled by Jesus' blood, and yet still has power over us because of the guilt or inner pain we feel. Our consciences *must* be cleansed.

Guilt causes emotional responses such as anger, nervousness, depression, low self-esteem, a lack of concentration, and excessive self-consciousness. We may be able to see the faults of others but be blind to our own. Our hearts harden when we refuse to deal with guilt, and a hardened heart leads to insensitivity to God.

We need a clear conscience if we are to function as peacemakers. We *must* be at peace with God and with ourselves before we can help others find peace. When we live with a guilty conscience, we usually live with hypocrisy, anxiety, and fear (e.g., fear of man or of intimacy). We may develop a mental illness. Guilt can cause believers to doubt their relationship with God. They feel they can never really please Him, which causes them to feel insecure with Jesus.

Causes of Doubt and Unbelief

- an unforgiving spirit (*see* Heb. 12:14-15). When we forgive others, we know the Lord forgives us, and we feel secure in our relationship with Him.

- an unwillingness to make past offenses right. We refuse to humbly seek reconciliation and restoration

- a particular sin we are unwilling to give up

God Provides For A Clear Conscience

God wants His people to have a clean conscience. What good news! Read 1 Peter 3:15-17. If you have a clear conscience, you do not have to defend yourself when you are accused. But if the heart is not purified and the conscience is not clear, there can be no genuine love (1 Tim. 1:5). Purity, faith, and a good conscience all go together as part of God's recipe for love.

If the devil can rob you of a clear conscience, he can steal your confidence towards God (1 Tim. 3:9). Sincere faith follows a good conscience; you cannot walk by faith if you do not have a clear conscience. **1 John 3:21-22** says, *"If our heart does not condemn us, we have confidence toward God."* When guilt in our hearts accuses us, we have trouble believing or receiving God's promises by faith.

What purges our consciences? Heb. 9:13-14 says it is the blood of Jesus, and Heb. 13:18 says it is honest, honorable living. We need both! We must apply Jesus' blood to our consciences, and we must choose to live honorably from now on (until eternity!). When the conscience is washed and cleansed, we can function as peacemakers.

Read 1 Peter 2:18-23. Your conscience suffers if you defend yourself when you are treated harshly. Allow the peace of God to fill you and do not react to wrong treatment, if for no other reason than to maintain a pure conscience before God. You find grace if you do well and suffer for it. God Himself comes to your defense. Which do you want the most—to be treated right by God or by man? A peacemaker is willing to suffer unjustly, to be mocked, and even to be openly rejected. He chooses not to retaliate, entrusting himself to God who judges righteously.

The Apostle Paul said in **Romans 16:20**, *"the God of peace will soon crush Satan under your feet."* It is significant that he said that it is the "God of peace" and not "the Lord of hosts" (Lord of armies) that crushes Satan. One person who abides in the peace of God has more power than armies do. King Solomon stated it well in **Proverbs 16:32**, *"He who is slow to anger is better than the mighty, and he who rules his spirit, than he who captures a city."*

Make Peace Through Dying To Self

Being a peacemaker is not so much something we do; it is something we are. Our mission on earth is to make God's peace available to others. This type of peacemaking comes through dying to self.

Look at what Paul wrote of Jesus in Eph. 2:14-15. Jesus became our peace through dying for us. We are to bring Him, Who is our peace, into the lives of others through willfully dying to self for their sakes. When we lay down our lives in love, others will see Who Jesus really is.

Philippians 2 is full of this principle, and clearly reveals what a true peacemaker looks like. Read this chapter in this light.

Vs. 1-2 – Unity comes through dying to self and being merciful to one another.

Vs. 3-4 – Esteem others as <u>better</u> than yourself, looking out for their interests.

Vs. 7-8 – Jesus, our example, laid down His reputation and emptied Himself of His privileges, taking a servant's role. He humbled Himself further to the point of shame and a painful death. His death made peace available to us.

Vs. 14 – Complaining shows that your carnal nature is still alive and has preferences about what it does. Joyfully accepting discomfort and inconvenience is part of dying to self. Do everything without complaining.

Vs. 15 – Peacemakers are blameless and innocent, children of God without fault, shining as lights in the world.

Vs. 17 – Paul described himself as a drink offering, which is a broken, surrendered offering. He was poured out, with no resistance. Paul was glad to sacrificially serve the believers.

Vs. 19-22 – Paul commended Timothy who did not seek his own will and way but the things of the Lord. He had the proven character of a servant.

Vs. 25, 30 – He commended Epaphroditus, a " fellow worker, fellow soldier." He told the Philippians to esteem him *"because for the work of Christ he came close to death, not regarding his life..."*

The Lukewarm Church

Read Rev. 3:14-22. Of all the churches Jesus addressed in Revelation 2-3, the church in Laodicea received the most severe words, with absolutely no praise or commendation. *"You say I am rich; I have acquired wealth and do not need a thing. But you do not realize that you are wretched, pitiful, poor, blind and naked"* (**Rev. 3:17**).

During His earthly ministry, Jesus warned people not to store up wealth for themselves on this earth and ignore God in the process (Luke 12:21). Here He told the Laodiceans that they were void of true spiritual wealth. They appeared to have it all, yet they had refused the call to take up their crosses and die to self. This church had become self-centered, lured away by the world. With comfort as her goal, she was oblivious to spiritual treasure, which could be obtained only by dying to self and serving others.

To the Laodiceans Jesus said, *"I stand at the door and knock. If anyone hears My voice and opens the door, I will come in and eat with him, and he with Me"* (**Rev. 3:20**). From outward appearances, these believers were rich and needed nothing. But they had everything but Jesus; He was standing *outside* knocking.

Jesus addressed their lukewarm situation. They did not want to be on fire for God, but they did not want to reject God and the faith either. They tried to fit in-between, embracing the gospel enough to get them to heaven and yet continue to indulge their flesh. They were unwilling to *fully* abandon themselves to God and yield to the Lordship of Jesus.

Sons of God

The term, *"sons of God"* implies maturity. God's sons are to model the only begotten Son of God, Jesus. Mature sons will be willing to lay their lives down to bring peace to others. The Laodicean church was lacking in this depth of commitment to God. In mercy, Jesus provided hope for them: the refining fire. His fire burns away pride, greed, lust, and anything else that is not of God. After a thorough refining, God's people should be able to manifest God the Father's character to the world.

Those who have signed a peace treaty with God have peace with Him. They also have peace within themselves and with others. They do the Father's work and are called by His name.

For Consideration and Prayer

Are you at peace with God? With yourself? With others?
Have you dealt with all guilt?
Is your conscience washed so that you have a good conscience before God?

Have you embraced death to self so that others can see and know the Prince of Peace?
Are you walking in the previous beatitudes so that being a peacemaker is your "natural next step?"
Are you a peacemaker?
Are you a mature son of God, reflecting His character in your behaviors and words?

Pray through these issues until you find a godly resolution to any discrepancy in your life.

"Blessed are the peacemakers, for they shall be called sons of God."

EXERCISE #8 – Matthew 5:10-12 ~ PERSECUTED

Memory verses: *Matthew 5:11-12*

1. Define persecution.

2. From Peter's words in 1 Pet. 3:13-17, 4:14-16, what should be the cause of any persecution we might receive?

3. Read 1 Peter 2:18-25. What kind of suffering finds favor with God?

Note what Jesus did when He suffered.

4. What does 2 Timothy 3:12 say about persecution?

5. How are we to respond to persecution according to these Scriptures?

    Psalm 31:14-16 —

    Matthew 5:44 —

    Romans 12:14 —

    1 Peter 4:19 —

6. What is our responsibility toward believers who are suffering or being persecuted? (Read Heb. 10:34, 13:3; Matt. 25:36-40, and 2 Tim. 1:8 for some ideas.)

7. What are some of the benefits of persecution and suffering? Consider 1 Peter 1:6-7, Mal. 3:2-3, and Rev. 20:4.

8. Be prepared to share with your discipleship group an experience of persecution for righteousness' sake that you have endured, and how the Lord helped you through it.

#8 – PERSECUTED FOR RIGHTEOUSNESS' SAKE

Matthew 5:10-12 *"Blessed are those who are persecuted for righteousness' sake, for theirs is the kingdom of heaven. Blessed are you when they revile and persecute you, and say all kinds of evil against you falsely for My sake. Rejoice and be exceedingly glad, for great is your reward in heaven, for so they persecuted the prophets who were before you."*

Jesus was light in the midst of darkness, but men preferred darkness rather than light because their deeds were evil. So they worked to put out the Light. Jesus was of the truth, but they were of the devil, the father of lies. So they crucified the Truth. Because of what Jesus was, they persecuted Him. *Because of what Jesus makes you, they will persecute you also.* If you walk in the character of the preceding beatitudes, you will manifest the same nature as Jesus, and you *will* experience conflict. Such a lifestyle makes you *radically* different from the rest of the world.

Persecution For Righteousness' Sake

Believers have been persecuted throughout history, but not *always* for the sake of righteousness. The key is the phrase: "for righteousness' sake." Are you being persecuted because you reflect Jesus and because His life in you convicts others, or are you suffering for your own sin or foolishness? (e.g., if you use company time for spiritual matters, and your boss is angry, you are not suffering for righteousness' sake. You are cheating the company.) Make sure your persecution is because you are living uprightly. Read John 15:18-22. Jesus was saying: "If life was not easy for Me, it will not be easy for you either!"

According to Romans 8:35-39, we may be persecuted for righteous reasons, but it cannot separate us from God's love. Read 2 Cor. 4:7-12. They were obviously persecuted for righteousness' sake (not for foolishness or because they deserved it). Verses 10-11 refer to *always* carrying about the death of Jesus so that the life of Jesus is manifested in us. We are delivered to death for *Jesus'* sake, so that His life is revealed in us.

Matt. 13:20-21 speaks of those who have stony places in their hearts. They may readily receive God's Word, but because their hearts are not cultivated and soft, they stumble when trials or persecutions come. They are happy with the Word of God until it causes them pain! This reveals that their motive of coming to Jesus was to receive something more or better than what they already had, and not to surrender their lives to Him.

Those of this description are not seeking hard after the Lord; they are seeking His blessings. Comfort matters more to them than the Lord does. As long as it is convenient, they will walk with God, but when things get difficult, they leave Him. Their conversions may have been weak, or maybe they were never personally discipled. Whatever the case, their hearts were unprepared for persecution. They loved self more than they loved God.

Why would Jesus consider us blessed for being persecuted (besides the fact that He is present with us)? The secret lies in <u>why</u> we are persecuted. When it is because of righteousness, it means that people are beginning to see Jesus in us.

Do People See Jesus in You?

Although God hurts with our pain, He is deeply gratified that people see His Son in us. Through the centuries, numerous unbelievers have come to the Lord as a result of seeing Jesus in the Persecuted Church. You are blessed when your life so clearly reflects Jesus that people are convicted of their sin. When He is so evident in your life that it makes people realize they are sinners, they may angrily attack you. Due to their guilt, they may believe you are condemning them. They feel justified in persecuting you even though you are just "being Jesus" to them.

A person who is persecuted for the sake of righteousness longs to reveal Jesus to others. That is his (or her) chief goal; whatever the person does to him in return is irrelevant. He looks at persecution only as an inconvenience or as an opportunity to die to self and probably considers it an honor.

Pain That Brings Life

Consider a woman who has just given birth to a baby. She is not bitter about the pain she had to go through; she just sees it as necessary in order to give birth. Similarly, we are sometimes called to experience the pain of persecution or rejection before a loved one or friend can be born again. As soon as that person receives salvation, the memory of our pain will be replaced with the joy of a new spiritual birth. We regard the pain we endured as a necessary part of the spiritual birthing process.

Consider Jesus as the other example. Read Hebrews 12:2. Jesus had two ways He could have viewed the cross: He could have considered it only personal torment and agony, or He could have seen it as a necessary and painful part in accomplishing the Father's goal—the redemption of mankind. He chose the latter: *"He endured the cross for the joy set before Him."*

If personal comfort is our objective and we have little or no desire to inconvenience ourselves for the sake of others, then we will not be able to see purpose in persecution because we have no joy set before us (their salvation). However, if we long to see others enter the kingdom of God, we will willingly suffer persecution as a part of their birthing process. **1 Peter 4:13** says, *"...to the degree that you share the sufferings of Christ, keep on rejoicing."*

From Obedience to Rejoicing

The greater the obedience, the greater the righteousness; the greater the righteousness, the greater the suffering; the greater the suffering, the greater the rejoicing!

Are you suffering for Jesus' sake? Do people lie about you or falsely accuse you? If not, does that mean you are not all that you should be for the Lord? Have you compromised His standard of righteousness? Are you so like the world that your life has no convicting power of sin? Are you so isolated and insulated in your atmosphere with believers that you have not stepped out into the world to be a peacemaker? Do you remember that you are an ambassador for Jesus? Have you forgotten that He commissioned you to reach the lost and disciple them? Have you refused to go where Jesus said to go because you did not want to endure hardness or suffer persecution (like Jonah)?

47

Harlan Popov in his book, *Tortured for His Faith,* wrote about what happened to the church as a result of the Communists' persecution:

> *As the fires of persecution grew, they burned away the chaff and stubble and left only the golden wheat. The suffering purified the church and united the believers in a wonderful spirit of brotherly love such as must have existed in the early church. Petty differences were put aside. Brethren loved and cared for one another and carried one another's burdens. There were no nominal or "lukewarm" believers. It made no sense to be a half-hearted Christian when the price for faith was so great. There came a great spiritual depth and richness in Christ I had never seen in the times before, when we were free. Every man, woman and youth was forced to "count the cost" and decide if serving Christ was worth the suffering. And to the Communists' great regret, this was the healthiest thing they could have done for the church, for the insincere gave up but the true Christians became aware of what Christ meant to them and became more dedicated than ever before."*

A God-fearing Attitude Toward Suffering

In 2 Timothy 1:8-12 and 2:9 Paul was saying, *"I am God's prisoner, not their prisoner, and I trust Him! My life is in His hands, not theirs. I face persecution and tribulation, knowing that He is in charge and has already overcome the world. My peace is in my Lord."*

The South African author and pastor, Andrew Murray, wrote a prescription for how we are to face suffering with a God-fearing attitude. We are to say, *"I am here by God's appointment, in His keeping, under His training, for His (appointed) time."*

I am here by God's appointment. He brought me here. I can rest, knowing that God has allowed me to be in this difficult place. I am here within the boundaries of His love, wisdom, and sovereignty.

I am here in God's keeping. His grace and protection are with me; He has not forsaken me. *"Though I walk through the valley of the shadow of death, I will fear no evil; for YOU are with me"* (**Ps. 23:4**). No matter how dark the valley, the Lord is with me.

I am here under His training. He will make my trials a blessing, teaching me lessons that He wants me to learn. He is working out His character in me.

I am here for His time. In His perfect time, He can bring me out of this trial—how and when He chooses. This season of testing is *seasonal,* and set by Him.

Our focus should not be on the end of the suffering, but on His salvation and glory that will be revealed in us through it. (*see* **1 Peter 1:6-9**) When we are persecuted for righteousness' sake, we are in good company—experiencing the same as His prophets who were before us!

> *"Blessed are the persecuted for righteousness' sake, for theirs is the kingdom of heaven."*

EXERCISE #9 – Matthew 5:13 ~ SALT

Memory verse: *Matthew 5:13*

1. Compare Matt. 5:13, Luke 14:33-35, and Mark 9:50. What can we learn about salt from these passages?

2. What are some practical uses of salt?

    "Spiritualize" your answers to show how we are to be salt in this world.

3. Read Lev. 2:13, Num. 18:19, and 2 Chron. 13:5. What is a covenant of salt?

    What does it symbolize?

4. As believers, we are privileged and responsible to be able and ready to share what Jesus has done for us (1 Pet. 3:15, Col. 4:5-6). Think about how you met the Lord. What were you like before salvation? How did you meet Jesus? How has He changed your life?

Using the following questions as a guideline, prepare to share your testimony in three minutes to your small group. Practice at home and time yourself so that you can keep it to the time limit. If you find this difficult, then you *especially* need the practice and opportunity! Come to the group ready to share. Use the space below to make notes for yourself.

a. What were you like before salvation?

b. How did you meet Jesus?

c. What difference(s) has He made in your life?

#9 – ARE YOU SALTY?

Matthew 5:13 *"You are the salt of the earth; but if the salt loses its flavor, how shall it be seasoned? It is then good for nothing but to be thrown out and trampled underfoot by men."*

Let's begin this study by looking at some of the Greek words and their meanings. The Greek word translated as 'loses its flavor' is **momos**; it means to blame, disgrace, or blemish. It is taken from the root word **moraino**, which means to be foolish. Jesus is saying that we lose our taste (our saltiness) by foolish, disgraceful words and behavior. Disgraceful behavior is anything that blemishes the Lord's reputation in us.

The Greek word translated 'good for nothing' means to be strong for no one or to have power for no one. If we act foolishly and cause disgrace, we lose our flavor and are strong for no one. Since we lose strength and power through disgraceful behavior, we can safely assume that we will gain strength through upright behavior!

Look at the last part of verse 13, *"thrown out and trampled underfoot by men."* In the time of Jesus, when salt lost its flavor and had crystallized, it was thrown onto the ground and used to make paths for men to walk on. The salt in those days was not the pure, refined salt we have today. It had different degrees of purity, and its uses were varied.

Value of Salt

Salt was and is used as a preservative, preventing the spread of corruption. It is used as an antiseptic to kill germs. Inferior salts have been used to decompose soil or to fertilize it. However, too much salt results in sterility so that nothing can grow. A conquering nation sometimes sowed salt over a city, demonstrating the city's irretrievable ruin (Judges 9:45). For example, in 70 AD Jerusalem was demolished, and in 71 AD she was sown with salt.

Salt has been so valuable in the past that there have been more wars fought over it than over gold! The final use of salt, when it had no value left, was for paths to walk on. **Luke 14:35** speaks of this final usage, *"Not good for the land (to decompose the soil) or for the dung hill (as a fertilizer), but only to be thrown out and walked on."*

A Believer's Responsibility

We who believe in Jesus are to have a distinct flavor. When we lose our passion for God, we lose our flavor. And when we lose our flavor, we lose our value. In essence, Paul wrote something similar: *"If my body is going to dominate me rather than God's Spirit, then God is going to have to disqualify me. Why? Because I am not what I ought to be as His child"* (**1 Cor. 9:27**). The message in Matthew 5:13 is the same: the life of a believer is not just a matter of doing, it is a matter of being. If you are not what God ordained you to be, then you have no value to the kingdom of God. You are good for nothing.

Pastor Rick Joyner in his book, *Epic Battles of the Last Days*, wrote, *"If corruption and darkness are spreading, it must be assumed that it is because the church is not doing what she was called to do."*

Dr. Charles Swindoll, in his book, *Improving Your Serve*, wrote the following:

> *Our very presence as salt in this earth halts corruption... it creates a thirst. It adds flavor, increasing the taste of most foods. Salt is amazingly beneficial "...but if the salt has become tasteless..." (Meaning: "if the salt has lost its bite, its uniqueness"), it is good for nothing. Jesus introduces not an imaginary warning, but a real one. Take away the Christian's distinctive contribution and nothing of worthwhile value remains. We become "good for nothing," exactly as the Lord put it. We must do a work of preservation... or we lose our influence and become as insignificant as a layer of dust on city streets.*

Trials Season Us

Mark 9:49a says, *"Everyone will be seasoned with fire."* The Greek word translated 'seasoned' is the word **artuo**, which means to make ready or to season. We are made ready and seasoned with fire. Fiery trials should motivate us to seek God desperately. They prepare us to carry His glory and to be salt in the earth. The fire of the trial purges us from the selfishness and sin that contaminate our flavor.

Read 1 Peter 1:6-7. Trials provide us with an opportunity to deal with our heart issues—the wounds, angers, and fears that influence what we do and how we speak. Maybe you have noticed that after a hard trial you are more careful with your words! Pain gives us proper perspective and matures compassion in us for others. Trials cause us to evaluate our relationships and priorities. When experiencing personal suffering, we realize that often we do not yet understand God's ways or even life itself as we might have thought we did. We learn that surface answers to deep problems can cause greater hurt to those who are suffering. Trials purge careless speech from us; they bring seasoning to our words and lives.

For our saltiness to increase, we usually *have* to go through difficult times. Only hard trials are sufficient to cleanse the impurities from our lives. Heartbreaks tenderize us; they motivate us to speak with gentleness, understanding, and wisdom.

Peace With Others

When salt loses its taste, how can its flavor be recaptured? Jesus gives us the answer: *"Have salt in yourselves and have peace with one another"* (**Mark 9:50b**). There is a close relationship between being at peace with others and being salty. When we are not at peace, we are easily irritated and offended. We disperse a negative fragrance and seasoning, rather than being salty with God's presence and joy. So, one of the chief ways to stay salty is to be at peace with others.

Romans 14:19 says, *"Pursue the things which make for peace and the things by which one may edify another."* The word translated 'edify' in Greek means "to build up or season." We cannot build up or add seasoning to others if our relationships with them are damaged. Our degree of saltiness and the anointing we carry, are limited or enhanced depending on the peace we have in relationships.

Words Release Life or Death

One way we season others is through the way we speak to them. *"Let no corrupt word proceed out of your mouth, but what is good for necessary edification, that it may impart grace to the hearers"* (**Eph. 4:29**). According to Prov. 16:24, 21, people learn better when we talk sweetly rather than harshly. Prov. 15:1-4 says words of comfort, mercy, and encouragement cause healing. And Prov. 8:6-8 says we should speak righteously, truthfully, and excellently.

Words that do not minister life and grace include:

- Talking too much (Prov. 10:19, 17:27-28)

- Complaining and criticizing (Phil. 2:14)

- Lying, exaggerating, and giving false impressions (Prov. 12:17-19)

- Slandering and gossiping (sharing character-damaging information) (Prov. 10:18b)

- Discussing 'works of darkness' (Eph. 5:11-12)

- Bragging or boasting (Prov. 27:2)

Walter A Henrichsen, the leader of a discipling ministry for believers in the American business world, suggests that Jesus said the words in Matt. 5:13 about salt as an illustration to the believer who refuses to be a disciple. He said, *"It is God's design that every believer be a disciple. But when one goes back on his commitment, he becomes good for nothing. You cannot save him; he is already saved. You cannot use him; he is unavailable. He is like savorless salt. Men throw it out."*

Rabbit-hole Christians

What about believers who do not salt the world they live in? Author John Stott calls them *rabbit-hole Christians*; they run from Christian friends to other Christian friends and from service to meeting, only to collapse in bed at night, exhausted from "reaching the lost for Jesus!" The rabbit-hole believer remains insulated and isolated from the world when he is commanded to penetrate it. How can we be the salt of the earth if we never get out of the saltshaker?

Salt must be spread out. It is shaken and sprinkled, not poured. Too much salt ruins food. Believers are to spread out rather than stay huddled together.

Salt adds flavor, but it is obscure. No one ever comments, "This is good salt." Instead, we say, "The food tastes good." As the Lord's disciplined servants, we should bring attention and glory to Him, not to ourselves.

Healing Barren Lives and Bitter Water

Read 2 Kings 2:19-22. The city looked good on the surface, but the water was bad and the ground was barren. Is that a description of us? Do we look good on the surface, while the living water within us is contaminated? Do our lives bear fruit or are we barren?

The waters were healed when salt was thrown into the source of the water; the salt purified the water. Do we need the Lord to throw salt on the source of our barrenness (wounds from the past, damaging words about us, or traumatic events)? Any of these painful experiences can cause us to be unfruitful.

Could the salt thrown in for healing also refer to the salt covenant? Perhaps God was saying to Jericho, *"Although you have disobeyed Me and been unfaithful, yet I remain faithful and I state again my everlasting covenant with you. I am faithful to our covenant even though you are unfaithful."*

For Consideration and Prayer

Are you salty? Does your presence around people cause them to thirst after Jesus, the Living Water?

Are you at peace with others?

Do you speak words of life and healing, or do you destroy hope, joy, and peace with your words?

Are you currently in a fiery trial? Are you seeking God fervently in it?

Are you zealous in your pursuit of God, or have you lost your passion for Him?

EXERCISE #10 – Matthew 5:14-16 ~ LIGHT

Memory verses: *Matthew 5:14-16*

1. What is the basic function of light? How does that apply to us as believers?

2. What do the following passages say about light?

Psalm 118:27 —

Psalm 119:105 —

Romans 13:12 —

1 John 1:5-7 —

3. After reading John 3:19-21, Eph. 5:8-9, Ps. 43:3, and 1 John 1:6-7, explain the connection between light and truth.

4. What do you understand Jesus to be saying in Matt. 6:22-23 and Luke 11:34-36?
(After praying for revelation, you might read cross-references or use Bible helps.)

5. From Eph. 5:1-16, how are we to walk as children of light?

6. For personal evaluation and prayer, answer the following questions:

Are you letting your light shine?

Referring to Matt. 5:16, what are your motives for the good works you do? Are they for God's glory or your own glory?

Are your good works motivated by your love for God or by your desire to *earn* the love of God?

#10 – LET YOUR LIGHT SHINE!

Matthew 5:14-16 *"You are the light of the world. A city set on a hill cannot be hidden. Nor do they light a lamp, and put it under a basket, but on the lampstand, and it gives light to all who are in the house. Let your light so shine before men that they may see your good works, and glorify your Father in heaven."*

God's first recorded words in Genesis 1 were, *"Let there be light."* This fact alone should speak to us of the importance of light. Many of the prophetic scriptures relating to the Messiah mentioned light. Read Isaiah 49:6 and 42:6. Jesus Christ came as the light, fulfilling the Messianic prophecies. He *is* God's salvation to all the earth! Read John 8:12, 9:5, and 12:46.

We Are Light!

Jesus has called us out of darkness into His light, as 1 Peter 2:9 and Eph. 5:8 tell us. The Scriptures say, *"You were darkness, now you are light."* Your basic nature is changed. Not "you had some darkness and now you have some light," but you were and you are. 2 Cor. 5:17 states that we are a new species in Jesus. The old is gone; the new has come!

The Apostle Paul prayed for the believers in Ephesus for *"the spirit of wisdom and revelation in knowing Jesus, the eyes of their understanding being enlightened"* (**Eph. 1:17-18**). Their eyes were already enlightened (past tense). Those of us who believe in Jesus are light and our eyes have been lit up!

Our Identity in Jesus

Eph. 2:1-3 – We were dead, disobedient, lustful, and children of wrath.

Eph. 2:4-10 – God made us alive together with Jesus, raised us up with Him, and made us sit together in heavenly places in Him. We are His masterpiece, created in Jesus for good works.

Col. 1:13 – We have changed kingdoms; now we are part of the kingdom of God's Son. Darkness has lost its power over us.

Col. 3:1-4 – We *have* died (past tense), and our lives *are* hidden with Christ in God (present tense).

Believe God's Truth

Now "Christ *is* our life..." This is who we are. Believing what God says about us does not make it true. It *is* true; therefore, we believe it. It is not prideful to believe what God says about us, but it *is* defeating if we refuse to believe what He says. What you do does not determine who you are; who you are determines what you do. You ARE light; you ARE in Christ. Believing God's truth about your identity will set you free to be who He says you are.

If we believe that we are part saint and part sinner, part light and part darkness, then we will live unfruitful lives with little to distinguish us from unbelievers. What we believe about ourselves defines us.

Read Luke 11:33-36. Now that you are lit up within, don't return to walking in darkness. Don't hide your light by sinning! Beware of secret sins of compromise. Do not give the enemy an opportunity in your life! John 14:30 says that there was no darkness in Jesus, making it impossible for the enemy to get a foothold to attack Him.

The eye is the lens of the soul, reflecting the orientation of one's life. Verse 34 mentions *"an enlightened eye"* which refers to a clear, healthy eye providing light throughout the body. A *"bad eye"* refers to that which is evil and unhealthy, resulting in darkness throughout the body. That darkness might look like racism, criticism, bitterness, prejudice or any number of other areas of sin.

Destruction of Unforgiveness

Read 1 John 2:9-11. A way we invite darkness to come into our lives is by allowing hate and bitterness to reside in our hearts. Even though we try to walk with God and hear His voice, the darkness of resentment can cause us to stumble. We must make sure we forgive quickly when we have suffered unjustly. There is a progression of unforgiveness to resentment to moral sin. It looks like this: *unforgiveness » resentment » bitterness » blame » hate » rebellion » deception » perversion and other moral sins.*

To avoid falling into deception and perversion we must release hurts and forgive those who offend us. Asking God to bless and prosper those who wounded us ensures victory in our hearts and blessing in their lives. It extends God's kingdom within us and in our sphere of influence.

Good Works Glorify God

In Matt. 5:14, Jesus calls us what He was when He said, *"You are the light of the world"* (**John 8:12**). We are the light of the world! What is true of Jesus applies to us because we are in Him. We are not only to stand up for what is righteous and just, we are called to *be* righteous. It is more than just having high moral standards and being able to teach them. It is being so much like Jesus that our righteousness reveals what is missing in the lives of others.

Matt. 5:16 says our good works should cause others to see God. According to verse 15, we are not to hide or limit our light (it should give light to *all* that are in the house). It is not the lampstand (vessel) that is important, but the lamp (light). We are the vessels, and Jesus is the light. Our good works must be done in such a way that they point to the Father and glorify Him.

Your light should so shine that others are convicted by your life because they see the Lord in you. Your mercy should convict others of their lack of mercy. Your brokenness over sin should cause others to see the hardness of their own hearts. Your kindness and good deeds should show others their self-centeredness. Your pure heart and clean conscience (and the peace and joy that accompany both) should convict others of their sin.

As unbelievers see your life and are convicted by and drawn by the Holy Spirit, they may call on Jesus for salvation. And as believers see God's holiness in you, they may be convicted to pursue more of His lordship in their lives.

Some distinctive characteristics of light are especially significant for us. Let's look at several and gain some insight:

Light is silent. It makes no noise; light simply shines.

Light gives direction. It does not preach; it speaks no words. Jesus said that others *see* our actions, but He said nothing about what they hear. (Light lives it; salt speaks it.)

Light attracts attention. Everywhere you are, you are a light in darkness. You communicate a distinct message with hardly a word being spoken. Initially some people may hate the light, but they are still attracted to it. Let it shine in such a way that God is glorified!

You Choose What You See

Look at Matt. 6:22-23. One interpretation of these verses is that you choose what you see—anger or forgiveness, peace or turmoil. Is the glass half empty or half full? How do *you* perceive life? Are you cheerful in spite of trials? Or, are you unhappy in spite of God's blessings? If you "see good," you will walk in light, experiencing and manifesting peace, hope, and joy. If you "see evil," you will walk in darkness, and be irritable and discontented with life.

Read Phil. 2:12-15. As God works His nature into you, work it out in your words and behavior! Do not complain (what a testimony that is)! You are to be blameless, innocent, without fault, shining as a light in the world. Your life will show others their need of Jesus!

Usually when we perceive Jesus in our devotional times of prayer and worship, we are convicted of our lack of righteousness and holiness. We then need to confess our failings to God, repent, and yield ourselves to Him again. We must absorb His life, and become one with Him. Then we can leave the prayer room as yielded vessels filled with His light and glory, ready to dispense His love to others.

Let There Be Light!

As you awake each morning, listen for the Lord's first recorded words spoken personally to you, "Today, My child, *let there be light* through you." At the end of the day as you prepare to sleep, may He with satisfaction and joy say to you, "There was light." *"And God saw the light, that it was good"* (**Gen. 1:4a**).

End this session by reading Isaiah 60:1-3. Hear God's exhortation to you: *"Arise and shine! Your light HAS come and the glory of the Lord HAS risen upon you!"*

EXERCISE #11 – Matthew 5:17-20 ~ GOD'S WORD

Memory verses: *Matthew 5:17-20*

1. Read Matthew 5:17. How did Jesus fulfill the Law?

2. What are some limitations of the law, according to Galatians 3:11, 21; 2:21?

3. Read Romans 13:8-10. How would you explain to someone that, *"love is the fulfillment of the law?"*

4. What do the following scriptures say about the Word of God?

    2 Tim. 3:15-17 –

    Heb. 4:12 –

    Ps. 119:89 –

    Ps. 119:105 –

    Ps. 119:140, 142, 160 –

    Ps. 19:7-9 –

    Matt. 4:4 –

    Isa. 40:8 –

5. According to Romans 12:2, we are transformed by the renewing of our minds. Most mind-renewal results from filling our minds with the Word of God. We do that in five basic ways: hearing, reading, studying, meditating, and memorizing. Evaluate a normal week in your life, and then note how much time (hours or minutes) you normally spend with the Scriptures in these areas:

Hearing (e.g. teaching tapes, preaching) _____

Reading   _____

Studying   _____

Meditating   _____

Memorizing _____

#11 – The Law and The Word

Matthew 5:17-20 *"Do not think that I came to destroy the Law or the Prophets. I did not come to destroy but to fulfill. For assuredly, I say to you, until heaven and earth pass away, one jot or one tittle will by no means pass from the law until all is fulfilled. Whoever therefore breaks one of the least of these commandments, and teaches men so, shall be called least in the kingdom of heaven; but whoever does and teaches them, he shall be called great in the kingdom of heaven. For I say to you, that unless your righteousness exceeds the righteousness of the scribes and Pharisees, you will by no means enter the kingdom of heaven."*

In these verses, we see clearly that Jesus did not come to do away with the law, but to fulfill it. The Greek word translated 'abolish' means to destroy or overthrow; the word translated 'fulfill' means to make full and complete. According to Luke 24:44, Jesus fulfilled all that was written in the Law of Moses, the Prophets, and the Psalms.

In this session, we will capitalize Law when it refers to the Ten Commandments. We will not capitalize law when it refers to the many laws in the Old Testament.

The Purpose of The Law

The purpose of the Law is to show us that we are sinners and in need of a Savior. Sometimes we hear the gospel preached without the laws of God being mentioned. However, it helps us to hear the Law in order to realize that we have broken it. Once we see that we are sinners in need of help, we are ready to cry out to God for salvation.

Ray Comfort, author and Bible teacher, writes that when we set aside the Ten Commandments in their function to show men their true state, we remove the sinner's means of seeing his need of God's forgiveness. It is as if we offer an antidote (the gospel) when the "problem sickness" (breaking God's Law) is not clear. The Law cannot justify us; rather, it exists to show us our need of Jesus Christ.

Explaining the Law

Suppose I said to you, "I have good news for you! Someone has just paid a $500 speeding fine on your behalf!" You would probably answer me, "What are you talking about? I don't have a $500 speeding fine!" The potentially good news is foolishness to you, and you might even be offended at my saying that you broke the law. However, if I gave the following explanation to you, you would then understand your transgression and the good news: "Today the police radar caught you traveling 50 mph in an area for blind children. You totally ignored four clear warning signs saying that the maximum speed limit was 20 mph. What you did was very dangerous! The fine is $500 or imprisonment. The law was about to apprehend you when someone you do not even know paid your fine for you. You are very fortunate."

An explanation of the law helps you to clearly see your violation and truly appreciate the good news of someone paying your fine. To tell a sinner the good news that Jesus died for his sins without showing him his sinful state makes no sense to him.

"For the message of the cross is foolishness to those who are perishing" (**1 Cor. 1:18**). Those who take the time to explain the Ten Commandments may well see a sinner become convinced that he is a transgressor. Once he sees his sin, the good news will neither be offensive nor foolishness to him, but rather the power of God that will lead him to salvation.

Jesus often quoted the Law to show people their sin (*see* Luke 18:20-21). The man to whom Jesus was speaking in Luke 18 already knew the Law, but Jesus still took the time to quote some commandments. The apostles James and Paul followed His example in James 2:11 and Romans 13:9.

Well-known theologians—John Wesley, D.L. Moody, Charles Finney, and Dr. Charles Spurgeon— were very effective in reaching the lost for the Lord. The key was in their careful and thorough use of the Law to prepare the way for the gospel. The Law is a mirror to show one his true state. The design of the Ten Commandments is to put the fear of God into our hearts so that we might know our need of a Savior. *"The Law was our tutor to bring us to Christ, that we might be justified by faith"* (**Gal. 3:24**).

Read Romans 10:1-4. The law in these verses refers to the system of a person earning righteousness in his own strength. The Messiah is the perfect fulfillment of everything the law requires, but He also put an end to the law as a way of achieving righteousness for everyone who believes. Verse 4 does *not* mean that a believer may ignore God's moral standards or commandments and live any way he pleases.

Under Law or Grace?

Read Romans 6:14. To be *under the law* is to try to earn salvation in our own strength by obeying the law; to be *under grace* is to be justified by Jesus' blood and to live by His indwelling resurrection power. Some wrongly interpret this verse to mean that it does not matter if believers disobey God's moral commands because they are no longer *under the law*. Such an interpretation is contrary to Paul's whole discussion of sin and to Jesus' own words about the law in Matt. 5:17-20.

Consider Romans 8:1-2. The *law of sin* means we have no option but to sin. As unbelievers, we sinned naturally, but as believers, we no longer *have* to sin. Jesus set us free from the law of sin by breaking the power of sin over us. He is our righteousness and sanctification, according to 1 Cor. 1:30. The *law of death* pronounces certain death without hope. Jesus refuted that lie by saying that He is the resurrection and the life (John 11:25-26). He went on to prove His victory over death by His physical resurrection from the dead.

From Romans 8:3-4 we see that the law has convinced us of our need of a Messiah, and we have come to salvation through Jesus. Our flesh cannot live up to the law's requirements, but God's Spirit within us empowers us to keep the righteous requirements of the law—those commandments of God summed up in love.

Love Fulfills the Law

Read Romans 13:8-10 and notice the two sentences, *"He who loves another has fulfilled the law,"* and *"Love is the fulfillment of the law."* If we truly understood and fully followed the command to love one another, we would fulfill every social duty fundamental in human relations.

We would be living out the fruit of the Spirit with one another—love, joy, peace, patience, kindness, goodness, faithfulness, gentleness, and self-control. We would humbly esteem one another and do nothing out of selfishness (*see* Phil. 2:3). Bible Teacher, Michael Eaton, from Nairobi, Kenya said, *"If we follow the Spirit deliberately, we will fulfill the Law accidentally."*

Righteousness That Exceeds

Look again at Matt. 5:20. *"Righteousness that exceeds that of the Pharisees"* and that which provides entry into the kingdom of heaven is to teach the Scriptures and to obey God's heart and purpose behind the law while cultivating a personal relationship with Him. The Pharisees knew the law and taught it, but did not know or obey God's heart behind the law. They had more relationship with the law than they did with God. Although they knew and taught it, they did not recognize the Messiah Who came to fulfill the law. We are not to be hypocrites like they were, pretending to be men of God and obeying the Bible without a heart connection to its Author. We are to have a solid relationship with the Father through the Lord Jesus, and our blood-bought righteousness should be obvious in our words and conduct.

Look at what Paul says in Galatians concerning justification by law, *"You have become estranged from Christ, you who attempt to be justified by law; you have fallen from grace"* (**Gal. 5:4**). In other words, "Don't even try to be justified by keeping the law. Stay in the grace of Christ!" The emphasis is on the relationship, not on religious activity. Paul closed most of his epistles with the blessing, *"The grace of our Lord Jesus Christ be with you."* He knew the importance of our knowing God's grace and favor!

Know the Scriptures!

Now we understand the Law's purpose: it shows us our need of a Savior. Does that mean we no longer need to know the Scriptures? No! Read 2 Tim. 3:10-17 to see what Paul says about the Word of God. Verse 16 shows how the Scripture confronts our problem areas and points us in the right direction in four steps:

1. The word teaches truth. [What is the commandment or principle?]
2. It shows us where we fall short. [How have we failed to live by it?]
3. It offers correction for that transgression. [What do we need to do?]
4. It instructs us how to walk in righteousness. [What is our specific plan to live it out daily?]

Let's consider the sin of worry as an example.

1. What does God's Word teach? We are commanded to trust in the Lord in Proverbs 3:5.
2. Where did we fall short? We recognize we sinned by worrying and not trusting God, revealed in Matt. 6:25-34 and Ps. 37:1-8.
3. What do we need to do? Steps of correction are found in Phil. 4:6. We are commanded not to be anxious about anything, but to pray about all things.
4. How do we walk in righteousness? We pray and trust God. We daily commit to God our needs and concerns. We thank Him that the answers are on the way and that He is in control.

64

Ingesting God's Word

Read John 8:30-32 and Hebrews 4:12. The Scriptures are powerful and will set us free to walk in God's ways. **Matt. 4:4** says, *"Man shall not live by bread alone, but by every word that proceeds from the mouth of God."*

Five ways to incorporate the Word of God into our personal lives:

1. Hear – We hear God's Word preached and taught through sermons and Bible studies. We remember 6% of what we hear.

2. Read – We read the Bible. We remember 10% of what we read.

3. Study – We study Scripture with commentaries and cross-references. We do word-studies and consider the context of passages (*see* 2 Tim. 2:15). We dig into God's Word for buried treasure; gems are always found below the surface. We remember 20% of what we study.

4. Memorize – Each verse we memorize gives the Holy Spirit more control in our lives. Memorized verses help us in prayer, spiritual warfare, and in sharing our faith with others. We remember 50-80% of what we memorize.

5. Meditate – We are freed from sin in greater measure as we meditate on God's Word. That makes it a part of our lives. (*see* Josh. 1:8; Ps. 119:97)

For Consideration and Prayer

• Are you under the law or under grace? Is your walk with God based on trying to keep the law or on a personal covenant relationship with God because of the blood of Jesus?

• Have you received His grace by faith?

• Is the Word of God a daily part of your life? Are you increasing in your knowledge and in your understanding of it?

EXERCISE #12 – Matthew 5:21-22 ~ ANGER

Memory verses: *Matthew 5:21-22*

1. Define anger.

   Anger is often linked with fear. Is there anything you are afraid of?

2. Read Eph. 4:26, 31. How can a person be angry and yet not sin?

3. Give two or three examples of justified anger. (For ideas, look at Mark 3:5; Neh. 5:6, 13:17,25; Gen. 31:36; Ex. 11:8, 32:19; Lev. 10:16, and Num. 16:15.)

4. What do these Scriptures say about anger?

   Eccl. 7:9 —

   Rom. 12:19 —

   Prov. 15:1 —

   Prov. 29:22 —

   Ps. 37:8 —

   James 1:19 —

5. How do you overcome anger?

How would you counsel someone to deal with anger?

#12 – ANGER

Matthew 5:21-22 *"You have heard that it was said to those of old, 'You shall not commit murder,' and whoever murders will be in danger of the judgment. But I say to you that whoever is angry with his brother without a cause shall be in danger of the judgment. And whoever says to his brother, 'Raca!' shall be in danger of the council. But whoever says, 'You fool!' shall be in danger of hell fire."*

We will begin this session with a Greek word study. The word translated as 'angry' in English in Matthew 5 is the Greek word **orgizo**, which means to be angry by natural impulse or disposition; to stay angry and plan revenge; to be unforgiving. The word translated as **raca** literally means "empty-headed," implying that one is dull, stupid, or foolish. It is an expression of contempt. The word "fool" in Greek is **moros**, which speaks of one who is lacking the maturity to be discriminating. It implies a very low development of reasoning abilities.

Carnal Anger Is Destructive

Both '**raca**' and 'fool' are derogatory, abusive words used with the deliberate intention of wounding or shaming someone. The principle Jesus was teaching is that not only is it wrong to murder someone, it is also wrong to be continually angry at a brother, to call him names, and to speak to him contemptuously. When we speak roughly and abusively, we dishonor that person and can cause emotional damage. When we lash out at others in anger, we hurt and humiliate them. Expressed anger is usually destructive to those it is directed against. It can kill joy, hope, and love; it can damage a person's spirit and wound his soul. Anger is a very strong passion, and can cause much destruction.

The anger Jesus spoke of in Matt. 5:22 is that which desires to harm someone. Jesus, more than anyone, knows the value of humankind. He desires for all people to be held in honor, and treated with respect and dignity. To murder is to carry out hate and anger to the full end. Jesus commands us to deal with irritating situations in righteous ways—to be patient and forgiving rather than angry and vengeful.

According to Matthew 5:20, our righteousness must exceed that of the Pharisees, who kept the law to the letter. Jesus says in verse 21 how our righteousness can exceed theirs—by not only obeying the command not to murder, but also by not retaining anger or hatred in our hearts. Jesus always dealt with heart issues, and in verse 22 He was confronting the issue of having a heart of anger.

God's Anger At Sin

In the Old Testament, God's anger is mentioned often and is usually linked to sin or to the jealousy He felt over the worship of His people. God's anger is righteous and holy; it is motivated by love. He is angry when we disobey Him and serve other gods because He knows that disobedience and idolatry will lead to our destruction. In His holiness and love for us, He cannot condone sin. It angers Him. God is jealous for our devotion. It is as if He says, *"In My love for you, I'm giving you borders (commands). Stay within these and you'll be happy, safe, and blessed."*

Self-centered Anger

Our anger, in contrast to the Lord's, is usually motivated out of our love for ourselves. We get angry when someone has crossed our boundaries, taken our rights from us, or blocked our goals. We are often angry when we feel threatened or frustrated, or when we have suffered physical or emotional hurt. Sometimes we use anger to get our own way. It is seldom motivated by love for others.

Greek Words For Anger

(1) **Orge** (mentioned earlier in another form) is a natural impulse or disposition of anger. **Orge** can be *righteous indignation* that is useful to God. It is an outward, active emotion that lasts a long time. It is used in connection with the wrath of man, punishment of human governments, God's anger with the Israelites, or God's anger towards those who disobey Jesus in His gospel (*see* John 3:36).

(2) **Thumos** is passion that quickly blazes up and then dies down. Sometimes **thumos** is an inward feeling rather than an active emotion. It is translated in the New Testament as 'angry tempers, rage, and wrath.' In Galatians 5:20, **thumos** is smoldering jealousy in the heart that leads to wrath.

(3) **Parorgismos** is irritation and exasperation. **Parorgismos** provokes to **orge**. It is the word used in Eph. 6:4 and carries the idea of "quivering with strong emotion."

Constructive Or Destructive Anger

Anger is a neutral emotion, neither innately good nor evil. Destructive anger is the desire to harm another person. Constructive anger is the result of being harmed by another. We see the difference in Eph. 4 where it says, *"Be angry* (constructive anger), *and yet do not sin* (destructive anger) (**Eph. 4:26**). Constructive anger takes place when we realize there has been a violation, and we use that hurt or violation as a springboard toward acts of righteousness. Love and holiness motivate this anger.

The Lord's cleansing of the Temple in Mark 11:15-18 is an excellent example of constructive anger. Jesus felt holy anger when He saw His Father's House being misused for man's profit. He noticed that the people who came to worship were being exploited and kept from offering their sacrifices. They were told that their animals were blemished, and were then sold "worthy sacrificial animals" at high prices.

Because some people could not pay the prices, they were turned away from giving an offering to the Lord. The greed of the Temple leaders kept the people from relating to God. Jesus was jealous for God's House to be revered, and for His Father to receive the worship due Him. His anger was motivated by His love for His Father and for the people.

A Den of Thieves

The phrase Jesus quoted referring to "a den of thieves" was one that the priests and scribes recognized from Jer. 7:11. This offended them! They knew the context of this verse, with which some of us might not be so familiar. For more understanding, read Jer. 7:9-11.

Jesus' accusations against the Temple leaders included theft, murder, adultery, swearing falsely, and idolatry. When He said, *"You have made it a den of thieves,"* they knew the charges against them, and yet they were standing in the Temple as if they were righteous. He was exposing their hypocrisy, and they knew it!

Guidelines for Righteous Anger

Righteous anger hates sin and injustice. God gave us the emotion of anger so that *His* purposes can be accomplished! Jesus was capable of righteous anger, but He was never guilty of destructive anger. When He faced sin (such as greed, pride, and hypocrisy), He allowed the passion of anger to arise in godly fear (*see* Ps. 7:6,11). When He was attacked, He did not react (*see* 1 Peter 2:23). Jesus had no self-protecting anger.

The Lord gives us clear directives regarding anger. Look at Prov. 19:11 and 17:14. Jesus warns us not to hurt others with our anger. Prov. 12:18 says a word spoken in anger can be like "the piercing of a sword." **Prov. 29:11** says, *"A fool always loses his temper, but a wise man holds it back."* And **Prov. 16:32** says, *"He who is slow to anger is better than the mighty."*

Passive and Aggressive Anger

We sin when we express destructive anger. We do that both passively and aggressively. Examples of *passively* expressed anger are irritability, exasperation, moodiness, withdrawal, sarcasm, a critical spirit, and resistance to authorities. When anger is expressed *aggressively*, it erupts in shouting, temper tantrums, abusive and violent language, disruptive behavior, and screaming.

A pattern of expressing anger openly and frequently can breed an angry personality. What does an angry personality look like? It looks like someone who is mad at everything! In Prov. 22:24-25, we are warned not to be good friends with people who are always angry.

For more help regarding anger management, go over the handout following this session entitled **Steps for Victory Over Anger**.

Steps for Victory Over Anger

When you realize your anger is building, there are some practical steps you can take to defuse it or to handle it appropriately.

1. *Get more information before you respond.* Sometimes we assume that certain things are happening when they really are not. When we get more information, our thoughts, feelings, and responses may change. We should ask ourselves, "Are my angry feelings justified?"

Before you react, ask the other person a few questions. This is a good way to gather more information to clarify words and actions. Here are some sample questions:

a. I am not sure that I understood what you meant. Could you please explain a little more?
b. I noticed you are _____. Could you please help me to understand why?
c. I may be wrong, but I feel there may be a problem between us. Is my perception correct?

2. *Go to your memory file.* If you are getting upset with someone, ask yourself, "Who does this person remind me of? Is this situation similar to another situation I've been in before?"

As you review your memories, you may be surprised as to how much hurt and anger you carry. Deal with the backlog of anger in prayer. Forgive those who hurt you in the past. Release all offenses so that you do not accumulate hurts and anger.

3. *Be aware of displaced anger.* Some counselors believe that 80-90% of all anger is displaced. Displaced anger is when we are angry about one thing, but we take it out on something else. What annoys us is often something other than the present event or person. It is like the boss who yells at his employee; the employee goes home and shouts at his wife who scolds the child. The child kicks the dog, and the dog chases the cat.

What do you do with *your* anger? Do you transfer your anger to the other drivers on the road? Do you play rougher with your children than you should? Are you cleaning house with quick and hurried movements? Are you short of patience? Do you find yourself wishing people would hurry up and get to the point in their conversation? If any of these are true of you, then you may have some displaced anger. Ask the Lord to help you to deal with the real cause of your anger rather than taking it out on others.

4. *Evaluate your angry feelings.* Ask yourself:

a. What is making me feel angry? Why am I feeling all this emotion?
b. Am I jumping to conclusions about the situation or person who is frustrating me?
c. Is my anger justified? Is it right for me to feel threatened in this circumstance?
d. Is there another way I could look at this situation?
e. Are there things I could do to change the circumstances in order to reduce my anger?

5. *Remind yourself that God is in control.* The Lord is not surprised by what is happening to you. Sometimes God allows unpleasant circumstances so that we might grow from them and learn to trust Him more. All of our trials have divine purposes behind them. (*see* James 1:2-4 and 1 Peter 1:6-9)

6. *Tell God how angry you are.* In dealing with your anger, you may find it helpful to read the Psalms. The psalmist often told God how angry he was and that he needed His help. (*see* Ps. 39:1-4)

7. *Learn to deal with the sin of your anger, using the following suggestions:*

a. Face your anger as sin! When you try to justify your anger or blame someone for it, you forfeit your victory over it. Usually a person will not gain victory over a wrong action until he is convinced it is sin. Consider God's commands to *"Cease from anger and forsake wrath"* and *"Let all bitterness and anger be put away from you."* Then, confess every angry thought or deed as sin as soon as it occurs.

b. Ask The Lord to take away the habit pattern of anger. 1 John 5:14-15 assures us that if we ask anything according to the will of God, He hears us, and grants our requests. Since we know it is not God's will that we bear destructive anger, we can be assured of victory if we ask Him for help.

c. Forgive the one who angered you. Eph. 4:32 instructs us to forgive others, as God for Christ's sake has forgiven us. When you have hostile thoughts toward someone, pray brief prayers of forgiveness for him. Gradually your *choice* of forgiveness will grow into *feelings* of forgiveness and love.

d. Give thanks for anything that annoys you (*see* 1 Thess. 5:18). Thanksgiving helps reduce anger. You will not be angry or depressed if in every insult, rejection, or injury you give thanks.

e. Think positively. People with positive thoughts are not plagued by anger or hostility. Submit every thought to Jesus and think about what is *"honest, just, pure, lovely, and of good report"* (**Phil. 4:8**).

Anger is often a habit—a temperament-induced, sinful habit—ignited through the years by unpleasant circumstances. It can control a person, causing him to react selfishly inwardly or outwardly. Unless you let the power of God within you change your thinking patterns, your condition will gradually ruin your health, family, relationships, business, and spiritual maturity. In addition, your anger grieves the Holy Spirit (Eph. 4:30), and robs you of the abundant life that the Lord wants to give you.

Repeat these steps when you are angry. Of the hundreds who claim that these steps have helped them, not one has indicated that it happened overnight. If anger is a problem for you, use this formula for sixty days. Gradually God will make you into a new person—which you and others will love.

EXERCISE #13 – Matthew 5:23-26 ~ RECONCILIATION

| Memory verses: *Matthew 5:23-26* |

1. According to Matthew 5:23-24, what relationship does Jesus consider of primary importance?

2. What principle do you understand Jesus to be teaching in Matthew 5:25?

3. Read 2 Corinthians 5:18-20. What ministry does each of us have?

What does this involve?

4. In Matthew 18:15-17, what are the steps that Jesus gave us for being reconciled with others?

5. How does the Apostle Paul tell us to interact with each other in Ephesians 4:1-3?

6. Read Romans 15:1-7. What are some of the instructions we are given for building unity with one another?

7. If someone came to you for counsel regarding a damaged relationship, what would you say?

#13 – BE RECONCILED!

Matthew 5:23-24 *"If therefore you are presenting your offering at the altar, and there remember that your brother has something against you, leave your offering there before the altar, and go your way; first be reconciled to your brother, and then come and present your offering."*

Read 1 John 4:20-21 and 2:9-11. Loving the Lord God is the proper motivation and foundation for reconciling damaged relationships. If we do not love the Lord as we should, we will not care enough to be reconciled to others. If we love Him, we will love His people.

Restore Relationships Before Worshiping God

In God's order, any spiritual activity is to come *after* restoration with others in His family. We cannot always force reconciliation with unbelievers who are angry with us, but those who are in the Lord's family should pursue peace with one another. Jesus may be assuming in Matthew 5 that *we* have nothing against anyone. In this verse, He is addressing the situation of someone having something against *us*, and tells us to take the first step to reconcile. *"If possible, so far as it depends on you, be at peace with all men"* (**Rom. 12:18**).

In 2 Cor. 5:18-20, the Apostle Paul speaks clearly about our ministry as Christ's ambassadors; all of us have the ministry of reconciliation. If you know that someone has something against you, you are to go to that person as soon as possible and be reconciled. Whether or not you *are* guilty is not as important as the fact that the wounded party has *perceived* you as guilty. Who is actually right or wrong does not matter as long as restoration occurs. If we insist on standing in our *rightness*, we might sacrifice walking in Jesus' *righteousness*.

You might say to the person, *"Are you at peace with me? I feel awkward when we are together. Have I offended you in some way? Please be honest with me; I value your friendship."* Make sure you do not use the word *"if"* in the reconciliation process (*"If* I hurt you...."*). This simple word makes the restoration more difficult because the wounded person feels your insensitivity to their hurt. Saying "if" demonstrates your sense of innocence regarding the offense.

Jesus' Instructions For Seeking Reconciliation

If someone has hurt or offended *you*, it is also up to you to initiate restoration. In Matthew 18, Jesus gives clear instructions regarding reconciliation and restoration. Before you even take the first step with the offending party, though, take time to be with God the Father where you pour out your heart to Him and receive His love and healing. Then you will be ready to approach the person who hurt you. Read Matt. 18:15-17.

1. Speak to the person alone. *"Argue your case with your neighbor yourself, and do not reveal the secret to another"* (**Prov. 25:9**). Do not tell others and get them on your side. The person at fault has the right to hear first (unless you need pastoral guidance). When you tell others first, you create three major problems:

a. You prove to God and to the ones you tell that you don't love the offender. You also prove that you don't love God, because you have disobeyed His scriptural guidelines. Jesus said, *"If you love Me, keep My commandments"* (**John 14:15**).

b. You tempt the other person to take up an offense against the offender, possibly damaging a friendship they had. *"A whisperer separates chief friends"* (**Prov. 16:28**). This could also lead to spreading discord and disunity, one of the seven sins that God hates, according to Prov. 6.

c. When you finally *do* approach the one who hurt or angered you, he may question your sincerity, and the potential for restoration is reduced.

"Absent Third Party Influence"

Never use an "absent third-party influence." Avoid quoting others to strengthen your point by saying things like: "Others have told me the same thing about you." Or "the pastor sees this in you, too." "Everyone has a problem with you." Quoting other people brings condemnation to the person and breeds discord in the Body of Christ. Our ministry is not to overwhelm, but to reconcile! Some reasons why we quote others in our arguments are:

Ignorance — We are not aware of the damage and complications it will cause.

Frustration — We see that the other person is not receiving what we are telling him, and we are frustrated at his inability to see from our perspective.

Insecurity — We are trying to strengthen our point of view.

In Luke 17:3-4, Jesus said to rebuke (to mention the offense) before you forgive. Immature love will forgive and move on without confronting. Mature love will confront and forgive because it desires wholeness in the offender and a restored relationship with him. When we forgive without reconciling, we close our hearts from trusting further, and the relationship is seldom as open and enjoyable again.

2. Take one or two mutual friends with you who can listen objectively and confirm what was said or done. Neutral friends can help achieve reconciliation. Throughout the confrontation and sharing time, make sure you maintain and exemplify the Lord's heart of mercy.

Be willing to forgive whether or not the other person repents. Jesus said God will forgive us as we forgive others. We all need mercy and forgiveness, so *we* must be merciful to those who need it. Our standard of extending forgiveness is found in **Eph. 4:32**, *"... forgive one another even as God in Christ Jesus has forgiven you."*

3. If the person refuses to be reconciled to you after you have taken others with you, tell the congregational leadership in order to enlist their help in achieving restoration.

Throughout the process, we must remember:

• Our goal is to be restored to the offender.
• We should involve as few people as necessary.
• We must examine ourselves before we approach the other person. Jesus tells us in Matt. 7 to remove the log from our eyes before we try to get a splinter out of someone else's.

The fruit of obeying Jesus' rules of reconciliation are amazing! When we realize the importance of restoring relationships within the Church and take proactive steps of doing so, we will see the Lord strengthen believers and save unbelievers. This will happen as we seek reconciliation in relationships:

• Gossip and slander in the Body of Messiah will cease.
• The Church will be strengthened and edified because we will speak graciously of one another.
• Expressed loyalties will build security and a defense against suspicion between believers.
• The world will believe that Jesus is God's Messiah (*see* John 17:21). When the world sees us being loyal and loving towards one another, they will recognize that Jesus is the Messiah.

Deal With Conflict Quickly

The phrase, *"Agree with..."* (Matt. 5:25) means "to think kindly of or favorably toward." Do not let unresolved issues go on indefinitely. Do not let grievances grow. Deal with conflict right away; do not procrastinate in seeking reconciliation. Merely hoping everything will eventually be resolved usually results in things *not* being acceptable for too long!

Notice the common exhortation in the verses we have read: YOU agree with your adversary, YOU pursue peace, YOU think kindly of and favorably toward your adversary. It is up to YOU! The responsibility for reconciliation is yours... *ours*.

So, make every effort to be reconciled with everyone! If it is a brother with whom you are at odds, be reconciled and restored to him before trying to minister to the Lord. If you are at odds with an unbeliever, deal with the situation as soon as possible to avoid future problems and repercussions. Restored relationships are often like soldered metal – they are stronger after bonding and healing than they were before the break.

Eph. 4:25 says, *"...We are members of one another."* We must cherish, protect, and take good care of each other in the family of God!

Read the next chapter on Reconciling Relationships for some practical guidelines in seeking peace and restoration in relationships.

RECONCILING RELATIONSHIPS

Dealing with hurt, anger, and offense is not a quickly learned skill; it takes time. There are some hurts and angry feelings we experience that can be adequately resolved in our personal time alone with God, such as matters of preferences or self-centeredness. Other feelings may need to be discussed with those who have upset us. We need to take responsibility for our reactions, rather than blaming others for making us angry. We need to learn to communicate with the one who hurt us in such a way that reconciliation can follow. In verbalizing our feelings, it is wise to follow some guidelines. Below are some that may help.

1. *Think and pray about what you are going to say before you say it.* You might want to write your thoughts down, which will help clarify your thinking and sort out your emotions. Also, pray for the right place and timing for the confrontation. *"When there are many words, transgression is unavoidable, but he who restrains his lips is wise"* (**Prov. 10:19**, NASB).

2. *Do not put off expressing how you feel for long periods of time.* If something is bothering you and you do not tell the person involved, you may find your angry feelings festering. Your feelings of mild irritation can grow into the poison of bitterness. *"If you are angry, don't sin by nursing a grudge. Do not let the sun go down on your anger. Get over it quickly; when you are angry you give a mighty foothold to the devil"* (**Eph. 4:26-27**, Living Bible).

3. *Do not withdraw into silence.* Silence does not settle issues; it only frustrates the solution. It is usually just an excuse when we say, "I don't want to talk about it; I might hurt her feelings," or "I don't think it would do any good; he would just get mad." Withdrawing does not bring about reconciliation and restoration.

4. *Be open to criticism.* No one enjoys criticism; it is painful and humbling to receive. But the truth is, no one is always right; we all have times of being wrong. When you begin to talk to someone about an issue that is bothering you, you may receive unexpected criticism in return. Listen to it; there may be truth in it. *"It is a badge of honor to accept valid criticism"* (**Prov. 25:12**, LB). *"Don't refuse to accept criticism; get all the help you can"* (**Prov. 23:12**, LB).

5. *Share only one issue at a time.* Beware of letting things build up until you are about to explode. Try to share how you feel at the time of the offense. Otherwise, when you talk with the other person, you will find it difficult to discuss only the present issue. You might empty your entire emotional load on him! Deal only with the issue at hand.

6. *Do not use the past to manipulate.* It is easy to bring up past offenses in order to make the other person feel guilty for something that is bothering you now. The past is past! Past issues only cloud the present problem you have. (Sometimes we bring up past issues because our present argument is not strong enough by itself.)

7. *Express your expectations for others verbally.* If you do not state your expectations, how will anyone ever know what they are or if the expectations are being fulfilled? You may find it helpful to write down your expectations before you share them.

8. *State your hurt or complaint objectively.* Try to keep as much emotion out of the conversation as possible. Emotions cloud the issue, causing reactions of anger, guilt, and confusion. It may be beneficial to read what you have written rather than to simply paraphrase it. If you have already prayed about the situation and expressed your emotions to the Lord, it will be easier to be objective with the person who hurt you.

9. *Share your complaint in private, not in public.* No one appreciates talking about personal issues when other people are around. **Matthew 18:15** says, *"If your brother sins, go and reprove him in private; if he listens to you, you have won your brother."*

10. *Let the person know that you are still committed to the relationship.* Tell him that you are happy with other aspects of the friendship. Talk about the one issue; do not destroy an entire relationship over a single problem. Rejection goes so deep in some people that they may fear the relationship is over when you share a grievance.

11. *Avoid a win-lose situation; look for a solution.* Are you after victory or resolution of the conflict? Sometimes we must live with compromise. Ask God to help you find a solution. *"If any of you lacks wisdom, let him ask of God, who gives to all liberally and without reproach, and it will be given to him"* (**James 1:5**).

12. *Do not make threats to terminate or leave the relationship.* Threats can be an intimidation technique used to get the other person to conform his behavior to your way of thinking. Determine not to escape the relationship. Commitment is a necessary quality in relationships.

13. *Be sensitive in your joking.* The book of Ecclesiastes says there is *"a time to laugh."* There is also a time not to laugh. Joking at a serious time can damage a friendship.

14. *Avoid accusing or attacking the other person.* Learn to use "I words" rather than "you words." "I words" are assertive; "you words" are aggressive. "You words" seldom settle issues; instead, they stir them up. We need to own up to our feelings. (Say, "I feel hurt when you arrive late without phoning to inform me," rather than "You never call when you are going to be late!")

15. *Do not exaggerate the issue.* We sometimes exaggerate in order to prove our case. Try to look at the issue from the other person's point of view.

16. *Allow for reaction time.* If you are the initiator of the discussion, you have had the advantage of thinking about the issue before you approach the other person. Give him or her some time to digest what you said before you demand a response.

EXERCISE #14 – Matthew 5:27-30 ~ OVERCOMING SIN

> **Memory verses:** *Matthew 5:27-30*

1. Author John MacArthur, Jr. writes that dying to sin is a way of life by which *"we seek to throttle sin and crush it from our lives, sapping it of its strength, rooting it out, and depriving it of its influence."* Read Romans 8:12-14. A characteristic of true believers is that they put the deeds of the body to death. How is this done?

2. Romans 6:11 says *"...reckon yourselves to be dead to sin but alive to God..."* What do you think that means and how do we obey it?

3. How would you practically obey Romans 6:12-14 (or counsel someone to)?

4. What are the commands given in the following Scriptures about resisting lust and dying to sin?

   1 Peter 2:11 —

   1 Cor. 6:18 —

   James 4:7 —

   Romans 13:14 —

5. After reading 1 John 3:6-10 and 1 Cor. 10:13, do you think it is possible to resist temptation? Why or why not?

6. According to these Scriptures, why is a sinful thought life hazardous?

   Titus 1:15 —

   Matt. 15:18-19 —

   Prov. 4:23 —

   Prov. 23:7 —

7. What was the principle Jesus was giving in Matthew 5:29-30?

#14 – OVERCOME SIN!

Matthew 5:27-30 *"You have heard that it was said to those of old, 'You shall not commit adultery.' But I say to you that whoever looks at a woman to lust for her has already committed adultery with her in his heart. And if your right eye causes you to sin, pluck it out and cast it from you; for it is more profitable for you that one of your members perish, than for your whole body to be cast into hell. And if your right hand causes you to sin, cut it off and cast it from you; for it is more profitable for you that one of your members perish, than for your whole body to be cast into hell."*

Put Sin To Death

Read Colossians 3:1-5. The Scriptures command us to deal with our sin by putting it to death. We cannot obey this command partially or half-heartedly when we really want to eliminate sin from our lives. Sin has a way of reviving old patterns and launching new and unexpected assaults on our most vulnerable areas.

Puritan John Owen from the 1800's wrote this about mortifying sin:

> *"Mortification abates sin's force, but does not change its nature. Grace changes the nature of man, but nothing can change the nature of sin. It may be destroyed, but it cannot be cured. If it is not overcome and destroyed, it will overcome and destroy the soul. Mortify sin. Make it your daily work. Be always at it while you live. Cease not a day from this work; be killing it or it will be killing you."*

Read Romans 8:1-11. Believers are "in Christ" when they choose to walk according to the Spirit and not according to the flesh. The Holy Spirit changes our basic disposition when we are born again. We become partakers of His divine nature (*see* 2 Peter 1:4), and our orientation to God changes. In the flesh, we could not and cannot please God, but now the righteous requirements of the Law *are* fulfilled in us, and we *are* pleasing to God. Our whole mind-set is new! As a result, our minds can and should be set on the Spirit rather than on the flesh. We are free from the bondage to sin. If our minds are set on the things of the Spirit, even when we yield to temptation, we still *"delight in the law of God in the inner man"* (**Rom. 7:22**). Our basic orientation is to love and obey the Lord.

The Word of God does not promise instant sanctification and immediate freedom from all sin. The Apostle Paul speaks of a continuous struggle with sin; we are persistently *"putting to death the deeds of the body."* We can never tame our flesh. Nor can we be gentle and playful with our sin; we must deal with it quickly and severely. We must see sin as our enemy and commit ourselves to destroying it any time it tries to gain a place in our minds or lives.

Read Matthew 5:29-30 again. Many have misunderstood this passage, thinking that Jesus meant it literally. Even the theologian Origen had himself castrated in an effort to fulfill this command. Jesus was not calling for self-mutilation, but for the denial of the deeds of the body.

Scriptural Guidelines For Overcoming Sin

The Word of God offers us some practical means by which we can overcome sin. Our growth in grace depends upon our obedience to these guidelines. This is not a mechanical formula; it is simply some instructions that allow the Holy Spirit to carry out His work of sanctifying us.

1. *Abstain from fleshly lusts.* If you want to put carnal lusts to death, stop entertaining them! **1 Cor. 6:18** says, *"Run from sexual immorality!"* You must do this; it cannot be done for you. Resist lustful thoughts, and refuse to accommodate fleshly lusts (*see* Romans 13:14). If you struggle with gluttony, do not buy foods that will tempt you to overeat. If alcohol is your problem, do not keep it in your home. If you have sexual lust, do not fill your mind with images that feed that lust.

If you do not want to fall, do not walk where it is slippery. Do not prepare for the possibility to engage in sin. Do not covet what you do not have and what is not yours. *"You are already free from sin; now stop sinning! You are dead to sin."* (**Rom. 6:6-7**) (If you continue to struggle in a particular area where you have applied spiritual disciplines, you may need a measure of deliverance from demonic oppression.)

2. *Fix your heart and mind on Jesus.* We become like what we worship. As we fix our minds on the Lord, we are conformed to His image (*see* 2 Cor. 3:18). It requires discipline for us to keep our thoughts on Jesus and on what pleases Him. But we must choose to do so if we want to live an overcoming life.

3. *Meditate on God's Word.* As the truth of God's Word penetrates your heart and mind, it will build in you a love for holiness and a hatred for sin and worldliness. Fill your mind with Scripture. Respond to temptation by quoting verses as Jesus did in Matthew 4. The Word of God is our most effective weapon for defeating the flesh and overcoming temptation.

4. *Watch and pray.* **Matt. 26:41** says, *"Keep watching and praying that you may not enter into temptation; the spirit is willing but the flesh is weak."* Prayer is a means of heading off temptations *before* they come! There is a realm of temptation we can avoid if we are people of prayer. Prayer draws us near to the Lord and focuses our thoughts on Him, which strengthens us against temptation and weakens the force of temptations we do face. Identify the circumstances that lead you into sin. Pray specifically for strength to face those situations and to find God's *"way of escape."* Pray for a holy hatred of sin.

5. *Exercise self-control.* Be self-controlled in all areas, such as: eating habits, rest, exercise, personal time with God, and the use of leisure time. John MacArthur wrote, *"Self-control is a watchful discipline that refuses to cater to the appetites of the body at the soul's expense."*

6. *Be filled with the Holy Spirit.* To be Spirit-filled is to be controlled by the Holy Spirit, just as being drunk is to be controlled by alcohol (*see* Eph. 5:18). Ask the Lord to fill you daily with His Spirit. Unite your spirit with God's Spirit through worship and prayer.

Working Out Our Salvation

Reflecting back on Romans 8, we put sin to death by the Holy Spirit. We cooperate with God by working out our salvation as He works it into us (Phil. 2:12-13). God molds our wills to obey and then gives us the strength to do what pleases Him. **Gal. 5:16** says, *"Walk by the Spirit, and you will not carry out the lusts of the flesh."* As we grow in the life of the Spirit, the works of the flesh will be strangled. We need to be wise in dealing with the deceitfulness of our flesh. We are not growing in holiness if we are playing games with our temptations and sins, deceiving ourselves. There are ways that we think we have dealt with sin when we really have not. Here are a few:

• *We cover our sin.* When we cover our sin to hide it from others, we give the impression that it does not exist. A false impression is a lie. Our goal is to walk free of sin, not to be good hypocrites! *"He who covers his sins will not prosper, but whoever confesses and forsakes them will have mercy"* (**Prov. 28:13**).

• *We internalize the sin.* When we forsake the outward practice of sin, but still enjoy the memories or fantasies of it, the sin has only become private; it has not been put to death. Jesus condemned that practice in Matt. 5:21-28 by saying that hate is the same as murder and lust is the same as adultery.

• *We exchange one sin for another.* When we put off one particular sin, but then embrace another that is similar, the sin is not denied and overcome; it has only changed its form.

• *We repress the temptation.* Sometimes we use diversions to deal with conviction, such as watching TV to drown out guilt or staying busy to avoid yielding to temptation. When temptations come, we need to rebuke them by quoting the Word of God as Jesus did, not just look for a temporary escape route. We should exterminate our sin, not merely subdue it.

Feel the Guilt

Feeling the guilt is a part of putting sin to death. It brings us to a place of confessing and repenting of our sin and hating it so that we never want to sin in that area again. Those who claim the promise of forgiveness and quickly acknowledge their guilt without having a godly sorrow for it run the risk of having their hearts become hardened. When we allow godly sorrow to produce honest and deep repentance in our hearts, our sin areas are severely weakened.

Author **Sinclair Ferguson** wrote the following in his book, *Taking the Christian Life Seriously*:

> *The Christian...knows that he cannot embrace the cross or the Christ who died on it... without renouncing all known sin. We cannot serve two masters—a crucified Messiah who died for our sin, and a sin for which He died. The more we rejoice in the way of salvation, therefore, the more we will mortify sin. That will not make us perfect, because there is no complete mortification in this life. But it will bring us joy in walking in the power of Christ and being delivered from the power of sin.*

Read Tit. 2:11-14 and 1 John 3:1-3, and ask the Holy Spirit to speak to you from these verses.

EXERCISE #15 – Matthew 5:31-32 ~ ONE FLESH

Memory verses: *Matthew 5:31-32*

1. Considering Matt. 5:31-32 and Gen. 2:20-24, why does God esteem marriage so highly?

2. Read Matt. 19:3-9. As best you can, explain the answer Jesus gave in verse 8 to the Pharisees.

3. What do you understand Malachi 2:13-16 to mean?

4. Read 1 Corinthians 7 completely, without stopping. This will enable you to see the context of what the Apostle Paul writes. Now answer the following questions:

In marriage, who has authority over the woman's body?

Who has authority over the man's body?

Is a believer expected to keep marriage vows when married to an unbeliever?

How should the believer handle it if his/her unbelieving spouse wants to separate or divorce?

Are we to be seeking a mate?

What is the difference between a married woman and one who is single?

5. Read Eph. 5:22-33 and 1 Pet. 3:1-7. Write down what behavior is expected of the wife and of the husband as commanded by the Lord.

Wife:

Husband:

#15 – ONE FLESH… GOD'S IDEA!

Matthew 5:31-32 *"Furthermore, it has been said, 'Whoever divorces his wife, let him give her a certificate of divorce.' But I say to you that whoever divorces his wife for any reason except sexual immorality causes her to commit adultery; and whoever marries a woman who is divorced commits adultery."*

From the beginning, God has viewed marriage as sacred. In fact, He planned marriage for both of His two natural sons, the first and second Adam. Both sons of God had marriage in their destiny—for Adam, it was a natural marriage; for Jesus, a spiritual marriage.

Although the subject of marriage may be more relevant for some than for others (like established singles), it is very important that we know what God says about it. He created and established this sacred institution. Unfortunately, over 55% of the marriages in the western world today end in divorce. Eighty percent of those divorcees will remarry; eighty-five percent of them will divorce again. (These statistics were given in 1997.) We need to know what the Word of God says about this issue so that we can have God's perspective on marriage.

The Law and Divorce

In the time of Jesus, the Rabbinical school of Hillel dominated Jewish doctrine and interpretation concerning the subject of divorce. This teaching gave the husband most of the rights and responsibilities regarding the option of divorce. The Pharisees interpreted Moses' teaching on divorce to mean that a man could divorce his wife for any reason, although he was required to repay the wife's dowry if he divorced her for a reason other than adultery. Jesus countered this abusive interpretation that victimized women, restricting divorce to the grounds of sexual immorality.

Read Deut. 24:1-4 to see the divorce procedure established by law. The one restriction placed on remarriage was that the original couple was not to marry one another again if one of them had been married to a third party in the meantime.

In Deut. 22:13-19, 28-29 we see the Old Testament restrictions on divorce. If rape preceded the marriage or if a man falsely accused his wife of immorality, divorce was not permitted. Although divorce and remarriage were not encouraged, they also were not denied under the law. It was assumed that remarriage would follow divorce.

The issue of divorce was raised a few times to Jesus, indicating that it was a much-debated topic among the Pharisees. Most of the debates were over the grounds for which a man might divorce his wife. Some said marital unfaithfulness was cause enough. Others said adultery was to be punished by stoning, not by a simple divorce.

Why was the issue of divorce debated so fiercely? The Jews understood that God through Moses had given His covenant people the law, and they were convinced that it was their duty and privilege to keep God's commandments. By the first century, most Jews were sure that their hope of salvation depended on keeping God's laws as faithfully as possible.

One who kept the law was considered a righteous person and would be able to enter the kingdom of God. Therefore, every law was important, and every legal question was debated intensely, including the law of divorce and remarriage.

The Mosaic Law and God's Ideal

In Matthew 5:21, Jesus introduced a series of *"you have heard it said"* sayings. In each saying, He quoted the Mosaic Law, and then He pointed to the ideal. Each of these sayings is intended to show that although the rulings of the law deal with outward behavior, God is primarily concerned about the state of men's hearts. The law is not the highest moral standard; it is actually a reduced standard! *Love* is the highest standard. Jesus was stressing the sacredness of marriage, reaffirming that it is a binding covenant and should not be broken lightly.

God's Intention for Marriage

Read Matthew 19:3-9. The first century Israelis knew that they could not commit adultery; that was against God's law. So, when they got tired of their wives, they merely wrote a bill of divorce and sent them away. Jesus declared that God did not intend marriage to be disposable; He intended marriage to last a lifetime. Jesus said in **Matt. 19:6**, *"What God has joined, let not man separate."* In this verse, He was referring to the institution of marriage. He was saying that God has ordained the marriage relationship, and that once it is entered into, mere men are not competent to break it apart.

In the first century, scribes and scribal courts were making pronouncements on when it was valid to divorce and when it was not. Mere men were making judgments on an institution that *God* had ordained; yet, the Old Testament granted no ecclesiastical court that privilege. The Pharisees and scribes were deciding for others when a marriage could be dissolved. But God has not made men judges over other men concerning the institution of marriage. Marital intimacy and the possible difficulties of the relationship are not open to the judgment of others.

In Deuteronomy 24, you will notice that no court of elders or priests was involved when a divorce took place. It was up to the husband and wife to determine if the marriage was over. The only legality involved was giving the wife a written bill of divorce and returning her dowry to her. The point that Jesus was making is *not* that a husband and wife are unable to divorce, but that *no ecclesiastical court* has any business saying, "you can" or "you cannot."

We need to realize that each of us bear the responsibility for our own choices. For example, if a couple feels that their marriage is destructive, and that divorce is the better option for them, then their future is their decision and responsibility. They are to seek God's will in the situation, knowing that divorce is the *last* option to be considered and that His grace is sufficient even in difficult marriages. Choosing to forgive and to live by a higher level of love is *far more* preferable than severing a covenantal union. However, if the couple does insist on divorce, that choice is theirs alone. They will be held accountable before the Lord, the Righteous Judge, regarding their decision.

God's View On Divorce

As we see in Malachi 2:11-16, God hates divorce. He does not want anyone to go through the agony of it—the sense of rejection, the emotional tearing and heartbreak, the disappointment, and the guilt and shame that usually accompany it. His goal in giving marriage to us was to strengthen and edify us, not to tear us down; to create a supportive union, not destructive isolation. So, God, Who loves us deeply hates divorce... for *our* sakes! Having said this, we must also realize that at times there can be greater hurt and damage to spouses and children by keeping the marriage together than by divorcing, such as in the case of severe abuse or brutality to family members.

Malachi 2:16 says that divorce is a violent act. It is violent to the spouse and to God's intention for marriage. God's ideal is for spouses to be faithful to one another and to their covenant before Him. He requires just and faithful behavior within the marriage bonds, and hates the selfish and hard-hearted attitudes that destroy this sacred covenant.

Kingdom View of Marriage

• God created marriage to be a uniting of two spirits, two souls, and two bodies.
• It is a divine union of two people and meant to be permanent.
• God expects godly offspring from the union.
• It is a primary cause for joy and gladness.
• It is the biblical metaphor for the coming union of the saints with Jesus.
• It is the most important and binding human commitment and covenant that is made.

Marriage demands toughness, tenderness, and maturity, all of which proceed out of commitment. No marriage will ever be stronger than the commitment that it is built upon. So, commitment is the essence and structure of marriage. Although many marriages begin as adventures in love, they will also, eventually, contain disappointment and hurt. Hopefully, forgiveness and reconciliation will follow the hurt, and love and commitment will deepen. *"Becoming one flesh,"* means that two lives are bound together in every respect. They share themselves physically, emotionally, and intellectually. They share their values and decisions. Through the sharing of all that they are, they become ONE.

Each Marriage Is Unique

Every marriage is as different as the two people involved. No one should compare his or her marriage with those of others. Some marriages are very romantic; others very compatible; some exemplify good teamwork; others produce wonderful children. Not all marriages have every good quality. The 'Hollywood ideal' of romance expressed in movies must be tempered with realism.

Read Hebrews 13:4. Marriage is to be respected and honored by everyone, by single people as well as by those who are married. It is a holy and binding covenant. Marriage partners are to be faithful emotionally, physically, and mentally to each other. They are not to covet another's spouse or flirt with someone else's mate.

Grace Available For Divorcees

For a believer, divorce will always be the last resort to a difficult marriage. Divorce falls short of God's ideal and His glory, and is therefore sin. Yet, God's forgiveness is available for those who fail in marriage just as it is available for those who fail in other areas of life. God's grace and mercy are consistent! Divorce is not the unforgivable sin, although it always carries painful consequences. As we search the Scriptures for guidelines regarding the issues of divorce and remarriage, we must also look through the eyes of grace as we consider those who have suffered the trauma of divorce. God is committed to work with us throughout our earthly lives with His redeeming grace—even in the face of our mistakes and failures. The grace that brings us to salvation continues to operate after we are saved. It is this grace that divorcees need from the rest of us in the Body of Christ.

Remarriage After Divorce

In conclusion, let us look briefly at the issue of remarriage following divorce. Rather than presenting a firm theology in this teaching, we, the writers of this material, would encourage you to talk with your own spiritual leaders. Find out what your congregation believes and why. Sort out this difficult question under the guidance of those that God has placed in leadership over you.

When Remarriage Is Justified

The Bible seems to speak most directly to individuals who initiate a divorce—some of whom do not care what God or His Word says. If, on the other hand, you are someone who had divorce forced on you, the picture is not as clear. We tend to believe that there are four sets of circumstances under which remarriage appears to be scripturally justified. It is when:

1. *the first marriage and divorce occurred prior to salvation.* The promise of all things becoming new in Christ (*see* 2 Cor. 5:17) applies to divorce as well as to all other sins committed in the believer's past.

2. *one's mate is guilty of sexual immorality and is unwilling to repent and live faithfully with the marriage partner.* Each case should be evaluated independently. Here, "immorality" refers to persistent, unrepentant behavior. Divorce and remarriage are an *option* for the faithful partner—not a command.

3. *an unbelieving mate willfully and permanently deserts a believing partner, and there is little or no hope of reviving the former commitment and salvaging the relationship.*

4. *one partner divorces another and remarries (wrongfully), leaving the other partner free to remarry (legitimately) since there can be no reconciliation* (Deut. 24:1-4).

We must not be so concerned about expounding biblical teachings on divorce (e.g., when it is or is not allowed) that we fail to show compassion for the individuals involved. Jesus did not come to burden a weak humanity with a stricter law, but to bring us a message of grace and truth. God is gracious to those who fail in marriage as He is to those who fail in general. We must be agents of healing and help in the midst of the tragedy of divorce, while still upholding the sacred institution of marriage.

EXERCISE #16 – Matthew 5:33-37 ~ INTEGRITY

Memory verses: *Matthew 5:33-37*

1. According to Matthew 5:33, what did the law say about making vows?

2. Look at the following verses concerning vows or oaths and note what you learn. Decide in each instance whether an oath (vow) was wrong.

   Lev. 19:11-12 —

   Num. 30:1-2 —

   Deut. 23:21-23 —

   Eccl. 5:4-5 —

   Psalm 24:3-4 —

   Psalm 15 (especially verse 4) —

3. Read 2 Cor. 1:15-22 a few times, asking the Lord to give you revelation and understanding into these verses. What do you believe God is saying here?

4. For your own evaluation and prayer time with God, answer these questions honestly:

Are you a man or woman of integrity?

Can others trust you?

Do you cheat (in anything! e.g., taxes or contracts)?

Do you tell the whole truth?

Do you exaggerate? Do you tell small lies? Big lies?

Are you failing in any way to let your "yes" be "yes" and your "no" be "no?"

Do you keep your word to your spouse and your children?

Do you keep your word to your friends?

Do you promise things you hope and plan to do, while being unsure that you can actually fulfill your promises?

How honest are you...*really*?

Ask the Lord to remind you to watch over the statements and commitments you make with your mouth. *"Set a guard, O Lord, over my mouth; keep watch over the door of my lips"* (**Ps. 141:3**).

#16 – INTEGRITY

Matthew 5:33-37 *"Again, you have heard that it was said to those of old, 'You shall not swear falsely, but shall fulfill your oaths to the Lord.' But I say to you, do not swear at all: neither by heaven, for it is God's throne; nor by the earth, for it is His footstool; nor by Jerusalem, for it is the city of the great King. Nor shall you swear by your head, because you cannot make one hair white or black. But let your 'Yes' be 'Yes' and your 'No', 'No'; for whatever is more than these is from the evil one."*

Before the coming of the Messiah, God's people were allowed to make oaths as long as they honored them. In Ruth 1:17 and 2 Kings 2:2-6, we see that Ruth and Elisha swore by the Lord, which was acceptable. A vow made an agreement binding. We see it in the incident of Abraham and his servant in Genesis 24:2-3. When his servant put his hand under Abraham's thigh, he was pledging himself by all of his strength that he would fulfill the word of his master. Oaths were a pledge to integrity. One who made a vow was saying, "I am sincere; I will carry out my commitment."

Integrity Makes Swearing Unnecessary

In Matt. 5:33-37, Jesus was conveying, *"The law says not to swear falsely but to do what you promise. I am telling you not to even swear. Your word should be good enough without your strengthening it with an oath."* Jesus was addressing the importance of honesty, declaring that the words 'yes' and 'no' should be able to stand alone because of the integrity of those speaking them. In God's kingdom, integrity makes swearing unnecessary.

In his book, *Sermon on the Mount*, Dwight Pentecost had these comments about Jesus' words:

> *Let your character, your reputation for honesty, your word be so obviously undefiled and true, that no man would think it necessary to put you under an oath because he suspects you of deception..."* Some words can have a double meaning, and some words can be interpreted in two different ways. But there is only one possible way of interpreting yes. Yes does not mean no. There is only one way you can interpret no. You can never interpret that as meaning consent. When you say yes, it means yes. When you say no, it means no. The Lord demanded that one's speech be so trustworthy that men would not have to debate what was meant and interpret what was said. They would know what was meant because he was an honest man.*

In *Dake's Annotated Reference Bible*, we read about James 5:12, that Jews and Arabs were notorious for swearing and taking oaths by heaven, earth, Jerusalem, the Temple, the altar, and different parts of the body. Even simple affirmatives were often accompanied by an oath. It was this practice that caused James to give this command. The phrase, *"...lest you fall into hypocrisy (judgment),"* refers to those who made oaths, believing that they could make them with the mouth while the heart canceled them. Oaths were often made with mental reservations to annul them, regardless of how solemn they were.

This explains why Jesus rebuked the Pharisees and scribes in Matt. 23:16-22. The Pharisees believed they were not responsible to pay vows sworn by the temple or the altar, but Jesus was saying that *all* vows had to be paid.

The Pharisees had developed an inconsistent and hypocritical system of taking oaths, some of which were binding and some which were not. Jesus denounced this system.

What Is Integrity?

God is *very* concerned with our integrity, the honesty of our words and actions. He would agree with the modern proverb, "Say what you mean and mean what you say." Integrity, as defined in the *American Heritage Dictionary*, includes the following meanings:

• moral or ethical strength; standing by principles
• the condition of being free from defects or flaws; possessing stability
• to be honest; having honor, and being upright
• being entirely whole; complete, unified, the same on the inside as on the outside

Read Acts 5:1-11; notice how seriously God takes lying. The couple created a false impression in order to deceive the apostles. We need to remember that everything we do to men, ultimately we do to God (verse 4), so we should live transparently and with integrity. Our lives must be able to withstand close examination by other people. We are to live uprightly—not pretending to be something we are not. *"The integrity of the upright will guide them, but the perversity of the unfaithful will destroy them"* (**Prov. 11:3**).

There are two essential standards for integrity: (1) Make sure everything you own was obtained honestly. (2) When you speak, speak the truth. There is no such thing as a "white lie." We know from John 8:44 that when we lie, we side with the devil. Col. 3:9 and Eph. 4:24-25 say that lying is a part of our old nature that we are to put off. Lying includes exaggeration, all deception, half-truths, hypocrisy, and silence that can imply an untruth.

Keep Your Word Faithfully

When we make a promise, we must keep it, even at our own expense if necessary (*see* Ps. 15:4). People need to be able to trust our word; it is our reputation. When you say you will do something, make sure you do it. Be someone that others can depend on. *"A good name is to be chosen rather than great riches"* (**Prov. 22:1**).

We should have the same testimony that God has in Ps. 89:33-35: He will not allow His faithfulness to fail, He will not break covenant, and He will not alter the words that He has spoken. God cannot lie; He will keep every promise He has made (in general and to us individually). *"God is not a man that He should lie, nor a son of man that He should repent. Has He said, and will He not do? Or has He spoken, and will He not make it good?"* (**Num. 23:19**)

To be godly men and women, we need to have integrity in every area of our lives. We are to speak honestly from a true heart, and to live uprightly without deceit. Before we were born from above, our hearts were deceitful and wicked according to Jer. 17:9. But now we are new creations! **2 Cor. 5:17** says, *"... if anyone is in Christ, he is a new creation; old things have passed away; behold, all things have become new."*

We Are Susceptible to Deception

We can deceive ourselves by hearing the Word of God and not applying it (James 1:22), and by believing there is no sin in our lives when there really is (1 John 1:8).

We can be deceived by people who lie, are argumentative, or cause divisions and offense (Rom. 16:17-18), and by those with extreme beliefs and views (Eph. 4:14).

We can be deceived by the devil when we proudly rely on our intellect rather than trust God and/or stray from the centrality of the gospel in our teaching (2 Cor. 11:3-4). We are also susceptible to deception when the enemy misquotes or misrepresents what God has said (Gen. 3:1).

How Can We Know When We Have Sinned (Since We Can Be Deceived)?

We can ask God daily to search our hearts and convict us, as we read in Psalm 139:23-24. And we can spend quality time in the Scriptures, devouring the truth (Hebrews 4:12). *Having* truth alone will not keep us from deception. We can know truth now and yet be deceived in the future. But *having a love for the truth* will protect us from deception! We must not be satisfied with our present knowledge and understanding of God. Every revelation of truth we have should be continually expanding and deepening into greater truth.

"Cease listening to instruction, my son, and you will stray from the words of knowledge." (**Prov. 19:27**). If we stop listening to instruction, we *will* stray. We need to keep pursuing more truth and revelation! We must never become content with our knowledge and experience of Jesus. Prov. 2:1-6 tells us to hunger and seek after wisdom, knowledge, and understanding.

"...purge out the old leaven, that you may be a new lump, since you truly are unleavened. For indeed Christ, our Passover, was sacrificed for us. Therefore let us keep the feast, not with old leaven, nor with the leaven of malice and wickedness, but with the unleavened bread of sincerity and truth" (**1 Cor. 5:7-8**). Choose to live with sincerity (transparent honesty and genuine purity) and truth (no darkness or hypocrisy). This description speaks of one who does not fear thorough examination of his motives and intents because he has nothing to hide.

For Consideration and Prayer

Are you a man or woman of integrity? Do you keep your promises? Do you tell the truth?

Do you cheat or steal?

Do you *love* hearing the truth – even when it hurts?

Examine your heart for any untruths, areas of hypocrisy, lying, or double standards. Confess these sins before God and ask Him for the gift of repentance. From now on, choose to live honestly and honorably.

EXERCISE #17 – Matthew 5:38-42 ~ EXTRA DISTANCE

Memory verses: *Matthew 5:38-42*

1. Where did the "eye for an eye, tooth for a tooth" law come from? Summarize what is taught in: Ex. 21:23-25, Lev. 24:17-22, and Deut. 19:15-21.

2. According to Mark 12:28-34 and Romans 13:8-10, what is the basis of the law?

3. Read the whole chapter of 1 Corinthians 13. What do verses 4-7 say about love?

4. Living in a fallen world, we will have times of being treated unjustly. In both the law and the gospels, we are forbidden to recompense evil for evil. To take private revenge is prohibited. Read Proverbs 20:22.

   Read how both the Old and New Testaments give the same principle in Prov. 25:21-22 and Rom. 12:20. The law of love is expounded here. Its obvious meaning is: seize the moment of distress to show kindness to the one who hates you.

   Pause and think about your life… In what areas do you avenge yourself?

   Ask the Lord to give you creative ways to show kindness to those who annoy or hurt you.

5. Our possessions belong to the Lord. We are to give or lend them with love and discretion. From these Scriptures, write the rules or truths you find about this subject.

Luke 6:30-34 —

2 Thess. 3:10-12 —

Prov. 3:27 —

2 Cor. 8:13-14 —

Eph. 4:28 —

1 John 3:17 —

#17 – GO THE EXTRA DISTANCE

Matthew 5:38-42 *"You have heard that it was said, 'An eye for an eye, and a tooth for a tooth.' But I say to you, do not resist him who is evil; but whoever slaps you on your right cheek; turn to him the other also. And if anyone wants to sue you, and take your shirt, let him have your coat also. And whoever shall force you to go one mile, go with him two. Give to him who asks of you, and do not turn away from him who wants to borrow from you."*

When Jesus Christ lived on earth over 2000 years ago, Rome occupied Israel. Roman soldiers could force an Israeli civilian to carry his burden the distance of one mile, but no more. The law was designed to keep a soldier from taking advantage of a civilian. Since righteousness is to be practical, Jesus addressed a current situation of His day, giving His listeners a practical illustration. He taught them through the example of "going the second mile" that love goes the extra distance, beyond what it is compelled to do.

God's Standard Of Justice

Read Deut. 19:15-21. God gave a clear standard of justice for the priests and judges to follow, which did several distinct things:

1. It protected against unjust retribution—getting more or taking more than what was fair. They were to take only one eye for one lost eye, not both eyes! Many times men want more than what is fair because of vengeance and greed. Just retribution kept the judge fair, prohibiting his receiving a bribe or showing partiality.

2. It was a deterrent, causing a man to think twice before committing a crime. He knew that the penalty would be exactly what he inflicted on his victim.

3. It held a man accountable for his behavior. Often when people break the law, they want mercy rather than judgment.

4. It protected innocent people, servants, and the poor from wicked men.

The judges were to judge and punish offenders. The offended person was not to get his own revenge. When we avenge ourselves, we foster resentment and violence, both of which Jesus never condoned.

The Law for The Ungodly

Read 1 Tim. 1:8-10. Anytime a judicial system protects the guilty and lets them go free, or allows the guilty to pay a lesser punishment than what their crime deserves, lawlessness is encouraged. Chaos abounds in the world today because of increasing humanistic philosophies that give freedoms without holding to absolutes. In our liberality, we are destroying ourselves. *"Because the sentence against an evil work is not executed speedily, therefore the heart of the sons of men is fully set in them to do evil"* (**Eccl. 8:11**).

Higher Law of Love

In Matthew 5, Jesus was not altering the law; rather, He was showing us that those who are righteous are controlled by a much higher law. He was calling for this higher law to be obeyed—the law of love as opposed to a law of legalism. Love has always been the true intent of the law. It is love for others rather than a fear of punishment that should keep us from mistreating and sinning against people.

In Matthew 5:39, Jesus said not to resist an evil person. He was preaching meekness and love. The word 'resist' is the Greek word, **anthistemi**, which suggests vigorous opposing while standing one's ground. This type of resistance reveals stubbornness and rebellion. We are to resist the devil (*see* James 4:7), but not resist a person out of our selfishness and rebellion.

"Love does no harm to a neighbor; therefore love is the fulfillment of the law" (**Rom. 13:10**). Since *"love is the fulfillment of the law,"* we are not *required* to demand an eye for an eye. We can fulfill the law by forgiving and turning the other cheek. A chief purpose of the law was to protect a person from unjust retribution, and to cause a man to think twice before committing a crime. But the higher law of love is fulfilled when we "turn the other cheek." This is expressing God's love.

If we are perfect as our Father is perfect, we have to go beyond the legalism of the law to the true intent of the law, which is love. We should respond in the grace of God to those who abuse our privileges and demand our possessions. We are to show them the meekness of Jesus and the mercy and goodness of God, which can lead them to repentance.

In Matthew 5:38-42, Jesus is not teaching the doctrine of pacifism. These verses are not dealing with the issues of going to war or settling national disputes. They apply to individuals, not to judicial systems or nations. God is also not saying that we are to keep turning the other cheek until we are battered to death! We are not to give away our possessions until we have nothing left. Allowing others to abuse us is enabling evil that will bring them under judgment, which is an unloving thing to do. Whatever we do, we are to do out of love. Love always desires the highest good of another.

Love Never Considers Itself

God calls us to live beyond the letter of the law. He is taking us beyond a legalism that wants to know how far it can go, to a love that *never considers itself at all*. Love will give up its rights to demonstrate the character of God. Love does not hold onto its personal possessions. It freely gives to him who asks or wants to borrow. Love is more concerned about another's need than about holding on to what it has. The giver then takes on the character of Jesus, whose nature is to give. Jesus did not say it would be more natural or easier to give than to receive, but that it would be more blessed (*see* Acts 20:35). When we turn the other cheek, give away our coats, give to him who asks, and love our enemies, then we are showing that we care more about others than we do about ourselves.

Revenge Is *Not* Ours

Not only are we to refrain from the act of retaliation, we must not even *desire* to get even! God requires holiness of heart as well as holiness of life. We are not only to refrain from returning evil for evil, but we are to return good for evil, to bless those who curse us, and to pray for those who use us.

Just as people take advantage of God, so they will take advantage of us when we imitate Him. And just as God's character never changes because of man's actions, so our character should not change because of what others do.

In this life, we will have times of being treated unjustly, and the Scriptures forbid us to take revenge. **Prov. 20:22** says, *"Do not say, 'I will recompense evil'; wait for the Lord, and He will save you."* We must allow Jesus, the Judge and Lord of the whole earth, to mete out justice and vengeance to those who wrong us. We do this because:

• God commands it.

• Vengeance belongs to Him (Rom. 12:19) and if we take it, we rob Him of His right.

• Jesus is our example, and He left judgment to God (1 Peter 2:23).

• If we do not forgive others, God will not forgive us (Matt. 6:15).

Do We Ever Resist Evil?

The Lord gave us instructions about how to deal with evil in other people. Consider Matt. 18:15-17. In dealing with a sinning brother, we are to challenge the wrong done, examine the offense, and discipline the transgressor.

Jesus dealt with sin in others through confrontation, as in John 2:13-17. In dealing with evil in the Temple, He did not show passive resistance. He demonstrated aggression against the sin. Read John 18:22-23. When struck by an officer, Jesus did not turn the other cheek, but challenged the man who hit him. He did not answer force with force, but He did expose and rebuke the wrong done.

If we never resist the wrongs imposed upon us, then we are allowing, condoning, and encouraging those sins. Lawbreakers are to be brought before the court. It is not our place to take vengeance into our *own* hands. However, it *is* our place to turn the lawbreakers over to God and to those whom God has put in authority.

We must not encourage evil in the wicked, yet at the same time, we must conduct ourselves as those whose values are eternal. We are not to take trifling matters to court (like suing someone who merely steals a coat), but we must know when evil men are to be taken to justice. We must know when to forgive a matter and let it go, and when to press charges while forgiving in our hearts.

Maintain a Generous Spirit

Ruling our own spirits is more important than clinging to our material possessions. Our time and strength can be devoted to eternal pursuits if we do not waste them over trifling matters. Holding on to petty hurts and resentments in our hearts will prevent us from being free to hear the Lord's voice and to serve Him wholeheartedly.

In all three areas that Jesus addressed, we are to resist returning evil for the evil we experience, whether it is insults to our person, attacks upon our possessions, or the deprivation of our personal liberties.

Looking again at Matthew 5:42, Jesus speaks of the generous spirit that we are to have. We are to generously return good for evil. It is better to give and lend to the undeserving than to cause strife by selfish refusal. Our possessions belong to the Lord and are to be offered (with wisdom) to those who need them.

EXERCISE #18 – Matthew 5:43-48 ~ LOVE

> **Memory verses:** *Matthew 5:43-48*

1. After reading Matthew 5:43-48, list the specific commands Jesus gives us in these verses.

2. Compare what you just read in Matthew 5 with Rom. 12:14-21. List any new insights or instructions you see.

3. Read Romans 13:8-10 and then rewrite verse 8 in your own words.

4. Read Lev. 19:16-18 and notice the clear guidelines that God gave concerning the treatment of neighbors. List them. Now read the story Jesus told in Luke 10:25-37. Who is our neighbor?

   Who is *your* neighbor?

5. Write down some practical ways you can love your neighbors. Ask the Holy Spirit for ideas and wisdom regarding this.

6. Read Matthew 5:48 again, considering the context of the passage. Rewrite the command according to your understanding of what Jesus meant.

#18 – INDISCRIMINATE LOVE

Matthew 5:43-48 *"You have heard that it was said, 'You shall love your neighbor, and hate your enemy.' But I say to you, love your enemies, and pray for those who persecute you in order that you may be sons of your Father who is in heaven; for He causes His sun to rise on the evil and the good, and sends rain on the righteous and the unrighteous. For if you love those who love you, what reward have you? Do not even the tax-gatherers do the same? And if you greet your brothers only, what do you do more than others? Do not even the Gentiles do the same? Therefore you are to be perfect, as your heavenly Father is perfect."*

The Pharisees of Jesus' day had misinterpreted Deut. 23:3-6 and Lev. 19:18 to say that the Jews were to love their neighbors, but were allowed to hate their enemies. But God had never said that! God has holy standards and blesses righteousness, yet He does not discriminate in whom He loves. He sends rain on the just and the unjust. John 3:16 says that God loves everyone in the world and wants *all* to have everlasting life. We are to love as God does—indiscriminately.

Committed To Love

In Matthew 5:44, the Greek word used for love is **agape**. Agape is defined as an unselfish affection or tenderness for another person without expecting anything in return. It chooses to seek a person's welfare and highest good, regardless of the worth of that person.

According to the Greek tenses used in this passage, the commands to love and pray are to be obeyed as one's general habit or committed lifestyle. It refers to a commitment to action (*"Love and keep on loving; pray and keep on praying. Do not stop! Keep it up as a habit."*). This is a different tense than we see in verses 46-47, *"If you love... if you greet..."* This tense indicates a single action, not continuous action. This refers to a one-time event. Anyone can show love once and greet someone once. But we are called to repeatedly love, bless, and pray for others! Even in the face of rejection, we are to continue to love!

Matthew 5:44 says, *"Love your enemies..."* Enemies are considered to be people who are hostile toward us, who are unfriendly, antagonistic, or argumentative. *"Pray for those who persecute you."* The Greek word translated "persecute" means to put to flight or intimidate. We are to pray for those who intimidate us! The *American Heritage Dictionary* defines 'persecute' like this: to harass or oppress with ill treatment; to annoy persistently; to bother. We have all had people in our lives that harassed or bothered us!

Sons of God Love As God Does

Matthew 5:45 says, *"prove yourselves"* to be mature sons of your Father. Offspring resemble their parents; there is an identifying likeness between them. We prove our close relationship to God when we resemble Him in character. We see that God blesses all men; He is as kind to evil men as He is to those who are good. As His sons and daughters, we are to be like Him in loving and caring for others whether they are good or evil.

Read Lev. 19:18, 34 again. God's people were commanded not to bear a grudge, and to love strangers as they loved themselves. Strangers in the ancient world were those from a foreign country or those who had a different nationality. How well do we love strangers today? Do we reach out to the foreign or transient people in our societies?

Mature Love

Return to Matthew 5:48. Each of us will give an account to God for our actions. No matter what others do, *we* are to be perfect in love the same way that our heavenly Father is perfect in love. The word translated 'perfect' is the Greek word **teleios**. **Teleios** refers to that which is finished, complete, or perfect. It denotes maturity when it is used in reference to believers. So, Jesus was saying that we are to be mature in our love for others; we should desire the good of all men. Our love should be complete, a finished product that reveals God's handiwork in our hearts and character.

According to Mark 12:28-31, loving God is to be the highest priority of our lives. Our second priority is to love our neighbor to the same degree that we love ourselves.

How Do We Love Ourselves?

Our love for ourselves is fervent, active, habitual, and permanent. A normal self-love respects one's own interests, especially spiritual and eternal interests. It prompts us to be concerned about our welfare, seeking it diligently and grieving for any personal calamity. In the same way, we should pursue our neighbor's welfare and have respect for his interests. 1 Pet. 4:7-10 exhorts us to love all believers fervently, and to have an open heart and open home toward them. We are to use our God-given gifts to serve one another.

Who Is Our Neighbor?

Our neighbor is anyone who has a need. Luke 10:29-37 reveals that the one who loved his neighbor was he who showed active mercy on him. He took care of the wounded man at his personal expense.

We are to be an extension of God's love to others. The Lord never said, "Love Me with all that you are, and that is enough." It is not enough to just read our Bibles and pray, praise the Lord, and attend worship services. We must also be available to serve others. Touching God without touching people is selfish, but touching people without having touched God first is lifeless! We need to daily receive grace from the Lord through prayer and reading the Scriptures, because He is the source of our life! We have nothing to offer others if we do not encounter Him.

Loving God Is Foundational

Read John 21:15-17. When Jesus commanded Peter to feed His sheep, He based that command on Peter's love for *HIM*, not on Peter's love for the sheep. Of course, Peter was to love the sheep, but the foundation of his ministry was a love for the Lord, not for the people. Our ability to love people springs from our deep love for God. But we cannot love God without loving man.

Read 1 John 3:16-17 and 4:20-21. Loving each other should naturally follow our loving the Lord, because the more we love God, the more we love what He loves. The closer we are to Him, the more our hearts beat in step with His, and what is precious to Him becomes precious to us. Because God's heart is for people, we love them, too.

Jesus said, *"It is enough for a disciple that he be like his teacher, and a servant like his master"* (**Matt. 10:25a**). Since God's nature is love, our focus in life should be learning to love as He does. All of our training here is training in love. We are not perfecting human love; we are embracing God's love. His love is not based on the performance of the loved one. Agape love arises from a heart of love, regardless of the worth of the recipient of that love.

Love Without Selfishness

1 Corinthians 13:4-7 gives us a description of the love that God wants us to offer others: unselfish love with no self-interest defiling it. All spiritual growth is growth primarily in one area, agape love. The first commandment is to love the Lord with all that we are, *then* to love others. If we love people or the ministry more than we love the Lord, we are guilty of idolatry. When we become jealous and possessive of those we care for, we are not able to have clear minds for discernment and righteous judgment. The more we love the Lord, the more we will be prone to *properly* care for His people.

Read Matt. 19:16-22. The young ruler obeyed all the commandments; he did everything right. Yet he did not love his neighbor as himself; he was unwilling to sell his possessions and give to the poor. He was *right*, but he was not *righteous*.

Notice in Ephesians 5 that after the Apostle Paul commanded the Ephesians to be followers of God, his first words of practical obedience were *"walk in love, as Christ also has loved us and laid down His life for us"* (**Eph. 5:2a**). It *is* possible to walk in love because God's Spirit is in us, His love is released in our hearts, and His abundant grace is available to us.

Jesus Requires More From Us

Jesus has good reason to require more from His people than from unregenerate men. We, His disciples, are recipients of His everlasting love, redeemed at infinite cost, and filled with the Holy Spirit. We *should* produce more love than others! We should be showing God's overwhelming, indiscriminate love through our lives.

Author **Rick Joyner** wrote about love in the end-times in his book, Harvest II:

The love that is to be revealed in the saints will be so profound that in the time of greatest darkness they will love every minute of every day. They will love every person, even those who kill them! As fear is the greatest power of the evil one, so love is the greatest power of heaven, and when they collide in their last and ultimate battle, love will win. This is the preparation for the saints for the last battle—to grow in love, faith, and obedience. This will bring power over all the powers of darkness that will be released in the last days, which will be rooted in hatred, fear, and lawlessness.

Referring to Matt. 5:48, to be mature and perfect in love is our goal. We are to have unconditional love for others as our Father does. Even though we may never love perfectly at all times, we must have the same attitude that the Apostle Paul had when he said in **Phil. 3:14a**, *"I press on toward the goal...."*

For Consideration and Prayer

Do you love unselfishly, unconditionally, and indiscriminately? Do you continue loving even in the face of rejection and/or persecution? How well do you love the stranger (foreigner) in your society?

Ask the Lord to give you a fresh baptism of love for others, and to help you express that love in ways that glorify Him.

EXERCISE #19 – Matthew 6:1-4 ~ THE GIFT OF GIVING

Memory verses: *Matthew 6:1-4*

1. Read through the entire chapter of Matthew 6. When you have finished, write down anything you sense the Holy Spirit wants to bring to your attention.

2. Ask the Lord to show you if you are practicing your righteousness to be seen of others rather than by Him only. Confess to Him any sin of which He convicts you.

3. Read Deuteronomy 15:7-11. What does God say about giving to the poor?

4. Rewrite Proverbs 11:24-25 in your own words.

5. According to Psalm 41:1-3, what are some blessings that will come to those who give to the poor?

6. What does Proverbs 19:17, 21:13, and 28:27 reveal to you about God's heart for those with needs?

7. After reading Mark 10:17-22 write down the spiritual principle(s) you see in this passage.

8. Explain Jesus' words to His disciples in Mark 10:23-25.

9. Examine God's example of extravagant, lavish giving in the following verses: John 3:16, Luke 12:32, Romans 6:23 and 8:32, 2 Cor. 9:15, and Eph. 2:8. What are some of the blessings He has freely given to us?

#19 – THE GIFT OF GIVING

Matthew 6:1-4 *"Take heed that you do not do your charitable deeds before men, to be seen by them. Otherwise, you have no reward from your Father in heaven. Therefore, when you do a charitable deed, do not sound a trumpet before you as the hypocrites do in the synagogues and in the streets, that they may have glory from men. Assuredly, I say to you, they have their reward. But when you do a charitable deed, do not let your left hand know what your right hand is doing, that your charitable deed may be in secret; and your Father who sees in secret will Himself reward you openly."*

Disciplines Toward Godly Character

In Matthew 6, Jesus teaches on five disciplines that will help us develop the attitudes that He talked about in Matthew 5. Giving, praying, fasting, storing treasures in Heaven, and trusting Him to meet our daily needs are the chief means by which we develop godly character and keep our hearts clean before God. These disciplines challenge wrong actions, attitudes, and motives, and keep us focused in our pursuit of the Lord and His kingdom.

It is not accidental that these disciplines follow after Jesus' teaching on having mature love for one another. When we fail to love, and thus keep resentment, prejudices, and judgments in our hearts, we block the flow of God's blessings toward us. We can pray, fast, and generously give, but if our hearts are not right with God and others, we lose the benefits of those disciplines.

Matthew 6:1 – The phrase, 'charitable deeds,' can also be termed 'righteousness acts.' In verses 2-4, the word translated as 'alms' in Greek is **elee–mosune**, which refers to mercy and pity, but specifically it points to money given to the poor.

Motivation for Giving

Jesus said, *"When* you give..." and not, *if* you give. It is as if Jesus says, *"Of course you will give to the needy. So when you do, do it like this... and don't do it like that..."* We are not to give for the purpose of receiving recognition or glory from man.

Read Acts 10:1-2. Cornelius' testimony was that he feared God, was sincerely religious, generously gave charitable gifts (alms), and prayed to God always. In Acts 10:4, 30-33, and 44-46, we see that God responded to the prayers *and to the alms*! Both prayers and alms are a memorial to God.

Give Generously

James 2:14-17 says faith without works is dead. An insulated faith that helps no one is not the same faith as that of the Messiah Who laid down His life for others. Our faith should motivate us to give to others as generously and freely as the Lord has given to us! Jesus said, *"Freely you have received, freely give"* (**Matt. 10:8**).

Read Luke 12:13-21, 31-34. A key for keeping our hearts free of covetousness and greed is to be a generous giver. Jesus exhorted His disciples to seek God's kingdom as their first priority. He told them to sell what they have and give alms, storing their treasure in heaven rather than on earth. Although it is wise for believers and unbelievers alike to prepare well for daily expenses as well as for retirement, believers in Jesus are also to prioritize storing treasures in heaven where they are eternally secure.

Read 1 Tim. 6:17-19. We are commanded to trust in God, rather than to trust in earthly, uncertain riches. God gives us many good things to enjoy, such as friendships, family, children, food, and nature. We are to be rich in good works, ready to give, and willing to share what we have. These are a few ways we can accumulate treasure in heaven.

Eternal Investments

If we are eternally minded, we will spend our time, energy, and finances building the kingdom of God on earth through sharing Jesus with others, discipling new believers, and supporting fruitful ministries. To hoard wealth here can be a waste of time and money, because this world is temporary. Investing in that which is eternal is of most value! Jim Elliot, a missionary who was murdered by the people he went to evangelize, wrote, *"He is no fool who gives what he cannot keep in order to gain that which he cannot lose."*

Two Principles Of Giving

Read 2 Cor. 9:6-9 and notice the two spiritual principles about giving. (1) We reap according to what we sow. Generous giving will result in plenty, and miserly giving yields feeble results. (2) God loves for us to give cheerfully, lavishly, and extravagantly! That is the kind of giver He is!

There was a millionaire in Texas who began regularly giving God 10% of his income when he first met Jesus. Then he increased his giving to 30%... to 50%... and to 75%. Eventually, he was giving 90% of his income to God, and keeping only 10%. Even then, he could not keep up with all the finances God poured in! As Evangelist Oral Roberts said, *"You cannot out–give God!"*

Giving To Alleviate Need

When God knows He can trust us not to hold onto or idolize any of His blessings, but to hold them loosely in order to share them with others, He will use us as channels of His financial and material blessings.

Read Luke 10:30-35 and notice the contrasting attitudes in this story. The attitude of the robber was *"What's yours is mine, and I'm going to take it."* The attitudes of the Priest and Levite were *"What's mine is mine, and I'm going to keep it."* The attitude of the Samaritan was *"What's mine is yours, and I'm going to give it."* Our attitudes should be like the Samaritan's! We must be willing to give when we see a need, and/or when the Lord prompts us. Our gifts need not be limited to finances; we can also give our time, talents, and practical help. Read 1 John 3:17-18.

"And though I bestow all my goods to feed the poor, and though I give my body to be burned, but have not love, it profits me nothing" (**1 Cor. 13:3**). Our giving must be motivated by love. Do not give hoping to receive in return, or to "force" God to give back to you. The Lord gives lavishly, hilariously, and loves it when His children do, too. When we do, we reflect one of His chief character traits – that of generosity. *Now* is always good time to invest in the kingdom of God and in the lives of others!

Suggestions For Prayer

Thank the Lord for His generosity towards you.

If you are guilty of covetousness, stinginess, or greed, confess that to God, repent and renounce those carnal attitudes.

Do you give? If so, why? What are your motives in giving?

Ask the Lord how you can increase your giving and where He would like some of your resources to go.

EXERCISE #20 – Matthew 6:5-8 ~ PRAYING IN SECRET

Memory verses: *Matthew 6:5-8*

1. As a believer in Jesus, you have been given a special privilege, according to Hebrews 4:16. What is it and why was it given to you?

2. After reading Matthew 6:5-8, write down the things Jesus told us *not* to do when praying. What are the reasons He gave?

3. Examine your prayer life: do you pray more in private or in public? Why?

4. Where did Jesus do much of His praying? For some clues, read Matt. 14:23, Mark 1:35, and Luke 5:16.

5. According to Matt. 6:8, the Father knows our needs before we ask Him. Why then should we bring our needs to Him in prayer?

6. What conditions for prayer do you find in the following verses?

Psalm 66:18 –

Mark 11:23-24 –

John 15:7 –

1 John 5:14-15 –

James 1:5-8 –

7. Author and preacher, Dwight Pentecost, wrote the following lines about Matthew 6:5-6:

"Two who are in love require privacy to properly communicate. Little real communication is possible in public. In the busyness of life, communication with the Father is impossible unless there is privacy. That's why the Lord said if we are to communicate with the Father we must go to our room and shut the door. As soon as we are conscious of one observer, the privacy necessary to intimately communicate is gone, and we become conscious of the observer rather than the Father with whom we are talking."

Private prayer will tremendously aid your growth in godliness. It strengthens your spirit and subdues your carnal nature. Ask the Lord how you can improve your prayer life; write down any instructions He gives you and a few goals you have for your devotional life.

#20 – PRAYING IN SECRET

Matthew 6:5-8 *"And when you pray, you shall not be like the hypocrites. For they love to pray standing in the synagogues and on the corners of the streets, that they may be seen by men. Assuredly, I say to you, they have their reward. But you, when you pray, go into your room, and when you have shut your door, pray to your Father who is in the secret place; and your Father who sees in secret will reward you openly. And when you pray, do not use vain repetitions as the heathen do. For they think that they will be heard for their many words. Therefore do not be like them. For your Father knows the things you have need of before you ask Him."*

If we engage in prayer in order to be seen by men, then we have our reward on earth, and God is not obligated to answer our prayers. We have received our reward—the attention and respect of fellow human beings. Jesus called those men who prayed in order to be seen by others "hypocrites." By definition, prayer is a means of communicating with God. To pray to God only to be noticed by man is pretense—pretending to meet with God, yet really only meeting with man.

Praying in public has its place (Jesus, Paul, and the disciples prayed in public), but we are cautioned against vainglory, which is seeking to commend ourselves to others. We are to pray to get God's attention, not the attention of man! We should pray in public with the same attitudes as we do in private–those of humility and sincerity–in order to see God's will come on earth and in the lives of men and women. Corporate prayer is powerfully effective, as we see in Matthew 18:19-20. The two main motives for true prayer are: (1) to enjoy communion with God while building a relationship with Him, and (2) to get things done; to work together with God.

Praying In Private

Read Psalm 62:8. Pouring out one's heart before God is usually done in private, intimate prayer. It is an expression of emotions and personal thoughts, an unloading of one's innermost self to the Lord. Although this kind of praying is often for one's own benefit, it may also be an expression of intercession on behalf of another. Generally, if we freely express ourselves in private prayer, we will find our public praying to be more concise and to the point. If we neglect private prayer, we may ramble and be unnecessarily wordy when praying in public.

When Jesus told His disciples to find a secret, enclosed place to pray, He was saying in effect, *"Shut out from your mind all thoughts of others and have respect for God alone. Do not be occupied with what is visible, but with what* (Who) *is invisible."* Jesus encouraged them to get away from all distractions and disturbances to find a quiet, secluded place where they could have unhindered communion with God.

Praying Before And After Ministry

As we look at the earthly life of Jesus, we see that He went from one place of prayer to the next. At the beginning of His ministry, He went out before daylight and prayed alone (Mark 1:35). In the middle of His ministry after feeding the 5000 men (plus women and children), He climbed a mountain to pray alone (Matt. 14:23).

At the end of His ministry (Luke 22:39-40), He went to a garden to pray. He even prayed on the cross. His death did not mark the end of His prayer life; even now Jesus is interceding for us in heaven (Hebrews 7:25).

If we are to be like Jesus, we must be a praying people! Jesus never reached a place where He could minister to others without an active prayer life. We, too, will never attain a place of spiritual maturity where we no longer need to commune with God. Jesus has given us the Holy Spirit to help us pray (*see* Rom. 8:26-27). One way He helps is by birthing in us a *desire* to pray. We also need to embrace the *discipline* of prayer. Prayer must become a natural habit for us. Jesus was disciplined in prayer, and as a result, the power of God flowed out from Him. If we want to see the power of God in our lives, we too must have a consistent prayer life. We need times in God's presence where we are renewed, refreshed, and refueled. No man is greater than his prayer life.

After we discipline ourselves to pray, prayer moves to the third level—from desire to discipline to *delight*. We delight in co–laboring with God in prayer. We love being in His presence, and we rejoice in His manifested power and provision. We find prayer to be exciting and fulfilling!

Look at Matthew 6:6 again. The Father waits in the secret place for us to meet with Him. He is *already* there, waiting! Notice that the singular second personal pronoun is used here eight times (e.g., you, your). This emphasizes again our need for personal time alone with God. The world must be entirely shut out. He loves corporate times of prayer, but those alone do not satisfy His heart. He longs for intimate times alone with each of us. Read Song of Songs 2:10, 14.

While we should avoid seeking the praise of men through our public prayers, we should also guard against intimidation and being unfaithful in public prayer because of the fear of man. The prophet Daniel continued to pray with his windows open, unafraid of being seen and punished for it. Praying over our food in public is expressing thanks and reverence to God, and we should not be afraid to do so. To pray publicly in order to be recognized for our spirituality is wrong, yet to fear man and thus avoid prayer in public is also wrong.

Persistent Prayer

In Matthew 6:7, Jesus was not speaking against our asking for the same thing again and again; He was condemning the practice of reducing the duty and privilege of prayer to that of performing religious acts. To repeat particular phrases over and over, thinking we will be heard for our religiosity is what Jesus condemned. God does not listen to us based on our performance—in this case, repetitious prayers—but because of our faith and motives.

There is validity in praying the same prayers many times. King David often asked God to teach him His statutes. The Apostle Paul asked three times for the thorn in his flesh to be removed. Jesus prayed three times in the Garden of Gethsemane concerning the cup of suffering He was facing. **Matt. 7:7**, written in the Greek continual present tense literally says: *"ask and keep on asking... seek and keep on seeking... knock and keep on knocking."*

There is a false teaching that says if you pray more than once for anything, you are not praying in faith. There ARE times that we pray in faith and then thank God, knowing the answer is on the way. There are other times when faithful, persistent, and ongoing prayer is what the Lord expects from us.

Read Luke 11:5-13. Persistent, bold supplication receives a response. Besides praying for our own concerns, sometimes God will give us a prayer burden for someone else, and we are to pray for that person until the burden lifts or the answer comes.

Matthew 6:8 says our Father knows our needs *before* we ask Him. Since God knows our needs in advance, why do we pray? When author C.S. Lewis was asked this question, he said, *"God could have chosen to do His work in any fashion He wanted, but He chose to do it (in part) in response to prayer."*

We also need to realize that we are *commanded* to pray! When we pray, we honor God by acknowledging His sovereignty and our dependence on Him. Prayer should be seen as a privilege rather than a duty. Instead of thinking, "How much time should I spend in prayer?" we should think, "How much time am I allowed to spend in prayer and not neglect the other responsibilities of life?"

The Secret of Victory

Prayer is the secret of powerful, victorious living. It is our communication with the Lord that sustains us and directs our steps. Communing with Him comforts our hearts, clears our minds, and gives us security and confidence. It is the means by which we become acquainted with God's heart. We enter into real prayer with all of our soul (mind, emotions, and will), and through this spiritual discipline (more than by any other), we become more like Jesus.

Revivalist author, Leonard Ravenhill, wrote, *"There is no place on earth where one can shake off the dust of this world like that of the prayer closet. There is no place where the glory of God so impregnates the soul as the prayer closet, where we are still and know that He is God. The most transforming experience to life and vision is prayer."*

Read Isaiah 50:4-5. Prayer involves two–way communication; we should be listening for God's voice daily in the same way that He listens for ours daily. Upon awakening in the morning, we should pray, "Lord, awaken, open my ears to hear as Your disciple. Give me a word to speak to those who are weary today."

In Psalm 5:1-3, King David promotes consistency and order in daily prayer. In verse 3, the word 'direct' is the Hebrew word, **arak**, which indicates an ordered strategy. David advocates a well–planned order to praying, a daily prayer strategy with purpose and meaning. In Matt. 6:9-13, Jesus gives us an ideal strategy, which we will look at in the next several sessions.

For Consideration And Prayer

Do you have a secret place of prayer? If so, where is it?

Do you regularly pour out your heart to God?

Do you give the Lord time to speak to you or do you do all of the talking when you pray?

Take some time to pray now that your prayer life will expand and deepen, become more effective, and increasingly bless the Lord and satisfy you.

Pray that God will increase your capacity for spending time in His presence and for co-working with Him in intercession to see His kingdom expand on earth.

EXERCISE #21 – Matthew 6:9 ~ BLESS HIS NAME!

Memory verse: *Matthew 6:9*

1. Read Matthew 6:9-13. Why did Jesus give His disciples a pattern for prayer?

2. What are some of the covenant names of God? In other words, what does He promise to be or to do for us who are in covenant with Him (e.g., Psalm 23:1 – The Lord is my shepherd: Adonai–Roi)?

3. Read Romans 8:15-16. What personal title are believers allowed to call God?

4. Explain how you feel about being in a personal/family relationship with the Almighty God.

5. Read Exodus 20:7 and 2 Tim. 2:19. What are some ways that God's name is taken in vain?

6. Psalm 34:3, 92:1, and 99:3 give us instructions regarding the Lord's name. What are they?

7. What are some promises that believers have regarding the name of the Lord? Consider Proverbs 18:10, 91:14, and 9:9-10. Do your own Bible study to find more answers.

#21 – BLESS HIS NAME!

Matthew 6:9-13 *"In this manner, therefore, pray: Our Father in heaven, hallowed be Your name. Your kingdom come. Your will be done on earth as it is in heaven. Give us this day our daily bread. And forgive us our debts, as we forgive our debtors. And do not lead us into temptation. But deliver us from the evil one. For Yours is the kingdom and the power and the glory forever. Amen."*

When Jesus gave this prayer to His disciples, He was giving them a model prayer of topics to cover. In the first century, a Rabbi generally taught by giving topics of truth. Under each topic he provided a complete outline. What we know as the "Lord's Prayer" is a group of six topics to be covered and expanded in prayer under the guidance of the Holy Spirit.

Overview of the Outline

1. *"Our Father in heaven, hallowed be Your name."* Jesus invites us to come into His Father's presence by acknowledging that He is our Father also. Through Jesus, we have entered into a blood covenant with the Father and have a personal relationship with Him. We praise the Lord's name and all that His name stands for regarding His nature and works.

2. *"Your kingdom come, Your will be done."* Pray for God's will to be done in your life, and in the lives of your family members and friends. Pray for His kingdom to come and His will to be done in the lives of the spiritual and national leaders of your country.

3. *"Give us this day our daily bread."* Bring to the Lord your needs and request His provision.

4. *"And forgive us our debts as we forgive our debtors."* Ask God's forgiveness for any sin you may not have confessed and repented of yet. Make sure you have forgiven anyone who has wronged you. Choose to walk in forgiveness and mercy with everyone all day.

5. *"And lead us not into temptation, but deliver us from the evil one."* Pray for a pure heart so that temptation will not appeal to you. Pray that you will not enter temptation through carelessness or rebellion. Ask the Lord to place a hedge of protection around you, your family, and your possessions.

6. *"For Yours is the kingdom and the power and the glory."* Return to praise as you end your prayer, acknowledging that the kingdom and all the power and glory belong to God.

In this session, we will consider the first part of the prayer in verse 9, *"Our Father who art in heaven, hallowed be Your name."* According to Psalm 100:4, we *"enter His gates with thanksgiving and His courts with praise."* We hallow and praise the Lord's name because it denotes His nature and character. When we praise His name, we praise Him for Who He is. **Deut. 32:3-4** says, *"For I proclaim the name of the Lord: ascribe greatness to our God. He is the Rock, His work is perfect; for all His ways are justice, a God of truth and without injustice; righteous and upright is He."*

We need to know the meanings of God's covenant name(s) and praise Him for what His names reveal about Him. When we praise His name, we praise Him for Who He is, not merely for what He does. His *doing* comes out of His *being*.

Adonai–Tsidkenu	–	"The Lord our Righteousness"
Adonai–M'kaddesh	–	"The Lord Who Sanctifies"
Adonai–Shalom	–	"The Lord is Peace"
Adonai–Shammah	–	"The Lord is There"
Adonai–Rophe	–	"The Lord Who Heals"
Adonai–Yireh	–	"The Lord Who Sees and Provides"
Adonai–Nissi	–	"The Lord my Banner"
Adonai–Roi	–	"The Lord my Shepherd"

We will look at these eight compound names to see how they reflect the salvation expressed in Jesus. As *Adonai–Tsidkenu,* Jesus became sin for us so that we could *"become the righteousness of God in Him"* (**2 Cor. 5:21b**). 1 Cor. 1:30 says He is our righteousness. Our sins—past, present, and future—are all atoned for because of Jesus' death and resurrection. His blood is more than sufficient for all of our sins; we receive His forgiveness by faith.

The second compound name of God, *Adonai–M'kaddesh*, refers to the Lord Who sanctifies, sets apart, and separates unto Himself. God's Spirit indwells us, empowering us to live holy lives (*see* 1 Cor. 6:11; 1 Thess. 5:23). The blood of Jesus not only takes away our sin, it also breaks the power of sin over us. His blood does not overlook sin; it *overcomes* it. Bless His name—the Lord Who sanctifies. We don't have to sin anymore!

God's compound name, *Adonai–Shalom,* means, "the Lord is peace." This represents the contentment, harmony, and wholeness the Lord makes available to us. Eph. 2:14,17 tells us that Jesus has broken down the dividing walls between man and God and between man and man. He *has* brought peace to us.

Adonai–Shammah signifies "the Lord is there." This name indicates that God is always with us. Hebrews 13:5 says He never leaves or forsakes us. We are the temple of the Holy Spirit and He lives within us (*see* John 14:17; 1 Cor. 3:16). He promises to stay with us, blessing us with His presence. Take time to thank God for the precious indwelling Holy Spirit. Ask God to fill you again with His Spirit! Pray and worship the Lord in the Spirit for a while, tuning your spirit with the Spirit of God. In Acts 4:31, we read of the disciples being filled *again* with the Holy Spirit and boldness.

Adonai–Rophe means "the Lord Who Heals." God restores, cures, and heals us physically, spiritually, and morally. Thank God for the healing available in Jesus, for sound mental and emotional health, for previous healings, and general good health. No matter how you feel right now, thank God for His gifts of healing, and receive His healing by faith.

Read Galatians 3:10-14. Man is cursed to failure because of his sin nature. Romans 3:23 says all men have sinned and fallen short of God's glory. No mortal man has ever fulfilled the requirements of the law, so according to Galatians 3:10, we all stand cursed before God. But Jesus redeemed us from the curse of the law at Calvary and fulfilled all the law's requirements for us. On the cross, Jesus took the curse of our failure, inferiority, and insufficiency. He saw our needs and provided for them.

Jesus became our provision so that the curse could be removed from us. As a result, we are free from the curse of moral, financial, social, and spiritual failure. We can do all things through the Messiah Who strengthens us. (*see* Phil. 4:13) We are free to walk without reproach as believers. Hallelujah! Jesus has set us free from every curse and continues to be our provision and provider.

God's name, *Adonai–Nissi*, means, "the Lord my banner." Banner is translated "ensign or standard." Ensigns and standards are a sign to God's people to rally to Him. They represent His cause or His battle and speak of deliverance and salvation. Thank God that He is your banner and has conquered death, hell, and the grave. He always leads us in triumph through our Lord Jesus Christ. We are more than conquerors through Him Who loved us. According to Isaiah 11:10, Jesus was the banner that Isaiah predicted. He is the banner of our redemption. He was victorious in life and death, and He gives us victory as we abide in Him (*see* 1 Cor. 15:57). Song of Songs 2:4 says His banner over us is love. Knowing and believing in His love enables us to overcome in the midst of our trials (*see* Romans 8:35-39).

Adonai–Roi means "the Lord my shepherd." We see a beautiful descripton of the Lord as our shepherd in Psalm 23. The primary meaning of the Hebrew word **ro'eh** is to feed or lead to pasture as a shepherd does his flock. It is also translated 'companion' or 'friend.' Jesus spoke of being our shepherd in John 10 where He said, *"I am the good shepherd. The good shepherd gives His life for the sheep"* (**John 10:11**).

Each of these compound names of God is a facet of His nature. Jesus fulfilled their meanings for us, giving us the right to claim the blessings and promises of each name. He said in **John 5:43**, *"I am come in My Father's name..."* and in **John 14:9**, *"he that has seen Me has seen the Father."*

It is through believing on Jesus' name that we are born again and can live in victory. We need to submit to His Lordship and His name in every area of our lives. He is our Righteousness and Sanctification, therefore we are to live out His righteousness and be set apart unto Him. He is our Peace, our Healer, and Provider. He is our Banner and Shepherd.

It is good for us to remember the eternal benefits of belonging to Jesus. We would be wise to praise His name(s) daily. He is worthy of our praise! As we repeat the blessings of the covenant we have with Him, our minds are renewed, our faith is strengthened, and our lives will show the fruit of that covenant expressed through us. We will live in the victory that our Banner, *Adonai–Nissi,* has won for us!

"Bless the Lord, O my soul; and all that is within me, bless His holy name" (**Psalm 103:1**).

PRAYER GUIDE FOR Matthew 6:9-13

1. Our Father in heaven, hallowed be Your name.
   a. Thank God that you can call Him "Father" because of the blood of Jesus.
   b. Praise Him, using His covenant names. Psalm 100:4 tells us to enter His gates with thanksgiving and His courts with praise. Thank Him for His covenantal blessings.

Name	*Meaning*
Adonai–Tsidkenu	"The Lord our Righteousness"
Adonai–M'kaddesh	"The Lord Who Sanctifies"
Adonai–Shalom	"The Lord is Peace"
Adonai–Shamah	"The Lord is There."
Adonai–Rophe	"The Lord Who Heals"
Adonai–Yireh	"The Lord Who Sees and Provides"
Adonai–Nissi	"The Lord my Banner"
Adonai–Roi	"The Lord my Shepherd"

2. Your kingdom come, Your will be done on earth as it is in heaven.
   a. Pray for God's kingdom to come and His will to be done in your life.
   b. Pray God's will for your family (spouse, children, siblings, other family members).
   c. Pray God's will for your congregation (especially for the pastors and leaders).
   d. Pray God's will for your nation (local and national leaders, spiritual leaders, and for salvation for the nation).

3. Give us this day our daily bread.
   a. Be specific and persistent in your prayers.
   b. Believe it is God's will to meet your needs.
   c. Be in the will of God. This includes areas such as your prayer life, congregational service, work habits, and financial giving.

4. And forgive us our trespasses as we forgive those who trespass against us.
   a. Ask God to forgive you for any known sin.
   b. Forgive and release others who have sinned against you.
   c. Choose in advance to forgive anyone who will sin against you today.

5. And lead us not into temptation, but deliver us from evil.
   a. Pray that God will teach you some other way besides through trials.
   b. Ask for strength to choose God's way when temptation comes.
   c. Pray that you will not enter into temptation through carelessness or disobedience.
   d. Pray for a pure heart so that temptation and evil will have no appeal to you.
   e. Ask for a soft and repentant heart.
   f. Pray a hedge of protection around yourself, your possessions, and your family.

6. For Yours is the kingdom and the power and the glory forever. Amen.
   a. Honor God as the King; thank Him for inviting you to share His kingdom with Him.
   b. Acknowledge that the power is all His, yet He shares it with you by giving you authority over the enemy. He also gave you the power of the Holy Spirit.
   c. Take time to worship Him. Worship is a key to all kingdom advancement.

Note: *According to this model prayer that Jesus gave us, we are to begin and end our times of prayer with praise and worship.*

EXERCISE #22 – Matthew 6:10-11 ~ HIS WILL; OUR BREAD

Memory verses: *Matthew 6:10-11*

1. Read Matthew 6:10. When we pray for God's will to be done on earth as it is in heaven, for what are we praying?

2. According to Romans 14:17, of what does God's kingdom consist?

   Are those elements real and active in your life?

   Take time to pray for an increase of God's rule in you and in your family.

3. After reading Isaiah 33:15-16, list the requirements God gives us for expecting our daily bread to be provided.

4. What are some of your daily needs? List intangible needs as well as material needs.

   Are any of the things you listed luxuries? (God only promises to meet our *needs*!)

5. Do you believe it is God's will for your needs to be met?

What do the following Scriptures say about that?

Philippians 4:19 –

Luke 12:32 –

Romans 8:32 –

Matthew 6:31-33 –

Matthew 7:7-11 –

Hebrews 11:6 –

#22 – His Will; Our Bread

Matthew 6:10-11 *"Your kingdom come. Your will be done on earth as it is in heaven. Give us this day our daily bread."*

In the Bible, we are told that the kingdom of God is *"righteousness, peace, and joy in the Holy Spirit"* (**Rom. 14:17**). The kingdom of God is His presence. When we pray, "Your kingdom come in me," we are praying for His peace, joy, and righteousness to be manifested in and through us.

Pray For God's Rule

Jesus is the King in God's kingdom. When you pray for His kingdom to come, you are praying for the Lord's governing power over you and for whomever else you pray. The four main areas into which you should pray are (1) yourself, (2) your family, (3) your congregation or fellowship, and (4) the harvest of souls. We will look at each of these in more detail.

1. Yourself – When *you* are in a right relationship with God, your prayers for *others* can be very effective. Invite Jesus to sit on the throne of your heart and life, and rule your spirit, soul, and body. Ask for His wisdom in all that you have to do and deal with today (James 1:5). You cannot properly administrate your home, business, or ministry without His wisdom and revelation! Pray over each concern that you have. Ask the Holy Spirit to empower you with ability and efficiency. You might want to pray in the Spirit for a while, allowing the Holy Spirit to pray through you for the situations that you will face. We are told in Romans 8:26-27 that He knows what we need and what God's will is for us.

2. Your family – Pray for God's righteousness, peace, and joy to be manifested in your spouse and children. Pray specifically for their needs. Pray for other family members as the Lord directs you. Bring before the Lord your relatives who do not know Him yet. You might spend more time praying for some than for others, as the Holy Spirit leads you. He knows who needs extra prayer; let Him direct your praying.

3. Your congregation

    a. the pastor(s) – Pray for God to anoint him/her and to speak to and through him. Ask the Lord to give your pastor the heart of a good shepherd, and to give him wisdom and revelation as he studies God's Word.

    b. other leaders – (deacons, worship leaders, youth leaders, Bible study leaders) Pray for the specific needs that you are aware of in the various ministry departments. Ask God to anoint each leader and to give them wisdom and strength to do His will. Pray that they will clearly hear God's voice. Ask God to bless every ministry of the congregation.

    c. congregational faithfulness – Pray for the people of the congregation to be faithful to Jesus and to the vision God has given the leaders. Pray for spouses to be faithful to their mates, and for the children to honor and obey their parents.

Pray that all will be faithful to give their tithes and offerings, time and talents to the work of the kingdom. Pray that the people will be planted in the Lord's house so that they can bear fruit for Him (Psalm 92:13-14) and serve Him gladly.

d. the harvest (Matt. 9:36-38) – Ask the Lord of the harvest to thrust laborers into every harvest field in your city. Pray for other mission fields as the Spirit leads you. Ask Him to give your congregation a burden for the lost and creative ways to reach them. Pray for individuals who have heard the gospel and have not yet embraced Jesus. Ask the Lord to give you a chance to speak to someone about Him soon.

4. Your nation – Pray *"Your kingdom come, Your will be done"* over your city and nation. Read 1 Tim. 2:1-4. Pray for those in leadership positions: the President, Prime Minister, congressmen and senators or cabinet members, governors and mayors. Pray that they will seek godly counsel and that they will be protected by God's power. Mention leaders and/or positions by name if possible.

Pray For Israel

God commands us to pray for Israel in Psalm 122:6. After praying for Israel and for the peace of Jerusalem, ask the Lord to show you a country He wants intercession for today (perhaps a country with famine, a nation that persecutes believers, a Muslim country, etc.). Let the Spirit of God enlarge the borders of your heart and enable you to love the world and its people as God does.

Live Your Prayer Priorities

After praying for these areas of priority, ask the Lord to help you *live out* these priorities.

1. Put Jesus and His kingdom first in your life.

2. Give yourself to your spouse and your family.

3. Be committed to your congregation and to the Lord's work.

4. Stand behind your national and local authorities in prayer and loyalty.

Petition God's Provision

"Give us this day our daily bread" (**Matt. 6:11**). This verse shows us how to appropriate God's provision in prayer. In Hebrew, the word 'daily' is actually translated "lawful" which gives the prayer a different slant. *"Give us this day our lawful bread."* We are told to ask for what we *need*, that which is *lawfully* ours by virtue of our covenant with God and because we are heirs of God and joint–heirs with Messiah.

While praying for daily bread, make sure you feed yourself with the true bread from Heaven, given by God! Read John 6:31-35. Jesus is our bread! His presence feeds and sustains us. As those who are hungry and desperate, we should feed on Him early and sufficiently in order to make it through the day.

Notice that in Luke 11:9-13, the son asks for basic food items; he does not ask for luxuries. We can ask God to grant us needed strength, wisdom, and guidance in addition to asking for material needs that we have. We can also ask for ears to hear His voice, for breakthroughs in relationships, and for salvation for loved ones.

Requirements For Praying In Your Needs

1. Pray specifically and persistently. The more specific your requests, more exact are God's answers. Though there may be a waiting period between your prayer and the answer, pray persistently (Luke 18:1). God hears prayers of faith. Continue to pray until you see your requests fulfilled (Dan. 10:12-14).

2. Believe it is God's will to meet your needs. According to Heb. 11:6, you need faith in order to receive from the Lord. Trust that your heavenly Father will take care of you (Luke 12:32).

3. Make sure you are in God's will in these areas:

   a. Maintain fellowship with the Lord through daily prayer and Bible–reading.

   b. Fellowship with a group of believers and be submitted to the pastor (Heb. 13:17; 10:24-25).

   c. Maintain diligent, balanced work habits (2 Thess. 3:10). Balance your work with devotion and rest. Refuse to let fear, worry, and insecurity drive you to overwork. Believe and live consistently with the truth that God is your source.

   d. Faithfully give your tithes and offerings (Malachi 3:8-10).

   e. Obey all that God has called you to or told you to do.

What we conceive in the Spirit can be lost if we cast away our confidence and refuse to wait on the Lord. Avoid miscarriages in prayer by faithfully presenting your needs to God until the answer comes. If you have been discouraged in praying and are struggling with unbelief, confess that to the Lord as sin. Then begin to actively take back the ground (e.g., faith and hope) from the enemy that he has stolen from you.

For victory and hope in the Lord, follow the steps listed in James 4:7: • Submit to God (repent of and renounce unbelief and other sins). • Resist the devil. • Draw near to God. Pick up the prayer burdens again and carry them before the Lord until the answer comes.

For Consideration and Prayer

Do you have a consistent prayer life? Do you pray specifically and persistently? Do you hold on in faith until the answer comes?

What prayer concerns do you need to pick up and faithfully pray about until God answers?

Do you read the Scriptures every day?

Are you a contributing, serving part of your local congregation?

What are your work habits like? (Are you lazy? Are you addicted to work?) Ask the Lord to help you with efficiency and balance in your work and rest.

Are you a good financial steward? Do you bring your tithes and offerings to the house of the Lord? Are you greedy, stingy, or a poor money manager? Do you pay your bills and have the reputation of an honest person who keeps his word?

Is there any deliberate disobedience in your life?

Are you obedient to what the Lord has told you?

EXERCISE #23 – Matthew 6:12-15 ~ THE GIFT OF FORGIVENESS

1. For us to be candidates for God's forgiveness, what do we need to do? Read Matthew 6:14, Acts 2:38, and 1 John 1:9.

2. Read Matthew 18:21-35 and then answer the following questions:

   a. How often did Jesus tell Peter to forgive his brother?

   b. What do you think Jesus meant by His answer?

   c. What truth(s) was Jesus teaching by the parable He told?

   d. What (or who) do you think the tormentors are that Jesus spoke of?

3. After reading Psalm 103:1-14, write down the phrases that have to do with God's attitudes and actions toward you and sin.

4. Is there anyone you have not forgiven for any offense against you?

5. Ask the Lord to search your heart for any unforgiveness. With His grace, forgive and release all debts. Ask Him if you should act on your forgiveness in any way (such as, give a gift as a token of forgiveness, make an appointment to talk, write a letter of reconciliation, or pursue restoration in some other creative way). Write down what actions you plan to take toward the one(s) you are forgiving. *The only people we should consider getting even with are those who have helped us!*

#23 – The Gift of Forgiveness

Matthew 6:12,14-15 *"And forgive us our debts, as we forgive our debtors. For if you forgive men their trespasses, your heavenly Father will also forgive you. But if you do not forgive men their trespasses, neither will your Father forgive your trespasses."*

Forgiveness is always twofold: we receive God's love and forgiveness by faith, and we offer love and forgiveness to others by faith. God expects us to forgive with the same great mercy that He offers us. He is not pleased when we give only small measures of mercy to others; He wants us to heap it onto them extravagantly—just as He lavishly pours out His mercy and forgiveness to us.

Jesus' Blood Is Sufficient

Read 1 John 1:9 and Romans 8:1. When we confess our sins to God and repent of them, He forgives us and cleanses us. He doesn't condemn us. We may suffer natural consequences of the sin, but His forgiveness toward us is complete. The devil condemns us by reminding us of our past failures; he loves to rob us of peace and joy. However, the blood of Jesus is sufficient for all of our sin—past, present, and future. We can lawfully resist condemnation as soon as we confess our sin, repent toward God, and receive His forgiveness.

Forgiveness Leads To Healing

Forgiveness is an important key to freedom, victory, and joy. In fact, *forgiveness is the key to all inner healing and transformation.* Once we forgive, we can be healed of emotional pain and receive deliverance from demonic strongholds and oppression.

Until we forgive, we are bound to the past and unable to live fully in the present. The bitterness we carry from past painful relationships will affect our present relationships, damaging and defiling them. When we retain resentment by focusing on the wrong done to us, we are bound to the person who inflicted the pain. This bondage limits God's work in both our lives and theirs. It is as if we tie God's hands. As soon as we forgive, God is able to work in everyone involved.

When we judge another for his or her sin, we run the risk of developing that same hated sin in ourselves. According to Romans 2:1, that which we are quick to see in others already has a foothold in us.

Refusing To Forgive Is Hazardous

Unforgiveness, according to Matthew 18:34-35, can open a door to the enemy in our lives. The tormentors who are assigned to the unforgiving include depression, fear, doubt, strife, and disease. When we refuse to forgive, we unintentionally *invite* oppression, demonic harassment, and particular physical ailments. Unforgiveness eats away at our emotional and physical health. If left unchecked, it will progress toward deception and perversion. The process is gradual, and it begins with real or perceived hurt.

If the hurt is not cleansed and healed through forgiveness, the unforgiveness will lead to anger, which grows into resentment. As resentment matures, it develops into bitterness. Bitterness leads to blame which results in hatred. Rebellion follows hatred, making one susceptible to deception and self–deception. Once a person is deceived, he moves into moral sins easily, including sexual perversion.

Bitterness is the seedbed for any demonic work! It is the result of unresolved revenge. The works of the flesh found in Galatians 5:19-21 can always be traced back to bitterness, and even further back to an area of deep hurt or rejection.

Bitterness Must Be Rooted Out

Resentment can sometimes be hidden, but once it has matured into a root of bitterness, it is revealed in our speech, actions, reactions, and attitudes. It defiles everyone around us. When a person has a root of bitterness, he tends to carry grudges and take on others' hurts easily, speak harshly or critically, overreact to minor injustices, and be ultra sensitive to rejection.

"Pursue peace with all people, and holiness, without which no one will see the Lord: looking carefully lest anyone fall short of the grace of God; lest any root of bitterness springing up cause trouble, and by this many become defiled" (**Heb. 12:14-15**).

We not only need to forgive those who wounded us, we also need to uproot the root of bitterness that has embedded itself in our hearts. Bitterness must be confessed as sin, repented of, and renounced for complete freedom. Otherwise, when the root is watered with a new offense or hurt, resentment will grow again quickly.

Forgiveness Is A Choice

Forgiveness is not a feeling; it is a choice of our will. We give it by faith, acting on our will to let the past go. We choose to forgive with Jesus' help and strength. We may not feel like forgiving when we choose to, but we will eventually experience positive feelings toward the person as we continue praying for and blessing him or her.

Worldly psychology may encourage us not to forgive (so as not to show weakness), and then try to tell us how to cope with the hurt and anger. But Jesus gives us the grace and strength to release the debt and to overcome! The word, *cope*, is not part of Jesus' vocabulary; the word *overcome* is! We must die to ourselves—our resentment and desire for revenge—in order to overcome. We have to allow Jesus to forgive others through us. If we wait until we feel like forgiving in order to do so, we never will because our fleshly nature loves to hold onto hurt and anger. Part of dying to self is learning to walk in forgiveness.

Read Colossians 2:13-14. Forgiveness is handling others' debts as God handles ours—He cancels them. We are to forgive even if we never receive an apology, explanation, or restitution. We release the offense, choosing never to look at it again. We "put it behind us" the same way that God puts our sins behind His back (*see* Isaiah 38:17).

Confront When Necessary

There are times when forgiving from our hearts without confronting the offender will not sufficiently restore the relationship. The general rule is this: we should forgive in our hearts and lovingly cover the sin as much as possible. If the offense still bothers us and robs us of peace a few days later, we should talk about it with the person alone, as Matthew 18:15 instructs.

When we repress and overlook offenses without confronting those who caused the pain, we tend to withdraw from them. Then, rather than growing in real relationship, we relate superficially and without trust. To be united in Christ, we need to have trusting relationships that involve transparency and forgiveness.

We must care enough to confront the person, talk out the hurtful situation, and be reconciled. Forgiveness should result in a restored, growing relationship. Whether we are the wounded party or the guilty one, we are to seek peace and restoration (*see* Heb. 12:14). It is always *our* responsibility to seek peace, no matter who is at fault.

Sometimes we have forgiven, but we still carry emotional pain. Our emotions may need some time and ministry from the Word to fully heal. **Psalm 107:20** says, *"He sent His Word and healed them and delivered them from their destructions."* Keep soaking in God's Word and His love, and in time the healing will be complete. Once you can pray for your offender with love and a welcoming heart, then you know your emotions have caught up with your choice of forgiveness.

What will hinder spiritual growth faster than anything else is unforgiveness! Do not allow yourself the luxury of retaining hurt and bitterness. It isn't worth it.

A Pattern For Forgiving Others

Ask the Holy Spirit to reveal to you your sins; then deal properly with them. You might want to list them, and then repent, asking God for forgiveness. (e.g., "I am sorry I _____ to _____ and I ask for Your forgiveness.") You must make restitution where necessary.

Release the unforgiveness. Make a list of the people who have offended you and write down the offense. Include family and friends, former employers, and even those who are deceased. (e.g., "I forgive _____ for his offense of _____.") Set your will to forgive and pray for those who offended you. Jesus will never ask you to do anything that He will not give you the grace to do.

Refuse to engage in self–pity. Make sure that you have dealt with all painful issues every day before you go to bed. *"...do not let the sun go down on your wrath, nor give place to the devil"* (**Eph. 4:26b-27**). When we hold onto inner pain and anger overnight, there is a cementing and sealing of that resentment that makes it much harder to get free from later.

If you have given ground to the enemy through unforgiveness and bitterness, then he has a legal stronghold in your life until you reclaim that ground for Jesus. James 4:7 tells us to submit to God (enthroning Him in our hearts) and then resist the devil.

Steps to Freedom From Bitterness

1. Acknowledge that bitterness itself is sin. Repent of it and renounce it in Jesus' name.

2. Ask the Lord to cleanse your heart from all bitterness with Jesus' blood.

3. Ask God to retake the ground of your heart (where the resentment was), to destroy the enemy's stronghold of bitterness there. Enthrone Him again as your Lord and King. In the authority of Jesus' name, tell any tormentors to leave you, such as fear, depression or sickness.

Make a decision at the beginning of every day to forgive others as God has forgiven you. Do not wait until you get into a confrontation or some emotional turmoil to decide how you will react. At that point, your flesh will resist all thoughts of forbearance and forgiveness! If you choose every morning to walk in mercy all day, then you will have the grace and strength at the time of a crisis to do so. Do not allow your spirit to be robbed of peace and joy. Live in the grace of forgiveness. You might pray, "Lord, I choose to forgive anyone who will hurt or offend me today. I forgive them in advance. Thank You for living in and through me, enabling me to love and cheerfully give mercy to those who need it."

Remember Jesus' words in **Matthew 6:14-15**, *"For if you forgive men their trespasses, your heavenly Father will also forgive you. But if you do not forgive men their trespasses, neither will your Father forgive your trespasses."*

EXERCISE #24 – Matthew 6:13 ~ Is Temptation Necessary?

1. Read Genesis 3:1-19 and answer the following questions:

   What lies did the serpent (Satan) tell Eve?

   Why did Eve yield to the temptation?

   Why did Adam yield?

   What did they do after they sinned? Why?

   What did God do?

2. Where did the devil originally come from? Read Isaiah 14:12-17 and Ezekiel 28:12-19 for some information.

3. According to 1 Peter 5:8, Job 1:7, and John 8:44, 10:10, what does the devil do?

4. What does James 1:12-15 say about temptation?

5. Read Luke 22:31-34. Why do you think Satan could *demand* to "sift" Peter?

6. How are we to resist temptation? See what Jesus did in Luke 4:1-13.

7. What does Hebrews 4:15 say about Jesus and temptation?

8. After reading James 5:16, think about the weaknesses or temptations you struggle with that you would like to share with your small group or trusted friend for prayer and accountability.

#24 – Is Temptation Necessary?

Matthew 6:13a *"And lead us not into temptation, but deliver us from the evil one."*

This verse could be paraphrased, *"Do not lead us into the devil's domain of temptation unnecessarily."* Temptation is sometimes necessary, such as when there is evil within us that must be purged out, when our faith needs to be strengthened, and when it serves as part of our training for mature godly character.

Temptations Can Reflect The Heart

Read James 1:12-16. Temptation is something we all face regularly, and yet as common as it is, it is also *individualized* to a large degree. What may be tempting to one person may not tempt another. The reason for this is given in James 1:14. Most of what tempts us is related to what is within our hearts.

The 'heart' in Scripture refers to a person's disposition and personality. It is the combination of all of his experiences and his perception of them. It includes his desires and motivations. Because we are usually tempted according to that which is in our hearts, our greatest defense against the devil is a pure heart. The temptations that are the most difficult to resist relate to something within us that needs to be cleansed, removed, or healed by the Lord.

Temptation From The Outside

The temptations Jesus overcame in Matthew 4 show us another side of temptation—that of being tempted from the outside. Not all of our temptations reflect our hearts. In John 14:30, Jesus said the devil could find no area of darkness in Him that could give him a foothold to attack him. Yet Hebrews 4:15 says Jesus was tempted in all areas.

Trials and Temptations

Read 1 Peter 1:3-7. The Greek word translated 'temptation' in verse 6 is the same word used in Matt. 6:13. It is **peirasmos**, which means "experiment, trial and temptation." In 1 Peter 1:7, the Greek word used for trial is **dokimeeon**. It means "to test, to prove trustworthiness." So, 1 Peter 1:6-7 can be understood to say: *"For a little while you are in heaviness through many trials, tests, and temptations, that the proving and testing of your faith will result in bringing glory to Jesus."*

A trial is both a test *and* a temptation: it is a test by God to see if we will obey His Word and practice righteousness, and it is a temptation by the devil to entice us to sin by gratifying our fleshly desires. In any circumstance, we face both tests and temptations, and have the option of pleasing God and standing firm in our faith, or of yielding to sin and pleasing ourselves.

In *The Final Quest*, author Rick Joyner writes, *"All of your failures will be the result of one thing, self-centeredness. The only way to be delivered from this is to walk in love for God and for others. Love does not seek its own will."*

Benefits of Temptations

Temptations can show us our helplessness and dependence upon God (Deut. 8:2-3). They teach us spiritual warfare (Judges 3:1-2), and help prepare us for God's will for our lives (as in Joseph's case in Genesis 39). They purify us and perfect our faith (James 1:2-4).

A parent or a spiritual leader who overcomes temptation gains greater victory in his life and can defeat the enemy's attack upon his family or congregation in those same areas of temptation. However, if he yields to the temptation, the door is open for the devil to more effectively tempt those who are under his care or authority. So, it is wise for us to strictly avoid situations where we are weak. Gal. 5:13 and Rom. 13:14 speak of not using our liberty as an opportunity for the flesh to sin. We must be aware of the enemy's desire and schemes to destroy us. Read 1 Peter 5:8-9.

Darkness Gives The Enemy Access

"Submit yourselves...to God; resist the devil and he will flee from you" (**Jam. 4:7**). A pure heart is subject to God and can resist the devil. Any area in which our hearts are impure or rebellious, the devil has the right to harass us. Satan is relegated to areas of darkness, such as hell, the system of this world, and darkness in human lives. Read Luke 11:35-36. Darkness in us gives the enemy access into our lives. Where we hide sin, we are vulnerable to the enemy.

In every area that we are not like Jesus, we will experience warfare. When Satan sees sin or the desire for sin in us, he goes to Jesus and demands the right to tempt us. The permission must be granted, but with limitations. Jesus referred to this sifting by Satan regarding Peter in Luke 22:31. God measures the sifting so that it is enough to surface the sin and/or lust, but not enough to destroy us. Paul speaks of a way of escape in 1 Cor. 10:13 that God provides so that we can bear the temptation and not yield to it. The way of escape is Jesus! He always provides for us a way to overcome our trials and temptations.

Purification Through Temptation

For temptation to appeal to us, there must be something in our hearts that welcomes it. We are susceptible in the areas where we have something in common with the enemy, or when we have needs or desires that have not been surrendered to God. After we have resisted the temptation (or given into it and repented), we can use it as an opportunity to search our hearts and surrender those regions to the Lord.

Satan seeks to exploit our weaknesses; God seeks to establish His nature in our weak areas, turning our failures into places of victory. He wants to deliver us from evil and to work godly transformation into us. When we fail, we need to repent quickly, and then ask the Lord to make us more like Jesus. Once His nature is established in us, we can strengthen others who are weak in the same areas in which we have struggled.

God is able to turn the temptations of Satan that entice us *to* sin, to the purging of our hearts *from* sin. He sometimes allows the devil to harass us with particular temptations, knowing that it will drive us to watchfulness and prayer. By doing this, God uses the temptation to one sin as a *preventative against another sin.* As we watch and pray, we become aware of tempting situations to avoid. If we are wise, we will use our temptations to discover our inner condition, and run to Jesus for deliverance and healing.

> *There is a realm of temptation we can avoid altogether if we are faithful to watch and pray. A prayerless disciple will be plagued with temptations.*

God uses temptation to promote the whole work of grace in our hearts. When we see our weak, sinful state, we should plead with God for full sanctification. Just as Peter said when Jesus offered to wash his feet, we can say, *"Not my feet only, but also my hands and my head"* (John 13:8-9)!

Temptation Is Universal

Notice in James 1:12 the words, *"when we are tempted,"* not *if*! We are *all* tempted! To endure a temptation means to continue to believe and act upon the Word of God in the midst of the conflict—whether that conflict is internal or external.

When Jesus told us to pray, *"Lead us not into temptation,"* He was instructing us to pray that forces beyond our control would not lead us into trials. He was also commanding us to watch and pray so that we will not enter into temptation through carelessness or disobedience. In Matt. 26:41, the disciples slept instead of praying, and in the hour of temptation, they deserted Jesus.

Jesus knows *our* potential weaknesses just like He knew those of His first disciples. He knows that our spirits may be willing, but our flesh is weak. He realizes that we can succumb to temptation as a result of our own carelessness and disobedience, and He knows of forces and circumstances beyond our control that can try us. Therefore, in His wisdom He commands us to pray, *"Lead us not into temptation, but deliver us from the evil one."*

Safeguards Against Temptation

• Identify and admit wrong behavior. Adopt a repentant, humble lifestyle (1 John 2:1). Be quick to acknowledge sin and renounce it.

• Set aside time daily to strengthen your spirit through praying, studying the Bible, and reading devotional materials. Seek a personal encounter with Jesus every day.

• Cultivate relationships where you share spiritual interests and passion for Jesus. Encourage and affirm growth in one another and be accountable to each other; confront any compromise you may see. Do not avoid asking hard questions when you notice signs of stress.

• Hold material possessions loosely. This will help you to avoid debt, covetousness, and pride. It will also keep you dependent on and secure in the Lord.

• Take time to rest; allow the Lord to restore you in solitude.

• Be filled with the Holy Spirit of God. He is our most powerful weapon to avoid sin.

We are more susceptible to temptation when we have a hard, unrepentant heart, refuse to embrace spiritual disciplines, isolate ourselves from others, are weary and stressed in mind and body, love worldly things, and lack the power of the Holy Spirit in our lives.

As we face temptations and trials, let us use them to search our hearts and to surrender more fully to the Lord our God.

EXERCISE #25 – Matthew 6:13b ~ IT'S ALL YOURS!

Memory verse: *Matthew 6:13b*

The model prayer Jesus gave us opens and closes with praise and with references to God's kingdom. As we study the Bible, we see that the kingdom, power, and glory belong to the Lord, and that He invites us to share them with Him. He allows us to participate in His kingdom, to receive and live by His power, and to share in His glory.

1. Read Luke 12:32, Col. 1:12-14, and 2 Tim. 4:18. Write a summary of these verses.

2. What does Psalm 66:7 and Jeremiah 10:12 say about God's power?

3. Read Psalm 145:10-13 to the Lord aloud, praising and thanking God for His power.

4. To whom does the Lord give His power?

    Psalm 68:35 _____

    Isaiah 40:29 _____

    1 Cor. 6:14 _____

5. Why does the Lord give us this power?

    Luke 10:19 _____

    Acts 1:8 _____

    Eph. 6:10 _____

6. Who is the King of Glory? (Psalm 24:8)

7. How do you understand John 17:22? (It helps to read the context.)

8. Reflect upon 1 Cor. 1:26-31. Thank God for sharing His kingdom, power, and glory with you.

#25 – It's All Yours!

Matthew 6:13b *"...For Yours is the kingdom and the power and the glory forever. Amen."*

The prayer that Jesus gave us opens and closes with praise and references to God's kingdom. After we bring our petitions to God in the words of this prayer, we are to return to praise. Even though the phrase, *"...Yours is the kingdom, the power, and the glory forever"* is not included in some ancient manuscripts of the Bible, believers worldwide consider it to be inspired by God. It is commonly used in Jewish prayers today.

Review of Topics In This Prayer

1. *"Our Father in heaven, hallowed be Your name."* We can enter God's presence by praising His name and thanking Him for the salvation Jesus purchased for us with His blood. Through Jesus, we have cut covenant with the Father and now have a personal relationship with Him. Psalm 100:4 commands us to enter His gates with thanksgiving and His courts with praise, so we begin our time of prayer with thanking and praising the Lord.

2. *"Your kingdom come, Your will be done."* We pray for His will to be done in our lives, in the lives of our family and friends, and in the lives of our spiritual and national leaders.

3. *"Give us this day our daily bread."* We ask Father God to provide what is lawful for us today.

4. *"And forgive us our debts as we forgive our debtors."* We ask God to forgive our sins, and we forgive anyone who has wronged us. We choose (in advance) to walk in forgiveness and mercy toward others all day.

5. *"And lead us not into temptation, but deliver us from the evil one."* Pray for a pure heart so that temptation will not appeal to you. Pray that you will not enter temptation through carelessness or rebellion. Ask God to put a hedge of protection around you, your family, and your possessions.

6. *"For Yours is the kingdom and the power and the glory."* We conclude the prayer with praise and worship, acknowledging that the kingdom, power, and glory belong to the Lord.

Jesus told us to end this model prayer with praise and worship, showing us that God wants us to move from petition to worship before we leave His presence. We do this by declaring that God is sovereign, powerful, and full of glory. In leaving our cares with Him, we are declaring our confidence that He loves us and is in control of all that concerns us. Our praise enthrones the Lord and makes the enemy flee from us. He cowers at the mention of the name of Jesus.

God created us with a natural inclination to worship. If we do not worship the Lord, we will worship someone or something else. God alone deserves our adoration, and worshiping Him is one of our most powerful spiritual weapons. Worship enables the Kingdom of God to advance. Besides blessing the Lord, worship also deeply affects our inner lives.

Personal Benefits Of Worship

1. *Worship releases an uninhibited expression of who we are.* The Lord wants us to worship Him freely. Whatever outward form our worship takes, we should engage in it with all that is within us. Uninhibited worship allows us to be completely transparent before the Lord.

Read Psalm 24:7. To what gates does the psalmist refer? One interpretation could be the gates to our hearts–barriers that each of us has put up inside. Too often we barricade ourselves from God and one another. Our cultures teach us to protect ourselves. We are preconditioned by society to erect inner walls toward anyone who might try to get close to us. Then when God attempts access to the deepest places of our hearts, our barriers go up. If we would be willing to lift up those ancient gates that guard our hearts, the King of Glory would come in (bringing healing and release to our souls)!

2. *Worship increases our faith.* As we confess God's Word in praise, acknowledging God for Who He is, we find that our faith rises to the level of our confession. We begin to believe that God is as mighty and marvelous as our praises declare!

3. *Worship causes growth in holiness.* Those who spend enough time with the Lord will become like Him, because we become like the person or object of our worship. (*see* Psalm 115:8 and 2 Cor. 3:18). When we worship the Lord with an open (unveiled) face toward Him, we reflect His glory, and we are gradually changed into His image. If worship does not change a person's life, it may be because he has not unveiled his face before God. Those who will lower their inner barriers and pour out their hearts to God with tears of repentance, contrition, and love will experience life–changing worship.

4. *Worship prepares us for any new thing God wants to do in our lives.* God wants to bring us into greater depths of divine revelation and relationship. He is always doing new things (*see* Isaiah 43:19). Part of our preparation for that newness lies in our worship. Worship softens our hearts and sensitizes our spirits so that when God moves, we recognize it. When God does something new, it often comes in an unexpected form. If we are not closely attuned to the Holy Spirit, we can easily reject the new thing that God wants to do. However, if we will gaze upon Him steadfastly in worship, we will see when He moves and which way He goes, and we will naturally desire to follow Him closely.

God's Kingdom (Greek: Basileia) – His Sovereignty and Royal Power

Jesus is the King in His kingdom, and He can operate His kingdom any way He pleases. According to Luke 18:17, we are to enter the kingdom of God as children—dependent, humble, openhearted, and grateful. We cannot enter in proudly, thinking too highly of ourselves and demanding our own way. We must recognize Jesus' Lordship and yield to it with humble hearts. Jesus' rule in us will be manifested by His righteousness, peace, and joy expressed through us (Rom. 14:17).

Intimacy with God should never cause us to be casual or impertinent with Him. We are never to take the grace of God in vain and turn it into license. We must beware of becoming so familiar with Jesus that we overstep boundaries that He has laid down for everyone.

Read 2 Samuel 6:1-7. Uzzah was obviously too familiar with the Lord's presence (the ark of the covenant). He may have thought he was above the law because the ark had been in his home. Maybe he thought he could touch it while others could not. He may have felt he was special to God and had extraordinary privileges, but God struck him for his irreverence. Beware of pride! Assuming privileges and responsibilities that are not yours can kill you.

God's Power (Greek: Dunamis) – Miraculous Might and Strength

According to 1 Cor. 4:20, the kingdom is expressed in power. God shares His power with us by giving us authority over the enemy (Luke 10:19), and by equipping us with the gifts of His Holy Spirit mentioned in 1 Cor. 12 and Romans 12. At times, God supernaturally allows us to use the power gifts (charismata) when specific needs or circumstances arise that require them. On other occasions, *only to the degree that we embrace God's kingdom (the sovereign rule of Jesus in our hearts and lives) can we walk in and live out the power of God.* When we are under Authority, we can carry authority. Resurrection power follows death. As we die to ourselves, the power of the Spirit is increasingly, consistently released in our lives.

God's Glory (Greek: Doxa) – Praise and Honor

Isaiah 42:8 says all the glory belongs to the Lord. Psalm 29:1-2 commands us to give to the Lord the glory and honor that are due Him. The Lord is willing to share His glory with us, but to do so, He requires us to share His suffering, also.

"The Spirit Himself testifies together with our own spirit, [assuring us] that we are children of God. And if we are [His] children, then we are [His] heirs also: heirs of God and fellow heirs with Christ [sharing His inheritance with Him]; only we must share His suffering if we are to share His glory. [But what of that?] For I consider that the sufferings of this present time (this present life) are not worth being compared with the glory that is about to be revealed to us and in us and for us and conferred on us" (**Rom. 8:16-18**, Amplified Bible).

Suffering For and With Jesus

Suffering with Jesus includes *anything* that requires a measure of death for us so that His kingdom can be established in us and extended in the earth and in the lives of others.

• Saying no to temptation. The flesh suffers when we deny it. The Lord Jesus refused to yield to temptation (*see* Heb. 2:18). He is our example and helper.

• Disciplining the flesh for the Lord's sake (1 Cor. 9:26-27), such as in fasting from food, sleep, or entertainment.

• Being persecuted for righteousness' sake.

• Interceding for others when it involves sacrifice.

• Doing the will of God when it is costly (e.g., going to the mission field, staying single, or studying further to equip yourself for ministry…).

God Shares His Kingdom, Power, and Glory

Although the kingdom, power and glory belong to the Lord, He graciously shares them with us. He allows us to participate in His kingdom, to receive and live by His power, and to share in His glory. However, these blessings have conditions attached to them! We only share in His kingdom to the degree that we surrender to Him and welcome His sovereign rule over us. We only consistently walk in His power to the degree that we die to our independence and embrace His Lordship. And we can only share His glory to the degree that we share in His sufferings. We are purified and sanctified by submitting to His discipline. We choose to die to the flesh so that we can live by the Spirit.

Each blessing builds on the other: embracing God's kingdom leads to a life filled with power and self–denial, which results in His glory. As Jesus exemplified in this prayer model, it is important for us to *begin* our prayers with praise and to *end* them with praise and worship. Having hearts full of adoration, we will be more than conquerors in the trials we face as we acknowledge His sovereignty and awesome power.

EXERCISE #26 – Matthew 6:16-18 ~ "WHEN YOU FAST..."

Memory verses: *Matthew 6:16–18*

1. Most people understand a fast to be refraining from eating for a limited period of time and for specific reasons. Fasting can also be understood in broader terms. Read Isaiah 58:1-10 and write down some aspects of fasting revealed there.

2. What principles for fasting are given in Matthew 6:16-18?

3. When do people fast? Write down what you see in the Scriptures listed.

   2 Sam. 1:12, Psalm 35:13 –

   2 Sam. 12:16, 21-23 –

   Ezra 8:21–23 –

   Jonah 3:5–10, Joel 1:14–2:13, 1 Kings 21:27-29 –

   Ezra 10:6 –

   Acts 13:2-3 –

   Daniel 9:3-19 –

   Luke 2:37, 2 Cor. 6:5 –

4. Have you ever fasted? What was (were) your experience(s) during or after the fast?

5. Why does fasting, when added to prayer, make prayer so powerful?

#26 – "WHEN YOU FAST..."

Matthew 6:16-18 *"Moreover, when you fast, do not be like the hypocrites, with a sad countenance. For they disfigure their faces that they may appear to men to be fasting. Assuredly, I say to you, they have their reward. But you, when you fast, anoint your head and wash your face, so that you do not appear to men to be fasting, but to your Father who is in the secret place; and your Father who sees in secret will reward you openly."*

Three Valuable Disciplines

In Matt. 6:1-18, Jesus taught on three practices that are very important to developing our spiritual lives: praying, giving, and fasting. Each of these disciplines requires us to deny our flesh and to engage in them "secretly" before the Lord.

Jesus knew that when giving, praying, and fasting are woven together, they strengthen and establish us in the faith. Fasting should be as much a part of our spiritual lives as giving and praying are. This sounds almost impossible if we think only in terms of total fasting, but it is realistic if we consider a variety of ways to fast. In this session, we will look at the spiritual benefits of fasting only, although there are tremendous physical and mental benefits derived from this discipline, also.

Reasons To Fast

Throughout history, people have undertaken fasts for many different reasons. Most of the fasts carried some religious significance. The people of God have viewed fasting as...

• preparation for waging a holy war (1 Sam. 14:24)

• a part of deep repentance

• a discipline to accompany casting out demons (Matt. 17:14-21)

• self–control against the temptation of the lusts of the body

• a means to end drought

• a way to strengthen prayer

• preparation for water baptism, baptism in the Holy Spirit, or for special ministry

• a practice to mourn sin, especially the sins of a nation (Joel 1:14)

Fasting Adds Power To Prayer

Read Isaiah 58:3-8. Verse 6 gives a list of the powerful effects of fasting. Verse 7 says that fasting is more than just refusing to eat food; it is a lifestyle of self–denial and caring for others. *Yet it is fasting from food that catapults us into a place of power with God and enables us to successfully war against the enemy.*

Because fasting requires tremendous discipline, it has been unpopular for a long time. Neglecting this spiritual discipline has resulted in diminished power in the Body of Christ individually and corporately. Too many of us have developed eating habits that we really do not want to change.

Food Is A Source Of Comfort

Because our minds are constantly thinking about food, we *should* fast—so that our minds are not controlled by food and our bellies do not become our gods. Consider Phil. 3:18-19. Today we build our social lives around eating. Businessmen have discovered an increased success in sales when customers have food placed in front of them. We hardly finish one meal before we plan the next. We seldom meet friends just to be together; we usually plan fellowship around food. Almost without exception, we add refreshments or a snack to the social agenda, even to church meetings.

We would all agree that eating is very enjoyable! The act of eating satisfies more needs than just hunger. It is a comfort to us. For example, our mothers fed us when we cried. We were rewarded with candy when we were good. When we received an honor, our mothers baked us a cake or cooked something special for us. In later years, we learned to nurture and comfort ourselves by indulging in our favorite meal when we felt deserving. And for many people, food is an anesthetic; it numbs their pain, depression, and disappointment.

Food Can Control Us

If we are honest, most of us will admit that food is a controlling force in our lives; it is a little god with a lot of power. In affluent societies, we often do not eat to live; we live to eat. The lives of some people have become unmanageable because of their addiction to food. In fact, there is now a support group available called "Overeaters Anonymous."

Read Ezekiel 16:49 and notice how overeating and idleness can lead to sexual sin, as in the case of the ancient city of Sodom. Any gluttony is sinful; it dulls the mind, stimulates the lusts, and leads to more carnality. Romans 13:13-14 tells us to *"make no provision for the flesh to fulfill its lusts"*—that includes a lust after food! We should eat moderately and healthily so that we are alert and able to carry out the duties God has given us.

Spiritual Benefits of Fasting

1. *Fasting makes us more sensitive spiritually.* As we deny the flesh and its demands for food, we more clearly hear the Lord's voice and discern His will. In longer fasts, our bodies are cleansed of toxins, so our minds are clearer and our energy is greater. We feel better and are sharper naturally and spiritually, which enables us to better serve others and obey the Lord's instructions to us.

2. *Fasting is a catalyst to transform us into the likeness of Jesus.* When we fast, we see our areas of carnality and selfishness that must be crucified. Fasting reveals controlling agents in our lives, such as pride, anger, jealousy, fear, and bitterness. We hide these sins (intentionally or unintentionally) with eating, entertainment, and busyness.

When hunger pangs increase, the hidden sins surface. We suddenly face fleshly attitudes we did not even know we had! As we confess our sin to God and allow Him to set us free, we move more toward Christlikeness.

3. *Fasting helps us keep our balance in life.* We tend to crave unnecessary things until they enslave us (1 Cor. 6:12). We too often allow nonessentials (coffee, entertainment, luxuries…) to take precedence in our lives. Fasting helps us to focus again on what really matters. Our desires are like a river that overflows its banks; fasting keeps the river in its proper boundaries. As we say no to eating, other carnal desires are reined in as well.

4. *Fasting softens our hearts and sensitizes our spirits toward God and the needs of others.* When we deny our flesh worldly delights, we see more clearly that *"life is more than food and the body more than clothing,"* as Jesus said in Matt. 6:25. In refusing to cater to our desires, we more quickly recognize the needs of others.

Fasting is the most serious and sacrificial way to devote ourselves to the Lord. The apostle Paul fasted to strengthen his ministry. In 1 Cor. 9:27, he spoke of disciplining his body. 2 Cor. 11:27 says he fasted often. Many of us follow Paul's teaching—except when it comes to fasting. Countless believers today have almost fully omitted fasting from their lives, although the Scriptures show that we have as much proof in support of fasting as we do for giving, and almost as much as for praying.

Different Types of Fasts

• The strictest biblical fast is the *total fast*. It calls for total abstinence from food and water.

• An *absolute fast* is a biblical fast that allows water only.

• The *partial fast* is abstaining from certain foods and drinks. Daniel abstained from "desirable foods," meat, and wine for 21 days (Daniel 10:3).

• The *proclaimed fast* (or *corporate fast*) occurs when two or more persons abstain from food together for a common cause. In the Old Testament, leaders often proclaimed a fast so that the people would call upon God for help in overcoming a serious problem, such as a plague or an advancing army (e.g., Joel 2:15). Leaders in the Antioch congregation in the first century declared a fast to seek the Lord. This resulted in the commissioning of Paul and Barnabas as the first missionaries (Acts 13:1-3).

• The *true spiritual fast* is essentially to strengthen repentance. It is sometimes for penance, and is initiated by an urging of the Holy Spirit. It may be a desire to deny self, and to bring the body and its lusts into subjection to the will and Word of God. It can also be initiated in order to receive answers to specific prayer requests.

• The most serious of all fasts, the *consecration fast*, is an absolute fast of extended duration undertaken for personal reasons. This fast differs from the other fasts in that only water is taken—usually for many days—as the person surrenders himself to God. During this fast, he sets himself apart from the world, food and drink, earthly pleasures, and comforts. It is a monumental act of supplication in which one's desires, goals, and very life are aligned with God's purposes.

A consecration fast is the best way to prepare to receive the fullness of God's blessings and anointing. It is almost certain that deep ministry in Holy Spirit power will not come until a person consecrates his life to God through a time of fasting and prayer. Only after Jesus fasted and overcame temptation in the wilderness did God release powerful gifts through His ministry.

An *ordinary fast* is one in which everyone can and should take part. It involves eating in moderation and not over-indulging natural appetites. The devotional author, Mr. Payson, wrote: *"Fasting is not so much by total abstinence from food beyond accustomed intervals, as by denying self at every meal, and using a simple diet at all times—a course well adapted to preserve the mind and body in the best condition for study and devotional exercises."*

Fasting and Passion For God

Fasting calls us out of mundane worldliness into deeper communion with the Lord. Most of us do not fast because we are too busy and too self–sufficient, the very reasons we *should* fast! Fasting is usually born out of a need to diligently seek the Lord. It is also a very effective discipline to engage in regularly if we are serious about being passionate for God. Regarding fasting for spiritual purposes and freedom, Pastor Frances Frangipane says, *"Fasting gets you there faster."*

Fasting strips us of carnal interests and aligns our focus on what is divine and eternal. When we feel God is distant, lack a sense of His presence, have no heart for worship, and/or lack enthusiasm for spiritual things, it's time to stop the busyness of our everyday lives and fast to restore our first love with Jesus. Fasting is a critical discipline especially for those who engage in healing and/or deliverance ministries; it strengthens faith and discernment, and increases effective, powerful ministry.

If you are not accustomed to fasting, you might start with missing one meal. Fasting for some people may entail skipping snacks between meals. Start small and work up to fasting one day, then two or three days. If fasting becomes a regular part of your life, you will notice its positive and powerful effects in your life and through you to others. Fasting positions and prepares you for what is to come.

EXERCISE #27 – Matthew 6:19-21, 24 ~ WHAT DO YOU TREASURE?

Memory verses: *Matthew 6:19-21, 24*

1. Spend some time thinking through your personal goals. Where are you headed? What are your desires, dreams, hopes and ambitions? Write them down.

2. Honestly reflecting on a fairly normal day, fill in the amount of hours/minutes you spend on each of the listed activities:

   devotions _____

   physical appearance (showering, shaving, applying make–up, dressing...) _____

   exercise _____

   preparation of food, meal times, and cleaning afterward _____

   housework and/or yard work _____

   work (secular or ministry job) _____

   family events and commitments _____

   friends _____

   telephone calls, texting, internet use _____

   hobbies (reading, painting, sports...) _____

   correspondence/homework/study _____

   travel time (bus, car, walking…) _____

   preparation for bed _____

   other _____

3. Looking at the ways you spend most of your "free" time, what are your first three priorities?

4. After reading Matthew 6:19-24, list the things you treasure most.

How do these treasures relate to your goals?

How do these treasures relate to the way you spend your time?

5. According to the following passages, on what things or areas should we focus?

1 Tim. 6:6-12 –

2 Cor. 4:18 –

1 John 2:15-17 –

#27 – WHAT DO YOU TREASURE?

Matthew 6:19-21, 24 *"Do not lay up for yourselves treasures on earth, where moth and rust destroy and where thieves break in and steal; but lay up for yourselves treasures in heaven, where neither moth nor rust destroys and where thieves do not break in and steal. For where your treasure is, there your heart will be also. No one can serve two masters; for either he will hate the one and love the other, or else he will be loyal to the one and despise the other. You cannot serve God and mammon."*

The Culture of God's Kingdom

In the Sermon on the Mount, Jesus was presenting the culture of God's kingdom to His followers. They had been longing for a Messiah who would lead a Jewish liberation force to overthrow the Roman Empire. They looked for someone who would restore their personal and national liberties to them. They expected him to give them worldly prosperity—riches, honor, and pleasures.

But Jesus spoke of a kingdom in which they were to turn the other cheek, love their enemies, and die to their personal ambitions and dreams. In these four verses, He exposed their wrong thinking regarding material wealth and riches. He also spoke of the spiritual fulfillment and blessing He would give them when they embraced His kingdom and yielded to His Lordship.

Communion with God Prepares Us for Trials

Look at the order of truth that Jesus gives us in this chapter. In the first 18 verses of Matthew 6, we are brought into the Lord's presence, and are instructed to have our lives occupied with Him "who sees in secret" through prayer, fasting, and giving. In verse 19 and onwards we come out of the secret place to face the trials and temptations of the world. This progression is parallel with what we see in the books of Leviticus and Numbers. In Leviticus, the children of Israel are told how to conduct the services and privileges of the Tabernacle. In Numbers, we see their warfare and walk in the wilderness.

This is the order we also need to follow. As we maintain communion in the secret place with God, we are equipped and empowered for the trials we will face on our journey to our "promised land." It is interesting and significant to note that the first test of the journey that Jesus addresses has to do with earthly treasures.

The phrase in Matt. 6:19 to "lay up or store up" means to "hoard or heap up against the future." The Greek word interpreted as "treasure" refers to abundant wealth and costly possessions such as property, gold, and precious stones. Jesus is warning against *hoarding* earthly and material treasures. He does not forbid us to provide what is necessary for our families and us, and for the present and the future as long as we acquire the wealth honestly. 2 Cor. 12:14 and 1 Tim. 5:8 support this truth. What the Lord speaks out strongly against is covetousness. Read Luke 12:15.

Forms of Covetousness

There are four common forms of covetousness that we see in God's Word. They are:

1. excessively seeking after worldly wealth when your needs are fully met. This shows discontent and insatiable desires (Luke 12:16-21, 1 Tim. 6:9-11).

2. pursuing worldly goods and despising true, eternal riches (Heb. 13:5).

3. trusting in riches rather than in God, which is idolatry (Col. 3:5, Prov. 11:28).

4. selfishly hoarding treasures for oneself only, not considering the poor nor supporting the preaching of the gospel (Matt. 19:21).

Righteous Attitude Toward Wealth

Read Prov. 30:7-9. The writer of this proverb had two requests: (1) make me honest, and (2) give me enough but not too much. This should be our attitude towards material wealth! We should pray, "Lord, give me enough for my needs and the needs of my family so that I do not steal, but do not give me so much that it turns my heart from You. My heart's pursuit is for You and for heavenly treasure."

It is not wrong to seek after the necessities of life for present or future use. However, it is wrong to yield to covetousness and to strive greedily after worldly riches. One of the blessings God often gives the righteous is financial wealth, especially if they use their finances for His kingdom and glory. Some Scriptures that support this truth are Psalm 112:1-3, Deut. 8:18, and Prov. 22:4.

God's Chief Rival

According to Matt. 6:24, mammon is God's chief rival. In the past, the term "mammon" referred to money that was entrusted to another for safekeeping. Later it began to signify money in which one trusted. Jesus viewed money as the chief thing that man drives himself to acquire and gives his energies to more than to God. According to **Mark 4:19**, it is the *"cares of this world, the deceitfulness of riches, and the desires for other things"* that choke the Word of God in our hearts, rendering it unfruitful.

To serve God as our top priority means there can be no competing loyalties; Jesus said no one can serve two masters. When unbelievers see us consider our money to be God's and available for His purposes, they will often be interested in the gospel. We can be a positive testimony to the world by our attitudes toward finances and possessions.

Author, Richard Foster, described the dominating spirit of mammon this way: *"When the Bible refers to money as a power, it does not mean something vague or impersonal. Nor does it mean power in the sense of "purchasing power." According to Jesus and all the writers of the New Testament, behind money are very real spiritual forces that energize it and give it a life of its own. Hence, money is an active agent; it is a law unto itself, and it is capable of inspiring devotion."*

Acquiring money can be addictive! Gambling is an obvious example. Consider, too, the businessmen who do well for themselves and yet keep striving for more at the expense of family and health. And what about the poor and the middle class who envy and covet? Money can seduce men to love it, cherish it, and sacrifice what is precious to attain it.

This American statistic is revealing: Most people who make $50,000 or more a year give an average of 1–2% of their income to the church. People earning $10,000 or less per year give an average of 10¬20% of their income to the church. It seems that the more money and material things we have, the more vulnerable we are to having our hearts drawn from a sacrificial love for God to a devotion to the wealth itself. But, if we will choose to forego accumulating treasures on earth in order to invest in the Lord's work, we will find treasures and riches in heaven.

Jesus Is Our Treasure

Our eternal treasure is found in the Lord Jesus! He is our gold and our delight, as we read in Job 22:23-26. In Him alone can we find lasting joy. **Psalm 16:11** says, *"You will show me the path of life; in Your presence is fullness of joy; at Your right hand there are pleasures forevermore."* And **Col. 2:3** says, *"...in Him (Jesus) are hidden all the treasures of wisdom and knowledge."*

Consider 1 Cor. 1:30 and Eph. 1:7. Whatever we need—forgiveness, wisdom, strength or comfort—can be found in Jesus. As God said to Abram in **Genesis 15:1**, so He says to us, *"I am your shield, your exceedingly great reward."*

Read Revelation 5:12. We need to see that all riches—spiritual (incorruptible wealth) or material (earthly wealth)—belong to Jesus! Any goods or wealth He entrusts to us are to be used for His glory. Knowing this will help us keep finances and possessions in the proper place in our hearts.

Your answers to the following questions will reveal what you prize more highly: earthly wealth or heavenly treasures.

• What does your soul prefer—the things of this world or the things of God?

• What do you consider your days of richest income?

• How do you consider your time well spent?

• What is dearest to your heart? What engages your most serious thoughts?

EXERCISE #28 – Matthew 6:22-23 ~ A GOOD EYE

Memory verses: *Matthew 6:22-23*

1. Read Luke 11:33-36. At the point of salvation, the eyes of our faith are opened, our vision is directed toward God, and our understanding is divinely enlightened. Think about when you made Jesus your Lord and He opened your spiritual eyes. How did you see things differently?

   How did the direction of your life change?

2. Matthew 6:22-23 follows verses 19-21 with the same thought pattern. Our character will conform to that which we treasure most. When our "eye" is good (healthy, single), we see with an eternal perspective, and our souls are full of light. What can we do to keep our eyes clear?

3. Read Revelation 3:15-19. Why were the Laodiceans blind to their true spiritual condition?

   To the best of your ability, define or explain the following phrases:

   "gold refined in the fire" –

   "white garments" –

   "eye salve to anoint the eyes" –

4. Only as a person's eye remains single does his body (soul) stay full of light. Meditate on Eph. 4:17-24 and Heb. 6:4-6 to see the seriousness of moving from spiritual enlightenment to darkness (willful rebellion). Write down any questions, thoughts, or convictions you have about this subject.

#28 – A GOOD EYE

Matthew 6:22-23 *"The lamp of the body is the eye. If therefore your eye is good, your whole body will be full of light. But if your eye is bad, your whole body will be full of darkness. If therefore the light that is in you is darkness, how great is that darkness!"*

Man was created to walk in communion with God, Who is Light. In the beginning, Adam's mind governed his soul in ways that glorified God. But because he sinned, the eyes of his offspring became evil and their understanding was darkened (Eph. 4:18). In order to walk in the light again, men and women must be born from above.

From Darkness To Light

At the point of our spiritual rebirth, our spiritual eyes are opened and our understanding is enlightened. We are immediately translated out of the kingdom of darkness into the kingdom of light. As a result, the way we perceive and approach life is (should be!) totally changed.

The eye refers to our aims and intentions. With our eyes we see our goals before us and direct our steps accordingly. If our eye is single, we will aim purely, desiring God's honor above all else. However, if our eye is evil, instead of aiming only at the glory of God, we will seek our own glory and the applause of man and/or we will yield to the desires of the flesh.

One who is developing a single eye will order his life aright and choose paths of righteousness. He will be zealous for good works. He will be in active communion with the Lord, walking in the light as God is in the light (*see* 1 John 1:7).

An Eternal Perspective

The Lord's disciples are to have one basic motivation for all that they do – to glorify Jesus the Messiah. The thoughts Jesus expressed in Matthew 6:22-23 correspond with what He said in the preceding verses, 19-21. A single eye refers to an eternal, spiritual perspective on life. Our characters conform to that which we treasure most.

In Col. 3:1-3, we are exhorted to set our minds on things above. By nature our minds are set on things of this earth. We tend to spend our time and energies storing our treasures in this life. We seek the honor of man and measure our success by our accomplishments and possessions. Before we are born again, our eyes are "evil" and our understanding is darkened. We have no spiritual perception, so we are easily deceived and captivated by false doctrines. We hold to our own points of view and to our rights to ourselves. Our judgment is usually distorted because of our infatuation with sin and love of this world. *"The way of the wicked is like darkness; they do not know what makes them stumble"* (**Prov. 4:19**). *"For all that is in the world—the lust of the flesh, the lust of the eyes, and the pride of life—is not of the Father but is of the world"* (**1 John 2:16**).

159

Lust of The Eyes Leads To Sin

For some of the Old Testament figures, it was the lust of the eyes that led to their sin. In Genesis 3:6, Eve's downfall came when she looked at something desirable that was forbidden. In Joshua 6-7, we read the story of Achan and his sin of covetousness and theft. Joshua 7:21 says, he *"looked... coveted, and took..."* What his eyes focused on caused him to sin. In 2 Sam. 11, when David saw Bathsheba bathing, he lusted after her and took her in adultery.

Psalm 101:3a says, *"I will set nothing wicked before my eyes."* The things we look at affect our inner lives. Our eyes have the power to lead us into life or death. The direction we gaze will determine the direction we walk. If we keep our focus on the Lord, our eyes will influence us for good. Seeing victory, peace, joy, and hope cause us to experience them! It is vital that we keep our eyes healthy.

Fear of God Dictates Behavior

Read 2 Kings 17:33, 41. This text says they feared the Lord, yet they served the images and gods according to the rituals of the land. Unfortunately, that description is often true of God's new covenant people. *We fear the Lord, yet we still value what the world values and live as the world does.* God calls us to express the character and conduct of His kingdom, and not to conform to this world. *"I urge you therefore, brethren, by the mercies of God, that you present your bodies a living sacrifice, holy, acceptable to God, which is your reasonable service. And do not be conformed to this world, but be transformed by the renewing of your mind, that you may prove what is that good and acceptable and perfect will of God"* (**Rom. 12:1-2**).

Measuring An Eternal Perspective

While the ungodly concentrate on attaining success in their earthly lives, as believers, we should concentrate our energies toward preparing for the next life. We are to be storing our treasures in heaven. There are a few good ways we can measure how well we are focusing on eternal things rather than temporal. These are the guidelines for rating your focus on eternity:

1. *How is your relationship with God?* Does it take first priority in your life? Do you listen for His voice? Are you communing with Jesus daily, *growing* in an intimate relationship with Him? Are you properly dealing with any known personal sin and trying to walk in holiness before the Lord and others?

2. *What is your relationship with material things like?* Are you storing up treasures here or in heaven? Do you hoard anything? Are you discerning the difference between real needs (what is necessary for life) and greed (coveting that which is not necessary)? Are you content with what you have?

3. *How are your relationships with others, especially within Church?* Do you show mercy cheerfully? Do you pursue reconciliation and restoration when there is strain in a relationship?

Do you try to build others up with your words? Do you encourage and exhort believers toward wholeness and godliness? Are you walking in patience and forbearance with everyone?

Finding Victory Over Problems

Read Mark 4:18-19. Our earthly problems have the potential of preventing us from being eternally–minded. Instead of soaring above our problems, we often drag beneath them. A common response to the question, "How are you?" is "Okay, under the circumstances." But what are we doing *under* the circumstances?! We need to remember John 16:33! In the world we *will* have tribulation, but we must keep our eyes on Jesus Christ who overcame the world.

A good way to throw off heaviness and get our focus onto Jesus and His victory is to loudly sing or shout praises to Him. Triumphant, loud praises cause our faith to rise, and release victory into our souls and circumstances. Declaring Jesus' authority over our situations can break through our anxieties and oppression quickly. Acknowledging His goodness and faithfulness reminds us that we can trust Him. He is far greater than every one of our problems! (If you do not know how to begin, open your Bible to the Psalms and read them aloud. Make sure the enemy and your mind and emotions hear the words you read.)

Light and Darkness Do Not Mix

The Lord Jesus said, *"A servant cannot serve two masters."* We cannot serve a holy God *and* an unholy world, light *and* darkness, or sin *and* righteousness. Both light and darkness want to dominate us, and we *must* choose light. We must say "yes" to God and "no" to the devil. "Yes" to obedience and "no" to rebellion. "Yes" to godly discipline and "no" to laziness. "Yes" to truth and "no" to lies, half–truths, and deception. "Yes" to purity and holiness, and "no" to immorality and worldliness. It is a matter of choice, and we must choose rightly. Every time!

Jesus said in **Luke 11:34**, *"The light of the body is the eye. Therefore, when your eye is good, your whole body also is full of light. But when your eye is bad, your body also is full of darkness."* We must be focused on living in the light if we are ever to become mature children of God. If we yield to darkness by being double minded or by dwelling on sinful/evil thoughts, our lights will grow dimmer, and darkness will win over our souls! Jesus went on to warn His followers in the next sentence: *"Therefore take heed that the light which is in you is not darkness"* (**Luke 11:35**).

"If then your whole body is full of light, having no part dark, the whole body will be full of light, as when the bright shining of a lamp gives you light" (**Luke 11:36**). This verse gives a clear picture of what mature holiness looks like—a life radiant with glory, just like a lamp shining at full brightness. What a tremendous hope we can have in Jesus—that we can be so completely illumined with the presence of God that there is "no dark part" within us!

If there *is* any darkness in us, we must not pamper or conceal it. We need to confess it and rid ourselves of it. We must hate and renounce the sin. As long as we allow darkness to remain in our hearts and lives, it will rule over us. But when we bring it into the light, its power is broken.

When we take our secret sins and boldly approach the throne of God's grace and confess them, He cleanses us from all unrighteousness (*see* 1 John 1:9). If we sin again, we must confess and repent again until the habit of sin is broken. *"He who covers his sins will not prosper, but whoever confesses and forsakes them will have mercy"* (**Prov. 28:13**).

Citizenship In Heaven

We need to remember that we are strangers and pilgrims on this earth. Our citizenship is in heaven, we are told in Phil. 3:20. Someday everything on earth will be burned up according to 2 Peter 3:10-13. Only those things that are done in accordance with God's Word and will and for His glory will last.

The devil tempts us to serve him and ourselves, rather than serve the King. He tempts us to sacrifice the eternal on the altar of the immediate and temporal. We must choose to live for our Master and for the future, rather than to settle for momentary pleasure and possessions that can rob us of what is eternal. **Psalm 90:12** says, *"So teach us to number our days that we may present to You a heart of wisdom."* A paraphrased version of that verse says, *"Teach us to use wisely all the time we have."*

For Consideration and Prayer

What is your heart set upon?

Do your relationships and does your lifestyle reflect an eternal perspective?

Is your focus straight ahead, fixed on Jesus, or are you distracted, looking in many directions?

Is there any sin or compromise in your life that you need to bring to the light in repentance and confession?

Lord, please heal us of double vision and cause us to seek You with single, genuine hearts. Free us from worldliness and earthly perspectives and set our hearts and minds on eternity! May we have a good eye that leads to life. We ask it in Jesus' name, Amen.

EXERCISE #29 – Matthew 6:25-34 ~ TRUSTING GOD

1. After reading Matt. 6:25-34, list the things about which we are to be worried or concerned.

   List the things about which we are NOT to worry.

2. What did Jesus mean when He commanded us to *"seek first the kingdom of God and His righteousness"* (**Matt. 6:33a**)?

3. According to Matt. 13:19-23, what will choke the Word of God, causing it to be unfruitful in our lives?

4. Think about your walk with God. What makes His Word in you ineffective? What robs it of power and life? (Examples: unbelief, fear, busyness, anger, greed, worry, self–pity, and love of this world)

5. How would you counsel someone who struggles with anxiety and worry?

6. What are we commanded to do in Prov. 3:5-6, and what will God do in return?

7. According to Phil. 4:6 and 1 Peter 5:7, what does God expect us to do with cares and concerns?

#29 – Trusting God

Matthew 6:25-34 *"Therefore I say to you, do not worry about your life, what you will eat or what you will drink; nor about your body, what you will put on. Is not life more than food and the body more than clothing? Look at the birds of the air for they neither sow nor reap nor gather into barns; yet your heavenly Father feeds them. Are you not of more value than they? Which of you by worrying can add one cubit to his stature? So why do you worry about clothing? Consider the lilies of the field, how they grow: they neither toil nor spin; and yet I say to you that even Solomon in all his glory was not arrayed like one of these. Now if God so clothes the grass of the field, which today is, and tomorrow is thrown into the oven, will He not much more clothe you, O you of little faith? Therefore do not worry, saying, 'What shall we eat?' or 'What shall we drink?' or 'What shall we wear?' For after all these things the Gentiles seek. For your heavenly Father knows that you need all these things. But seek first the kingdom of God and His righteousness, and all these things shall be added to you. Therefore do not worry about tomorrow, for tomorrow will worry about its own things. Sufficient for the day is its own trouble."*

In the verses preceding this discourse on trusting God for provision, Jesus had warned against covetousness, the hoarding of earthly treasures, and the love of money. In these last verses of chapter 6, He says that anxious care about temporal needs, such as food and clothing, is wrong. It is dishonoring to God, our loving Father, Who is aware of our needs and promises to provide for them. Jesus was directing His disciples' focus onto higher, eternal things. He was saying, "Trust God with all of your life, even with your most basic needs."

Worry or Trust?

There are two kinds of concern: a proper concern to provide for our families and ourselves, and a tormenting concern of fearful worry in spite of being a child of God. When our foresight degenerates into foreboding and our diligence into worrying, we have entered into sin.

Psalm 131 (author's paraphrase) says, *"As a weaned child does not cry and fret but is content just being with his mother, so my soul is weaned from discontentment and fear, and is waiting and hoping in God."* The attitude of King David in this psalm is one of worshipful trust. He had relinquished his life into his Master's hands and was at rest. Knowing that the Lord could handle every area of his life, he did not try to understand His dealings or to dictate to Him. David placed his hope and trust in the Lord and admonished God's people to do the same.

We who are called by the Lord's name should fully trust Him. Unfortunately, we often don't; instead, we try to figure Him out. We look back on past experiences (ours and those of others), and we judge God based on His performance. We consider whether or not God can be trusted in each situation we face. We wrongly form our perceptions of God and His ways from what we have experienced and seen in life rather than from what the Scriptures tell us about Him. Our environments, cultures, and education influence our understanding of God. What we believe about Him directly affects our trust in Him.

Understanding of God Influences Faith

Most of us would say we trust the Lord, but many of us are guilty of having only *selective* faith. Instead of having an *overall* trust in God, we trust Him in only certain areas and situations. For instance, we might trust God to protect us, but not to choose our friends or spouse for us. We might trust Him to meet our financial needs, but not to guide our decisions. We may trust Him in small areas, but not in major ones. We may trust Him for healing, but not for the grace necessary to endure suffering. Our dependence on God is often partial rather than all–inclusive.

The sad truth is this: we tend to believe God to be Who we *think* He is, rather than trust Him to be Who He reveals Himself to be in His Word. We form an image of God, and we trust Him within that image—the framework of our observations, culture and education, and personal experiences. However, God wants to be known and trusted for Who He is. Just as we dislike being expected to live up to someone's ideas and opinions, so does God! He does not want to be put in a box and limited to our perceptions, *often distortions,* of Him!

God's Word Is Reliable

God reveals Himself in the Bible. What He says about Himself is true; there is no deception or pretense in Him. We can trust the Word of God to reveal God's character to us. In fact, when we question the Scriptures, we are guilty of what Heb. 3:12 calls *"a wicked heart of unbelief."* Unbelief is at the root of our anxiety and worry.

Read Heb. 11:6. If we are to please God, we must put our full confidence in Him. He is a good Father and will do what is best for us. To have faith in Him is to believe in His integrity and His ability to do what He has promised. **Psalm 9:8-10** (author's paraphrase) says, *"Those who know Your name, Your reputation and character, who know You are trustworthy and have tasted of Your goodness, will confidently put their trust in You."*

God Is Our Refuge

We grow in our knowledge of God by reading and studying the Bible and through prayer. We become intimately acquainted with Him as we seek Him in the midst of personal pain or hardship. We find that He really *is* a refuge in times of trouble. We do not merely have head knowledge about God's faithfulness; rather, we *know* He is faithful because we have proven Him in our lives.

At the beginning of our walk with God, we looked forward in faith to His proclaimed faithfulness. Now that we have known Him personally over a period of time, we have experienced that faithfulness and can fully attest to it. We have found Him to be all that He promised He would be!

Trusting God's Faithfulness

Proverbs 3:5a says, *"Trust in the Lord with all your heart..."* The heart is the soul, the seat of our affections, our beliefs and values. It is our inner man. This verse says, "With *all* that you are, trust in the Lord!"

The Amplified Bible defines faith as *"the leaning of the entire human personality on God in absolute trust and confidence in His power, wisdom, and goodness."* Trusting God does not mean that we do not experience pain or difficulties. It means that we believe God is at work through our pain for our ultimate good. It means that we fully abandon our lives to His care, not just in some areas, but in *all*. If He gives us a pleasant cup to drink, we drink it with gratitude. If it is a bitter cup He chooses for us, we drink it by His grace and in communion with Him.

Trusting God is like signing a blank check and saying, "Here, Father, please fill it in." We relinquish our rights to Him to choose our vocation, marital status, housing situation, a ministry... anything! We may not always understand His will and way for us, but we can trust Him because we know He is good. *"He will not be afraid of evil tidings; his heart is steadfast, trusting in the Lord"* (**Ps. 112:7**).

Psalm 27:13-14a says, *"I would have despaired unless I had believed that I would see the goodness of the Lord in the land of the living. Wait [in faith] on the Lord..."* On earth we have limited vision, almost like tunnel vision. We can only see so much and so far. Our knowledge and understanding are finite, but God can see the big picture; He knows the end from the beginning. From His vantage point, He knows exactly what is best for each of us. When we can't trace His hand, we can trust His heart.

Believe God's Love

Read 1 John 4:16-18. We are to *know* (with our minds) and *believe* (in our hearts) that God is love. When we really know and believe the Father's love for us, we will not fear trusting Him. We will trust His choices for us because we know that they are motivated by love. Even in the midst of problems, we can rest in the knowledge that our Heavenly Father is sovereign over all that concerns us. We are His responsibility. We can have peace through our trials because His love gives us victory over anxiety and insecurity.

This peace does not come from being so "spiritual" that we fail to notice hardships; it comes from being so confident in God's love that, regardless of the battle, we know His charge over us is motivated and energized by His tender love. His love, when perfected in us, creates a shield that fear cannot penetrate! Perfect love casts out fear.

Trusting God includes many unknowns because there are no boundaries involved. Obeying God has boundaries; He speaks and we obey. But trusting Him is open–ended. It is a decision of our will to put our lives fully and unreservedly into His hands. It is a lifestyle of worship, where we acknowledge that our Creator is greater than we are and worthy of our trust.

It is to our wisdom to entrust our future to the Lord, allowing Him to choose our way for us. As the Apostle Paul said in **2 Tim. 1:12**, *"I know Whom I have believed, and am persuaded that He is able to keep what I have committed to Him until that Day."* It is safe to commit our lives to the Lord. *"Oh, taste and see that the Lord is good! Blessed is the man who trusts in Him"* (**Ps. 34:8**).

Psalm 56:3, 9, 11 say, *"Whenever I am afraid, I will trust in You. When I cry out to You, then my enemies will turn back; this I know because God is for me... In God I have put my trust; I will not be afraid."*

For Consideration and Prayer

Do you trust God with your life and your future?

Do you really believe He loves you?

Confess to Him any unbelief and fear, and choose (again) to put your trust in Him.

EXERCISE #30 – Matthew 7:1-5 ~ JUDGING OTHERS

1. According to Matthew 7:1-5, there is a problem with your brother's eye and your eye. Note what is in your brother's eye and in your eye, explaining what Jesus meant in these verses.

2. Does the above passage allow you to take the speck or the mote out of your brother's eye? If so, under what circumstances?

   How does this compare with Galatians 6:1-5?

3. Write in your own words the warning Jesus gives in Matthew 7:2.

4. What does Jesus call the person who tries to take the speck out of his brother's eye before taking care of his own eye? Why do you think Jesus chose this word?

5. Read Romans 2:1. How does this verse relate to Matthew 7:1-5?

6. When Jesus and Satan view sin in our lives, they both take action. What does our Lord do? (Heb. 4:14-16, 7:25; Luke 22:32)

What does the devil do? (Rev. 12:10)

What should *we* do when we see weakness in someone?

7. After reading Romans 14:1-23, list the instructions given for relating to one another.

#30 – JUDGING OTHERS

Matthew 7:1-5 *"Judge not, that you be not judged. For with what judgment you judge, you will be judged; and with the measure you use, it will be measured back to you. And why do you look at the speck in your brother's eye, but do not consider the plank in your own eye? Or how can you say to your brother, 'Let me remove the speck from your eye,' and look, a plank is in your own eye? Hypocrite! First remove the plank from your own eye, and then you will see clearly to remove the speck from your brother's eye."*

The Greek word translated *judge* is **krino;** it means to assume the office of a judge, to condemn, to undergo the process of a trial, or to execute judgment upon someone. In the Lord's command, *"judge not,"* He is forbidding the unlawful judging of others. There are numerous ways in which we are *not* to judge. Here are the most common:

- *Judicially* – prying into official or civil affairs of others without authority. This refers to that which lies outside the prerogative of a private individual.

- *Presumptuously* – judging suspicions or unconfirmed rumors as facts.

- *Hypocritically* – detecting minor faults in others while being unconcerned about our own sins; pretending to be righteous while indulging in lust or compromise.

- *Hastily* – thinking the worst of someone before making a full investigation and obtaining clear proof that the suspicions or reports are correct.

- *Unjustly or unfairly* – ignoring what is good and right in a person and seeing only what is unsatisfactory.

- *Unmercifully* – being unmerciful in passing judgment on another.

Read John 7:24. Our judgment of others is wrong when we judge according to our own standards of behavior or on the basis of appearance or personality. Our judgment must be like that of the Messiah's as prophesied in Isaiah 11:2-5. Under the anointing of the Spirit of the Lord, the Messiah to come would judge with righteousness, equity, and faithfulness. He would not judge according to what He saw or heard in the natural realm. Now that the Messiah, Jesus, *has* come and is living within us as believers, we are to judge others as He does… righteously and faithfully.

Micah 6:8 says God requires us, *"…to do justly, to love mercy, and to walk humbly with God."* We are not only to *be* merciful; we are to *love* being merciful to those in need of it!

In **Luke 6:36** Jesus said, *"Be merciful in the same way your Father in heaven is merciful."* We in the Body of Christ are often lacking in mercy. In fact, unjust and unloving criticism of one another has been called *"the peculiar sin of the saints."* Instead of being known for our grace towards others, we are often known for our "disgrace."

171

Satan Uses Slander and Criticism

Author and theologian, Paul Billheimer, wrote, *"Disunity in the Body probably sends more people to hell than open sin; it binds the hands of the Holy Spirit and thwarts His work of convicting of sin, righteousness, and judgment. The most important prerequisite to world evangelization and revival is the unity of the Body of Christ."*

The most common tools that the devil uses to fragment the Church are accusations and criticism that come from *within* the Body. Throughout history, the Church has thrived under outside persecution, but it has disintegrated under inside persecution. If the devil cannot destroy God's people from outside attacks, he comes inside using the tools of gossip, slander, criticism, and betrayal to divide and conquer.

It is tragic when we are more willing to share weaknesses and question motives of others than we are to speak affirmatively of them! To criticize and find fault with someone is not a sign of spiritual maturity; it's a sign of immaturity. It reveals a lack of love.

Condemning fellow believers wounds and scars the Body of Christ and destroys its testimony to the seen and unseen worlds (both of which look to the believers to represent God). Every time we accuse another, we are putting into motion a death process that affects the Lord's Body, the testimony of the Church, and ourselves personally.

In his book, *Epic Battles of the Last Days*, Rick Joyner writes, *"Accusation has been the devil's most effective and deadly tool in destroying the light, power, and witness of the Body of Christ."*

Prayer Unites The Body of Christ

What *should* we do when we see weaknesses and sin in each other? We should intercede! While harsh judgment increases the lack of love and unity in the Body of Christ, prayer moves God into action and becomes a uniting force. When we choose to pray rather than to criticize, we will see the Church become whole and be the light to this world that She is called to be.

The greatest threat to Satan's domain is unity in the Church. Unity does not just increase our spiritual authority; it multiplies it. (Unfortunately, the enemy has understood this much better than believers have.) In **John 17:21** Jesus said, *"When they are one in Us, then the world will believe that You sent Me."* When the world sees the love and unity we share with each other as His disciples, they will believe that He is God's Messiah. It will be because of our unity, not by amazing signs and wonders, that the divinity of Jesus will be authenticated.

We are a part of one another, and we need to lovingly care for each other. We can exhort and encourage one another to be faithful to the Lord, but we are never given permission to condemn or slander each other. These activities sow discord in the Lord's family. In Proverbs 6, God says *"sowing discord among the brethren"* is an abomination to Him. It breaks down the very thing (His Body) that He is trying to build up. The enemy is the accuser of the brethren; we must never join him in accusing others. We need to cover one another's vulnerabilities and weaknesses, not expose them.

The Danger Of Hypocrisy

Look again at Matthew 7:1-5. Jesus was denouncing the hypocrisy of those who were judging others while having serious problems of their own. They were not perfect and yet they were expecting others to be. Notice the contrast between the plank and the speck. Those with the planks were judging those with the specks. What hypocrisy!

The Lord's disciple is to judge himself carefully and thoroughly (1 Cor. 11:28, 31), refusing to invade God's judicial office concerning others. The more strictly we judge others, the more strictly God will judge us. The Apostle Paul wrote in **Romans 14:4**, *"Who are you to judge the servant of another? To his own master he stands or falls; and stand he will, for the Lord is able to make him stand."*

Choose To Love

Read James 4:11-12 and Romans 13:8-10. The Law finds its fulfillment in love, not in judgment. It is interesting to note that much of our judgment of others concerns the gray areas of life. We often do not actually judge sin; we judge personalities and cultural or traditional differences. If we would choose to walk in love and seek to edify others, then we would not need to worry about breaking Jesus' commandment in Matthew 7:1.

"Therefore do not go on passing judgment before the time, but wait until the Lord comes who will both bring to light the things hidden in the darkness and disclose the motives of men's hearts; and then each man's praise will come to him from God" (**1 Cor. 4:5**).

For Consideration and Prayer

As we have looked at the Word of God, you may have thought of people that you have criticized or treated unmercifully. Ask the Lord to search your heart and show you what you need to confess and where you need to repent.

Are you guilty of slander or gossip? If you have been guilty of sowing discord in the Body of Christ, ask the Lord for forgiveness and cleansing. After praying for those you have slandered, make concrete plans to bless them in some way.

Read Romans 2:1-4 and examine yourself. Are you judging others and yet doing the same things they are doing? Are you going after specks in another's eye when you have planks in your own?

Ask the Lord to whom you should actively show extra measures of mercy and grace.

EXERCISE #31 – Matthew 7:5-6 ~ REMOVE THE PLANK!

Memory verses: *Matthew 7:5-6*

1. According to Matthew 7:15-20, how are we to judge others? Are there any other ways?

2. What is the meaning of the term *"dog"* referred to in 1 Sam. 17:43 and 2 Sam. 16:9?

   How does this relate to Matthew 7:6?

3. After reading Matt. 7:5 again, examine yourself for planks or logs that you need to remove from your eyes so that you can see clearly. (If you do not see any, ask the Holy Spirit or a close friend to help you.) Consider prejudices, bitterness, selfishness, angers and fears. All of these can be filters that influence how we perceive people and situations.

4. According to the following verses, what is our responsibility to one another in the Church?

   Heb. 10:24-25 –

   Phil. 2:1-4 –

   Eph. 4:1-3 –

   Gal. 6:1-2 –

#31 – REMOVE THE PLANK

Matthew 7:5-6 *"Hypocrite! First remove the plank from your own eye, and then you will see clearly to remove the speck out of your brother's eye. Do not give what is holy to the dogs; nor cast your pearls before swine, lest they trample them under their feet, and turn and tear you in pieces."*

Jesus said, *"First remove the plank from your own eye...."* Before trying to help others with their obvious sins and weaknesses, deal with your own! Examine yourself before God, and repent of anything that you know to be displeasing to Him. This is the prerequisite for judging others, and if we follow this rule, we will not unlawfully judge anyone.

Common Planks

It is easy to hate the sin and its consequences that we see in others, and yet at the same time, love our own sin. God wants us to hate sin altogether, especially in ourselves! Read Psalm 97:10a, Psalm 119:104, 128, and Prov. 8:13. In relation to this text in Matthew 7, there are two things that are commonly a "plank" in the eyes of God's people: hypocrisy and spiritual pride.

Hypocrisy is pretending to be something we are not. It reveals our desire to please man, even at the cost of displeasing God. It is living a lie, and because our own state of being is untrue, we cannot adequately discern the true state of others.

Spiritual pride causes us to be proud of our spiritual maturity or performance and, at the same time, look with disdain on others. We assume a superior posture when we judge someone. From that lofty position, we are ineffective in restoring a fallen brother due to our lack of grace. Because pride robs us of humility, it also robs us of the grace that comes with humility.

Other "planks" can be any particular sin or lust that we allow in our lives. These sins can distort our judgment. Unless we put them to death, we are not qualified to reprove sin in others. The psalmist David prayed, *"Create in me a clean heart, O God...* Then *will I teach transgressors Your ways"* (**Ps. 51:10, 13**).

For Whom Are We Responsible?

"...remove the speck out of your brother's eye" (**Matt. 7:5b**). We are to help those we would consider our "brother." In order to remove a "speck" from another's eye, we must be in close relationship to him. Jesus tells us that we should seek to correct the faults of those who are near to us—members of our family, intimate friends, and the people we are close to in our congregations. We are not to bring correction to mere acquaintances or to try to clean up the inner life of anyone with whom we come into contact.

My responsibility is first to myself, then to those with whom I am close. The necessity of close-ness to remove a speck from another's eye not only suggests a nearness of relationship, but also a *moral nearness* (having a place in his affections and esteem).

I must win the right to speak into a person's life. I cannot get close to him while towering over him in pride or while being so distant from him that he does not sense my genuine care for him.

Levels of Friendships

American seminar speaker, Bill Gothard, teaches on four levels of friendships, defining the freedoms on each level. Those levels are:

1. Acquaintance – one with whom you have occasional contact. With him, you may share public information or ask general questions.

2. Casual friend – one with whom you share common interests, activities, or concerns (e.g., a classmate or a sport team member). You may ask a casual friend specific questions.

3. Close friend – one with whom your friendship is based on mutual life goals. This level allows for genuine soul fellowship.

4. Intimate friend – one with whom you have a deeply committed and trusted relationship. With him or her, you may share secrets and emotions, and give honest, constructive criticism.

It is on level four that we are able to most freely speak to people about their weaknesses or sins. The exception to bringing correction to someone other than an intimate friend is in the area of spiritual authority. The authority figure has the concern and responsibility to address sin in those under his authority. This is an accepted role of ministers, pastors, and counselors/therapists.

Judgment or Discernment

Read Romans 2:1-3. The phrase 'to pass judgment' in Greek is **krino**. It means to give a verdict with no intention of personal involvement in the guilty person's life. There are distinct characteristics of someone who judges another. Here are five:

- He forms opinions with only a few known factors.
- He shares conclusions with people not related to the solution of the problem.
- He has not yet overcome the same problem.
- He rejects the sinner as well as the sin.
- He reminds God of the shortcomings of the offender (with accusatory, negative prayers).

Read 1 Cor. 11:31 and 14:29. There are two Greek words used for the words 'discernment' or 'proper judgment.' They are **diakrino**, which means, "to distinguish" and **anakrino**, which means, "to investigate." Here are six characteristics of one who distinguishes or investigates others:

- He asks questions until all factors are understood.
- He studies all factors to discover root causes and motives for the problem.
- He accepts the offender as he is and waits for the right time to approach the problem.
- He looks for a comparable problem in his own life.

- He gains the confidence of the other, then shares how he overcame a similar problem.
- He assumes responsibility for restoring the offender or needy person.

Restore With Humility

One who *discerns* the faults of another is willing to get involved in the healing process. Part of our responsibility in the Body of Christ is to help one another toward more godliness. To do this, we need to spiritually discern situations rather than make human judgments. We must meekly approach those in sin and gently admonish them. Ideally, we should already have a relationship of love and trust with that person, which allows open, personal sharing. Our motive must be love, and our goal should be to see God's kingdom and glory released more fully in him or her. This ministry to others calls for preparatory prayer, sensitivity, and spiritual wisdom.

The Holy Spirit will *only* reveal to us what is wrong in others for the purpose of intercession, *never* for the purpose of criticism and accusation. When we see sin in others, we are always to pray, sometimes to confront, and never to gossip! *"If anyone sees his brother sinning a sin which does not lead to death, he will ask, and He will give him life for those who commit sin not leading to death..."* (**1 John 5:16a**).

Share Gems of The Kingdom Wisely

When Jesus said, *"Do not judge"* He was not calling us to disregard the unrighteous behavior of others, nor to close our eyes to sin. He was not advocating tolerance of false doctrines or indiscriminate acceptance of those who teach them. He *was* telling us not to take the beautiful gems of the gospel and throw them before mockers. He was commanding us not to share the truths of God's Word with those whom we know would ridicule them. We are to discern whether or not a person is ready before we share eternal truths with him or her. *"Do not give what is holy to the dogs; nor cast your pearls before swine, lest they trample them under their feet, and turn and tear you in pieces"* (**Matt. 7:6**).

Devotional author, Oswald Chambers, wrote, *"Over and over again men water down the Word of God to suit those who are not spiritual, and consequently the Word of God is trampled under the feet of 'swine.'"*

Jesus said in **Matt. 5:17**, *"Think not that I am come to destroy the law, or the prophets: I am not come to destroy, but to fulfill."* What was the teaching of the Law and the Prophets concerning this subject? Under the law, dogs and swine were unclean and unholy animals. The Israelites were prohibited from using them for food or sacrifices. The term "dog" was applied to persons of worthless character (*see* 2 Sam. 16:9) or to those outside the camp of God's people.

In looking at Matt. 7:5-6 together, we see that we are to try to restore those with specks in their eyes after we deal with the planks in our own. We are to discern who is willing to be admonished, as some will resent our interest in them and reject us, treading our admonitions under their feet.

"Speak not in the ears of a fool, for he will despise the wisdom of your words" (**Prov. 23:9**). *"The ear that hears the reproof of life will abide among the wise. He who disdains instruction despises his own soul, but he who heeds reproof gets understanding"* (**Prov. 15:31–32**).

Read Prov. 27:5-6 and notice how committed love for another will sometimes include reproof and correction. When we care enough to confront a serious sin or weakness in the life of someone with whom we are close, we prove our love.

Suggested Prayer

Lord, please help me to walk in humility, discernment, and unconditional love with others. Show me when I can share my testimonies and pearls of insight and revelation, and when it is to my wisdom to refrain from sharing. Help me to get the planks out of my eyes so that when the time comes, I can help those who will welcome my assistance. In Jesus' name, amen.

EXERCISE #32 – Matthew 7:7-11 ~ SUPPLICATION

Memory verses: *Matthew 7:7-11*

1. Read Matt. 7:7-11. What sort of prayer is the Lord referring to in these verses?

2. Explain the element of trust that seems to be implied in the above verses.

3. From what Jesus said in Luke 11:8, what are prayers of *importunity* or *persistence?*

4. What does it mean to prevail in prayer, and why is this type of prayer necessary?

5. From the following passages, write down the kinds of prayer that are mentioned:

Matt. 21:22 –

Acts 12:5 –

Rom. 8:26 –

Eph. 6:18 –

James 5:15-16 –

6. If there is someone or something you are persistently praying about, consider sharing with the others in your group so they can pray with you.

#32 – SUPPLICATION

Matthew 7:7-11 *"Ask, and it will be given to you; seek, and you will find; knock, and it will be opened to you. For everyone who asks receives, and he who seeks finds, and to him who knocks it will be opened. Or what man is there among you who, if his son asks for bread, will give him a stone? Or if he asks for a fish, will he give him a serpent? If you then, being evil, know how to give good gifts to your children, how much more will your Father who is in heaven give good things to those who ask Him!"*

The tense used in Greek for the verbs ask, seek, and knock is the continuous present tense. Jesus was saying, *"ask and keep on asking, seek and keep on seeking, knock and keep on knocking."* Keep on bombarding heaven until the answer comes!

Although the Scripture is clear that God wants to answer our prayers, He does lay down some scriptural conditions for our receiving from Him. We are to: (1) seek first God's kingdom (Matt. 6:33), (2) believe in God's goodness and desire to give (Heb. 11:6), (3) pray according to God's will (1 John 5:14-15), and (4) maintain obedient fellowship with Jesus (John 15:7).

Persistent Prayer

Read Luke 11:5-8. The Greek word translated "persistence" in verse 8 is **anaideia**. It refers to the believer who presses God boldly and persistently until He answers. Importunate prayer pleads for *others*; it is not usually a prayer for one's own needs. In the story Jesus told in Luke 11, the man was obtaining bread to give to someone else. Persistent prayer does not yield to discouragement, weariness, or impatience. God delights in boldness that will not take "no" for an answer.

Read Genesis 18:20-33. God was planning to destroy Sodom and Gomorrah because of their wickedness, but Abraham pleaded with God to save Sodom for the sake of the righteous in the city. The last request Abraham made was in verse 32; God agreed to save the city for the sake of ten righteous people. If Abraham had made one further request, asking God to save the city for the sake of five righteous ones, perhaps the city would have been spared. *He quit praying too soon!* In his intercession before the Lord, Abraham did not "ask and keep on asking." Right up until he finished praying, God had agreed to every request of Abraham's. How often are we guilty of the same thing? We stop praying too soon! Perhaps God would have answered our prayers positively had we pressed in and pleaded with Him for the sake of others!

There is an aspect of prayer that involves sweet conversation between two intimate friends. The prayer mentioned in Matt. 7, however, is not just relational conversation; it is prayer that prevails to move the hand of God on behalf of another. P.T. Forsyth, author of *The Soul of Prayer*, warns us not to reduce all prayer to talking to God or even conversing with God. He says if we do this, we may lose the aspect of spiritual wrestling and prevailing. Prevailing prayer is intensified intercession that presses in until the answer comes. God wants our prayers to be effective! Prevailing prayer is one of the most important ministries in God's kingdom. It is His ordained means for extending His kingdom and will on earth, and for defeating the devil and his hosts of wickedness.

The secret of prevailing prayer is simply to pray until the answer comes. The length of time is immaterial, as it is God's answer that matters. This kind of praying always involves a price.

Levels of Warfare Praying

There are increasing levels of prevailing prayer. Supplication may begin as simple petition, but it can escalate to waging war in prayer as led by the Holy Spirit and energized by compassion. Here are the steps leading from asking to spiritual warfare:

1. Asking – This is a basic prayer of petition.

2. Seeking – The asking becomes longer and more intense.

3. Knocking – Interceding becomes more urgent and insistent; one's perseverance is tested.

4. Fasting – Fasting is added to the intensity of intercession.

5. Praying with a burden – A burden may come suddenly and be intense, lifting only as we pray it through to victory. Other times a prayer burden may extend for a while and need to be prayed over daily for weeks or months until the situation yields to God's will.

6. Wrestling in prayer – This very intense praying may include demonstrative acts in the spirit or pacing about while fervently interceding. The intensity may be felt in the intercessor's body and soul, and his words of prayer may give way to groans of travail. Food and rest may easily be forgotten as he wrestles with God to a place of victory. An example of this kind of prayer is when Jesus agonized in the Garden of Gethsemane.

7. Waging war in prayer – When an intense spiritual battle lasts for a long time, the praying usually includes fasting, proclaiming God's Word over the situation, resisting or binding the enemy, and/or engaging in victorious praise. This is most often done with a group of like–minded believers who are willing to pay the price in time and energy to "get the job done."

The basis for prevailing prayer is our constant, instant access to God's throne. The Lord wants us to take a responsible and active role in His will being accomplished on earth. We are given power and authority through prayer because we are *"seated with Christ,"* according to Eph. 2:6. To actualize this privilege we must be consecrated to the Lord, filled with the Spirit, and endeavoring to live victoriously. We are to be so identified with Jesus that we are one with Him in His death, resurrection, and on His throne. Both the crucified life and the victorious life should be natural expressions of our daily walk with God.

People of prayer are usually normal in their homes, businesses, and churches. But in the hidden place of prayer, they have power with God; they exercise spiritual authority. They are not usually unbalanced or fanatical, but they do carry a special portion of God's presence. They walk in quiet power, intense commitment, and active faith. They maintain a disciplined and devoted prayer life.

To be a man or woman of effective prayer, we must learn to prevail over anything that does not yield to God's will. That may include something in ourselves, our circumstances, in those who resist the gospel, and over the enemy.

Prevail Over Yourself

A person who is spiritually healthy will love to pray. He will often hunger for *more time* to be alone with Jesus. He is eager to sacrifice other things in order to commune with the Lord and intercede for others. If that does not describe you, you may need to ask God to deliver you from being unwilling to pay the price for victory. You cannot *earn* answers to your prayers, but there is a price in discipline, effort, and prioritizing that you must pay. You must be willing to sacrifice self–interests so that God's will can be done.

You may need to prevail over…

… *your schedule of activities.* You'll need to adjust your priorities so that you can make time to be alone with God. You may have to sacrifice good and urgent activities in order to give adequate time to intercession. (Satan always seems to manipulate circumstances or people to interrupt us when we want to concentrate in prayer.)

… *weariness and pain.* When you are tired, the best thing to do is to rest before you begin praying. You can also pace about or vary your posture to stay alert as you pray. Physical pain seems like a good reason to pamper yourself, but if you can overcome the pain, you can wage a good fight in the spiritual realm. As you concentrate on eternal issues in prayer, your focus on pain will often give way and you'll lose your awareness of it.

… *laziness.* You might need to confess laziness to God as a sin and practice self–discipline. You may need to tell yourself to "rise up and pray!" Nothing is as important as praying.

… *doubts and wandering thoughts.* Resist the spirit of unbelief and actively focus your thoughts on Jesus and your subject of prayer. Read or quote 2 Cor. 10:4-5.

… *food.* God may lead you to add fasting to your intercession for a time. (It is interesting that often when we want to meet with God in prayer, we suddenly feel hungry.)

Prevail Over Situations and People

The situations we pray about are often complex and may require considerable prayer before they yield to the will of God. Repeated roadblocks can be frustrating and cause hopelessness, but all things are possible with Jesus! God is sovereign over nature and people. He acts in wisdom, grace, and power until the answer comes and His will is done. Never doubt the possibility of a miracle.

God has created each of us with a free will. People for whom we pray may be resistant to change and stubborn, but our hope is in the Lord. He can change what appears to be impossible. God can speak to a person's conscience, or bring new thoughts to his mind.

The Lord will never treat people as robots, manipulate them, or violate their free will, but He has ways of coordinating events and the actions of others until the most stubborn people do change. It may take continuing intercession over a long period of time, but prayer can prevail. Take courage and keep praying!

Prevail Over The Enemy

Satan tries to keep us from praying, but if that fails, he tries to shorten our prayer time and distract us while we pray. He wants to discourage us before we prevail. He would rather have us busy *working for* God than *praying to* God. Prevailing prayer has the potential to hinder Satan and free his captives. We have not prevailed until Satan is defeated! The defeat begins in the unseen world of the spirit, but becomes visible as our prayers are answered.

Pastor Samuel Chadwick wrote, *"The one concern of the devil is to keep the saints from prayer. He fears nothing from prayerless studies, prayerless work, and prayerless religion. He laughs at our toil, mocks at our wisdom, but trembles when we pray."*

Dr. Charles Spurgeon, whose preaching and writing impacted multitudes, said, *"He who knows how to overcome with God in prayer has heaven and earth at his disposal."*

Changes Follow Supplication

In Genesis 31, Jacob left his father–in–law, took his wives, children, and animals, and headed for home. Esau, his angry brother, was on his way to meet him with 400 men. Jacob desperately needed a miracle! In Genesis 32:24-30, we read that Jacob struggled (the Hebrew word, **sarah**, means 'to persist, exert oneself, and persevere') with the Man (many believe He was Jesus pre-incarnate), determined to receive a blessing. Jacob prevailed; he received a blessing and a name change. Jacob and Esau reconciled the next day, but the battle was won the night before in prayer.

Two truths we can learn from this account: (1) A name change indicates a character change. When we prevail with God in prayer, not only will our situations yield to His will, but *we* will yield to His will! Our characters must change as we encounter the Master. A name/character change through a divine encounter can also be a birthing into a new calling or anointing. (2) Jacob prevailed in prayer before he prevailed in the natural realm. He had the answer by faith, having prayed through to victory. We, too, must wrestle with God in prayer before we try to be successful with men. Prevailing in the invisible realm makes prevailing in the visible realm possible.

For Consideration and Prayer

In what areas do you need to prevail in order to intercede effectively?

Have you laid down a prayer burden that the Lord once gave you? Have you stopped praying because you were discouraged? The Lord wants you to pick that prayer burden up again! Pray for the grace to persevere in prayer until you see the victory come!

EXERCISE #33 – Matthew 7:12 ~ THE GOLDEN RULE

1. As you read and memorize Matthew 7:12, explain in your own words what Jesus was saying to His disciples in this verse.

2. Why is it difficult for man to live by what Jesus commanded in Matt. 7:12, commonly known as "The Golden Rule?"

   What would make such a lifestyle possible?

3. If you really do to others as you want them to do to you, what will that require of you?

4. What are some possible wrong motives for obeying Jesus' command in Matt. 7:12?

   What is the correct heart motivation for obeying this commandment?

5. What do the following Scriptures tell us to do?

   Luke 6:31 –

   Romans 13:8-10 –

   Galatians 5:13-14 –

#33 – THE GOLDEN RULE

Matthew 7:12 *"Therefore, whatever you want men to do to you, do also to them, for this is the Law and the Prophets."*

The Golden Rule

The words of Jesus in Matthew 7:12 have often been called "The Golden Rule." This verse is the key to understanding the Sermon on the Mount. It is such a familiar verse that even unbelievers know it without knowing Who said it!

Jesus said that He did not come to abolish the Law or the Prophets, but to fulfill them. The Greek word for fulfill is ***pleroo***, which means "to complete, to fully carry out, to bring to fullness." Jesus fulfilled the Law by teaching it and by living out its full expression. Let's look at some Scriptures from the Old Testament that Jesus could have been referring to when He commanded His disciples to do for others what they would like done for them.

Lev. 19:18 *"You shall not take vengeance, nor bear any grudge against the children of your people, but you shall love your neighbor as yourself: I am the Lord."*

Exodus 23:4 *"If you meet your neighbor's ox or his donkey going astray, you shall surely bring it back to him again."*

Deut. 15:7-8 *"You shall not harden your heart nor shut your hand from your poor brother, but you shall open your hand wide to him, and willingly lend him sufficient for his need, whatever he needs."*

Righteous With God

When we look at the Ten Commandments, we see that the first four laws are directed toward God and the following six toward man. The commandments begin with instructions to love God and have no idols before Him, to honor His name by not taking it in vain, and to keep the Sabbath day holy. From there, the focus of the commandments turns toward man's relationship to man: honoring parents, not murdering, not committing adultery, not stealing, not bearing false witness, and not coveting a neighbor's possessions.

What is revealed by the order of the commandments is that we are to be righteous before God before we can live righteously before others. What we are in action we are to first be in heart. When we live righteously with God, it should be evident in the way we relate to those around us. In our human strength, we can never fulfill the Law and the Prophets. However, if we allow God to fill us with Himself, then we *can* do for others as we would like them to do for us. As we walk in His Spirit and listen for His voice, we can know what to do and have the love and courage to do it. We need to be filled with and led by the Spirit of God!

Choose To Do Good

Read 2 Kings 6:8-23. Elisha's prayer for his servant is good for us to pray, *"Lord, I pray, open his* (my) *eyes that he* (I) *may see"* (**2 Kgs. 6:17a**). It is vital that we see what is happening from God's perspective; then it is easier for us to receive and understand His strategies for our situations. In verses 22-23, we see how well the king of Israel treated the enemy Syrian troops. He did them good, which resulted in peaceful relations between Israel and Syria for a time.

Read Prov. 25:21 and Romans 12:20-21. When we do good to those who mean evil against us, the situation can turn out for our good, resulting in peace, reconciliation, and healing.

Live Sacrificially

Read 2 Cor. 8:9 and John 10:17-18. Jesus chose to lay down His life and die so that we can live. He became poor so that we might be rich. Just as He had the power to lay down His life and take it up again, in a sense, so do we. We can choose every day to take up our crosses and follow Him, to lay down our preferences and put others' interests above our own. We can deny ourselves by living and giving sacrificially.

Doing for others what you would like done for you means that you go the extra mile. For instance, you smile at others when you are weary and in pain, knowing that you would appreciate a smile from someone. You cook for others when you are busy and tired because you would like someone to cook for you. "The Golden Rule" can touch on the very area that you personally need loving ministry yourself. In obeying this rule, you give to others exactly what you need. Maybe you need patience, but you are in a position that requires you to be patient with others. Maybe your own home needs cleaning, but you offer to help a friend clean hers. You may feel pressed for time, but you sacrifice a few hours to listen to someone who is facing a difficulty.

It costs us to do for others what we would like them to do for us. It means we give away that which we need and want ourselves. We choose to be sensitive to others' needs and concerns. We see their pain and compassionately help them even when we are struggling ourselves. *"...let each esteem (regard, consider) others better than himself. Let each of you look out not only for his own interests, but also for the interests of others"* (**Phil. 2:3-4**).

Be Gracious

Look again at Matt. 7:12. The word "therefore" looks back to what Jesus said in the previous section (verses 7-11). Since we expect good gifts from our fathers, we should give good gifts to others. Privilege and duty always go together; we receive blessings from the hand of God, so we are responsible to bless others. The goodness we receive from God enables us to better perform our responsibilities to men.

"Be followers [imitators] of God, as dear children" (**Eph. 5:1**). God has been gracious and kind to us, so we should be generous and kind to others. Do not let your conduct be determined by the way *people* treat you, but by the way *God* treats you.

Bible Commentator, Matthew Henry, wrote, *"Christ came to teach us not only what we are to know and to believe, but what we are to do. What we are to do, not only toward God, but toward men; not only toward those who are like us and who we like, but toward men in general."*

Read 1 John 4:20-21. We usually find it easy to voice our love and adoration to God, but what if He were to test that love by asking, "Do you love your brother?" God is attracted to our worship, but is repelled by any lack of love toward others that He sees in us.

Obey the Golden Rule

When the Scripture does not give us specific commands from God in our dealings with men, we are to obey the commandment given in Matthew 7:12. We are to search our consciences as to how we would have others deal with us in similar circumstances, and then do the same for them. That being the case, we would never be unkind to others, as we would want kindness from them. We would not be inconsiderate, for we appreciate consideration. We would be faithful because we want faithfulness from others.

In our modern age, "The Golden Rule" is sometimes stated negatively, *"Do not do to others what you do not want done to you."* By stating it positively, Jesus made it more significant. It is not so difficult to refrain from doing harm to others; it is much harder to take the initiative by doing something good to them or for them.

This rule, as Jesus stated it, is the foundation of active goodness—the kindness, goodness, and mercy that God shows to us every day. **Psalm 23:6** says, *"Surely goodness and mercy shall follow me all the days of my life; and I will dwell in the house of the Lord forever."*

If we obey Matt. 7:12, we will reflect the heart of our heavenly Father. Remember the words of Jesus in **Matt. 5:44-45**: *"...love your enemies, and pray for those who persecute you in order that you may be sons of your Father Who is in heaven; for He causes His sun to rise on the evil and the good, and sends rain on the righteous and the unrighteous."*

EXERCISE #34 – Matthew 7:13-14 ~ THE NARROW GATE

Memory verses: *Matthew 7:13-14*

1. Read Matthew 7:13-14. What is the narrow gate?

Why is the *"way which leads to life"* difficult?

2. Some believe that Jews have a special door to salvation because they are the First Covenant people of God. Read the Scriptures below and write what the Bible says about the way to the Father and to eternal life.

   John 3:36 –

   John 10:9 –

   John 14:6 –

   Acts 4:12 –

   1 Tim. 2:5 –

   1 John 5:12 –

3. Read Luke 13:22-30. Why will many not be able to enter the Master's house?

What is a *"worker of iniquity?"*

189

What will happen to those who fail to enter in?

4. Read Psalm 1 and write down the descriptions of a godly person that you see there.

5. Ask the Lord if you are guilty of worldly thoughts and actions. Is there compromise in your life? Do you need to return to the way of holiness? Is Jesus Lord of your life, or is "Lord" just a name you call Him? Think and pray about these issues until you have settled them with Jesus.

#34 – THE NARROW GATE

Matthew 7:13-14 *"Enter by the narrow gate; for wide is the gate, and broad is the way that leads to destruction, and there are many who go in by it. Because narrow is the gate, and difficult is the way which leads to life, and there are few who find it."*

The Righteousness Gate

The narrow gate that Jesus alluded to in this passage represents strict observation of the command He gave in the preceding verse, *"Do unto others as you would have them do unto you."* The wide gate is an allusion to the careless sinful ways of the wicked. It is easier to be vengeful and covetous, to take advantage of others, and to live for oneself than to walk according to Matt. 7:12. *"The way which leads to life"* refers to a lifestyle of righteousness. This lifestyle is difficult because to live it, we have to deny our carnal desires and yield to Jesus in all areas of our lives.

Jesus' words about the narrow gate contradict common theological understandings of our modern, selfish generation. Some preachers say that we can reach heaven through numerous avenues and that there is no suffering in acquiring it. This contradicts Acts 4:12 and 14:22. We hear that we can be disciples of Jesus without denying ourselves and taking up our crosses, and that we do not have to put to death the deeds of the body in order to live. This is contrary to Romans 8:13. Many believe we can serve two masters and please both! In short, modern teaching and thinking holds to the belief that the gate is not as narrow as Jesus declared it to be.

To be born again, we must come to Jesus, confess and repent of our sin, and receive His forgiveness. We must surrender our lives to His lordship, and, by faith, receive the eternal life that He promises. At the point of receiving the new birth, we begin the process of sanctification, which is transformation into the likeness of Jesus. We enter the gate (Jesus) into eternal life, and the way that we begin to walk is a narrow one of righteousness toward holiness.

Strive To Enter

In Luke 13:24, Jesus tells us to *strive* to enter, which indicates that there are difficulties and obstacles to overcome. The Greek word for strive is **agonizomai**, which means "to agonize, to struggle, to contend for a prize." We see the same word in 1 Cor. 9:25, referring to the fierce competitions in which athletes take part. They willingly undergo extreme disciplines to be in the best shape. The same Greek word is translated "to labor earnestly" in Colossians 4:12. From these verses, we understand that it requires fervent effort to the point of agony to take up our cross and deny ourselves!

We must be determined to master all difficulties and to overcome every obstacle that would hold us back from God's kingdom and rule in our lives. Yet, in the midst of our determination and fervent efforts, we must remember that it is *all* a work of grace! It is only through abiding in Jesus that we can make any progress *at all*. As we yield to Him, embracing the new covenant and all that it entails, He accomplishes the sanctifying process in us.

The Narrow Gate

To "enter the narrow gate" means to recognize that we need God's salvation, acknowledge that the Bible is true, and put our trust in Jesus as the only way to God. It means to exercise true repentance by abandoning our sin and anything that separates us from the Lord. We must not only mourn our past sin, we must also be sincere in standing against future sin. **Psalm 119:128c** says, *"I hate every false way."* We must repent of all of our rebellion against God, accept His rule over us, and completely surrender ourselves to the Lord.

Dr. C.H. Spurgeon said, *"You and your sins must separate, or you and your God will never come together. No one sin may you keep."*

Jesus is the great prophet, priest and king. We receive Him as a prophet to instruct us, as a priest to atone for us, and as a king to rule over us. It is by *completely* surrendering to the Lord Jesus (in all three areas) that we pass through the narrow gate.

The Wide Gate

The wide gate refers to the course of this world (Eph. 2:2); it leads to the bottomless pit. Unregenerate man walks on this path of self–will and self–gratification. The path is "wide" because those on it know no restrictions. They do not obey God's commands and do not practice self–denial. Their way is downhill and easy; it is crowded with many people walking in the same direction. It is attractive to the carnal mind because it allows lust and unlimited self–indulgence. It is a deceptive road; few know and understand where it is taking them, according to Prov. 14:12. Psalm 1:6 says that the road is fatal; it leads to destruction.

We are all born in sin and are on that road unless the grace of God reaches us. We can only abandon the road leading to destruction by receiving God's salvation. We must turn to Him from sin, and then live in a way that pleases Him. Saving faith not only trusts in Jesus; it also obeys Him. It not only believes God's promises; it also holds to His precepts. Godliness must be our chief concern and our main business in life. Otherwise, we will become like so many who prefer sin to holiness; they indulge the lusts of their flesh and choose the world over choosing the Lord. They are unwilling to forsake their old sins, to turn their backs on the world, and to surrender to Jesus. They embrace the broad way rather than the narrow gate and difficult way.

Called To Holiness

Many of us in the Body of Christ have severely strayed from the holiness that God requires of us. Generally speaking, we do not maintain holy lifestyles. Activities that are unnatural in God's eyes have become natural in ours. For instance, many believing couples get involved sexually before they marry. Some believers look at pornography; others watch movies in which God's name is taken in vain. Still others are guilty of deception (e.g. cheating on taxes) and bribery. They may appear to be righteous, but their lives contain compromise.

Read 2 Peter 1:5. The first thing we are to diligently add to our faith is virtue, which is moral excellence. Are we trying to build moral excellence into our lives? Do the things that we read, watch, or listen to encourage and increase moral excellence? Do our close relationships and associations inspire us toward moral excellence?

Read Romans 13:13-14. Rather than make provision for the flesh, put on Jesus! Feed on Him and His Word. Practice self–control against fleshly lusts. For instance, if you have a TV addiction, get rid of the TV or put it out of sight for a few months. Do not nourish your flesh; starve your flesh and feed your spirit.

Discern Satan's Strategies

When we get involved in worldly activities, we lose the fighting edge of discernment in our battle against Satan. God has placed within His redeemed people the ability to perceive His nature and the things that please Him. When our minds and spirits are dulled by worldliness, we lose our keen sense of discernment.

Jesus told His disciples to "watch and pray" in Matthew 26:41. We need to be alert concerning the tactics of the enemy. It is chiefly through prayer that we discern his strategies. We must distinguish what Satan is doing and pray so that we will not fall into his traps. Our prayer life keeps that discernment in check; as we draw near to the heart of God, our spirit is tuned to God's Spirit. When we do not engage in prayer as we ought, we do things that are contrary to the life we are supposed to be living.

Resist Worldliness

Every blood–washed, Spirit–filled believer in Jesus should realize that intimate involvement with the world is contrary to the life God wants him to live. *"Do not love the world or the things in the world. If anyone loves the world, the love of the Father is not in him. For all that is in the world— the lust of the flesh, the lust of the eyes, and the pride of life—is not of the Father but is of the world. And the world is passing away, and the lust of it; but he who does the will of God abides forever"* (**1 John 2:15-17**).

Satan wants to tear down the nature of God within us by seducing us to embrace the world. If we cannot break away from its lusts and attractions, we will be powerless to live holy lives, no matter how much spiritual warfare we engage in. Satan will win the battle if we cannot let go of our love for the world and our involvement in it.

"... gird up the loins of your mind, be sober, and rest your hope fully upon the grace that is to be brought to you at the revelation of Jesus Christ; as obedient children, not conforming yourselves to the former lusts, as in your ignorance; but as He who called you is holy, you also be holy in all your conduct, because it is written, 'Be holy, for I am holy' " (**1 Peter 1:13-16**).

Present Your Body to the Lord

Read Romans 6:11-15, 18. To be free from past sin and shame, present yourself to the Lord for a fresh cleansing with His blood. Verbally apply the blood of Jesus to the members of your body that you have used in sinful activities. Symbolically wash those areas as if you had a bowl of the Lord's precious blood in front of you. Then offer afresh your body as a sacrifice to God. Dedicate the parts of your body that were used as instruments of unrighteousness to be used in the present and future as instruments of righteousness.

"I beseech you therefore, brethren, by the mercies of God, that you present your bodies a living sacrifice, holy, acceptable to God, which is your reasonable service" (**Rom. 12:1**).

By God's grace, may we be numbered among those who find and follow the narrow path that leads to life!

EXERCISE #35 – Matthew 7:15-20 ~ BEARING FRUIT

1. Read Matthew 7:15-20. What is the fruit of our lives? How is that fruit revealed?

2. Explain what *"the good treasure of a man's heart"* is, mentioned in Luke 6:45.

3. After reading James 3:2, Prov. 18:20-21, and Psalm 12:4, why do you think Bible authors spoke of the tongue so strongly?

4. Read John 15:1-8. What does Jesus do with the branches that bear fruit?

What does He do with the branches that do not bear fruit?

What is the key to bearing good fruit?

5. According to John 15:16, what are we chosen and appointed to do?

6. List the fruit of the Spirit found in Galatians 5:22-23.

Take time to pray for the fruit of God's Spirit to be revealed more fully in your life. Confess any resistance to His fruit in you, such as unbelief, fear, anger, resentment, or pride.

#35 – BEARING FRUIT

Matthew 7:15-20 *"Beware of false prophets, who come to you in sheep's clothing, but inwardly they are ravenous wolves. You will know them by their fruits. Do men gather grapes from thorn bushes or figs from thistles? Even so, every good tree bears good fruit, but a bad tree bears bad fruit. A good tree cannot bear bad fruit, nor can a bad tree bear good fruit. Every tree that does not bear good fruit is cut down and thrown into the fire. Therefore by their fruits you will know them."*

Jesus told His disciples to test their teachers by looking at the fruit of their lives and of their teachings. As His disciples today, we are also to test our Bible teachers and preachers by their fruit. The fruit of a man's life may look good, but he may be teaching a doctrine that ultimately bears bad fruit in the lives of his hearers. Likewise, a man may be teaching sound doctrine, but the fruit of his personal life is foul.

Please note this word of caution: in judging the doctrines or lives of others, we must be careful not to allow carnal suspicion to take the place of Spirit-inspired discernment. We must be patient, and wait for fruit to manifest itself. During winter seasons when there is no fruit to see, we could easily mistake a rose bush for something else. We need to wait before passing a verdict on others. In time, wrong teaching produces its fruit just as right teaching does.

It is easy to believe that our personal convictions are the Lord's standards. We might be tempted to condemn those who do not agree with us. However, the Bible never instructs us to walk in the light of convictions, but in the light of the Lord Himself.

Created To Bear Fruit

Read Matt. 21:18-19. Jesus cursed the fig tree because it bore no fruit. Since the branches of the tree were filled with leaves, Jesus expected there to be fruit, too. He expects the same of us; we are created to bear fruit, not to merely produce leaves. God clearly states that this is His will for every one of His servants. In **John 15:16** Jesus says, *"I chose and appointed you that you should go and bear fruit..."* And in **Matt. 3:10** He says, *"Every tree which does not bear good fruit is cut down and thrown into the fire."*

Read John 15:1-5. Fruit–bearing is the manifestation of an intimate relationship with the Lord. Intimacy results in the reproduction of life. As we abide/remain in Him in close communion, we cannot help but bear good fruit. When our roots go deeply into the Lord, we receive life–giving nourishment, and we will naturally bear fruit that resembles Him.

At least three areas of fruitfulness should be evident in the lives of believers:

1. the fruit of the Holy Spirit revealed in personal holiness
2. the fruit of good works
3. the fruit of salvation—introducing others to Jesus

Personal Holiness

In **Galatians 5:22-23** we read, *"...the fruit of the Spirit is love, joy, peace, patience, kindness, goodness, faithfulness, gentleness, and self–control."* **Eph. 5:9** says, *"the fruit of the Spirit is in all goodness, righteousness, and truth."* These traits are to be clearly seen in those who spend time in the presence of God and are led by His Spirit.

Our lives should reveal God's life within us. Our words should communicate His love and truth because we are filled with His love and truth. Our inner lives are revealed by our words. Jesus said in Matt. 12:33-37 that the mouth speaks of what fills the heart.

"The mouth of the righteous is a well of life" (**Prov. 10:11a**). For our words to give life, we must make sure that our hearts are pure. We need to repent of all unbelief, lust, pride, and bitterness. We need to allow the Lord to touch the wounds in our souls that cause us to react defensively and angrily. We cannot afford to allow grievances to accumulate; resentment contaminates us. We must walk in forgiveness with everyone. Any contaminant within will make its way out in our words, attitudes, actions, and reactions, all of which demonstrate the fruit of our lives.

Read Prov. 10:21. Do our lips feed others? Are we worth listening to? The key to having valuable, life–giving things to say is to be filled with the Lord! If we will fill our lives with God and His Word, then what we say will be an overflow of His life within us. As we worship the Lord and commune with Him throughout the day, our conversations with others will contain the overflow of our life with God. We will increasingly speak words of life—words that refresh, inspire, and encourage. Our words will draw attention to the Lord and will glorify Him. *"Death and life are in the power of the tongue, and those who love it will eat its fruit"* (**Prov. 18:21**).

We must also be careful not to talk too much. G.D. Watson, in his book, *Soul Food*, wrote,

> *Being talkative is utterly ruinous to deep spirituality. The very life of our spirits passes out in our speech, and hence all superfluous talk is a waste of the vital forces of the heart. In fruit growing...excessive blossoming prevents a good crop, and often prevents fruit altogether; and by so much loquacity the soul runs wild in word–bloom and bears no fruit. [Talking too much] is one of the greatest hindrances to deep, solid union with God.*

According to Mr. Watson, there are three negative effects of excessive talking:

1. Spiritual power is lost. The more condensed the thoughts and feelings of the soul, the greater their power.

2. Time is wasted. The hours spent in useless talking can better be used in prayer or devotional reading.

3. Unwise and unprofitable words may be spoken. *"When there are a multitude of words, transgression is unavoidable"* (**Prov. 10:19**). We frequently begin our conversations led by God's Spirit, but we conclude them speaking from our souls.

To speak words that give grace and life, we must guard our speech. Some things we are only to say in God's appointed timing and in harmony with His Spirit. Sometimes it is good for us to withdraw from the company of others in order to sit quietly in communion with Jesus, where we can be restored and refreshed. Engaging in these disciplines of solitude and silence will result in greater holiness.

Good Works

Read Col. 1:9-10 and notice the phrase, *"...being fruitful in every good work..."* If our works are done in the Holy Spirit, they will accomplish much and the fruit will remain. But if our works are done in the flesh, they will profit nothing (*see* John 6:63). We must make sure that everything we do is birthed and energized by the Spirit of God.

God has destined each of us to do specific good works. He created us for them, according to Eph. 2:10. Part of our fruit–bearing is doing these good works. Because of our love for God and our place of abiding in Him, we naturally want to be a blessing to those around us. Our hearts should be moved with compassion for the needy; we should want to alleviate their need. Consider 1 John 3:16-17. The apostle Paul encourages us to be rich in good works, ready to give, and willing to share (1 Tim. 6:18-19).

The Pruning Process

"Every branch that bears fruit He prunes, that it may bear more fruit" (**Jn. 15:2b**). In the pruning season, our roots go deeper into Jesus in our desperate need for answers and spiritual nourishment. In this God-imposed rest, we press in closer to Him. It is a time of separation to God from our ministry to people so that we are available to Him alone. His purpose in pruning us is so that we can bear more fruit of better quality.

Pruning is usually painful. It may take the shape of a closed door to our spiritual gift(s). We might be in a place where our ministry is not needed or recognized. We may need to stay home to care for a child or an elderly parent. Perhaps a physical weakness or disease robs us of energy and the ability to actively serve others. During these seasons, the enemy may tell us that God was not pleased with our ministry, and that He is punishing us in removing us from active service. According to John 15:2, however, Jesus *was* pleased with our fruit–bearing, and has pruned us back in order to make room for more fruit in the next bearing season.

The pruning season is often a time of refocusing or moving into different or specialized areas of ministry. God may be narrowing down our ministries and trimming back our areas of service in order to make room for the more specific works He is calling us to do. He might be moving us from excessive work in order to put us in a position of a richer and greater anointing.

If you are in a pruning season and seemingly bearing no visible fruit, don't be discouraged or impatient. Use this time to seek the Lord; determine to be more firmly and deeply rooted into Him. The next fruit–bearing season will come!

Psalm 1 mentions the righteous personal bearing seasonal fruit, *"He shall be like a tree planted by the rivers of water, that brings forth its fruit in its season..."* (**Psalm 1:3**). Be careful not to judge the fruit of your life or of the life of others by what you can see only in the natural realm. Some fruit is visible only later.

Winning Souls to Jesus

We read in the book of Acts that the apostles bore fruit in seeing people repent everywhere they went. In Acts 2, it is recorded that Peter preached, and 3000 people came to faith in Jesus. **Acts 11:24** says, *"A great many people were added to the Lord."* **Acts 17:12** mentions, *"...many of them believed..."*

In 1 Cor. 9:19-23 we see that the apostle Paul was willing to do whatever it took to win men to Jesus. He especially had a passion for the Jews to meet their Messiah, as we see in Rom. 9:1-3. As believers in Jesus, we should eagerly want others to know the Lord. Besides growing in personal holiness and engaging in good works, we should be fervent in winning people to Jesus. Salvation for the world is the reason that He went to the cross! If we stop at our own salvation and sanctification, then we have missed His heart and purpose in coming for all who are condemned to hell and need eternal life. **Proverbs 11:30** says, *"The fruit of the righteous is a tree of [eternal] life, and he who wins souls is wise."*

Psalm 92:13-14 gives us a promise regarding bearing fruit: *"Those who are planted in the house of the Lord shall flourish in the courts of our God. They shall still bear fruit in old age; they shall be fresh and flourishing."* We will never get too old to bear fruit for God!

EXERCISE #36 – Matthew 7:21-23 ~ DOES HE KNOW US?

1. Read Matt. 7:21-23, Rom. 2:13, and James 1:22. Paraphrase what the Lord says to you through these Scriptures.

2. How can we prophesy, cast out demons, and do wonders in Jesus' name (Matt. 7:22-23), and He justly say to us, *"I never knew you; depart from Me, you who practice lawlessness"*?

3. Lawlessness and iniquity are similar. Read 2 Tim. 2:19 and Psalm 5:5, 6:8 to see how God feels about those who are lawless. Compare that to Psalm 119:1-3. Pen your observations.

4. Read John 14:15, 21-23 and 1 John 2:3-5. How can we demonstrate our love to the Lord?

5. In Matt. 7:21, Jesus says those who do the will of His Father will enter the kingdom of heaven. What do you understand God's will to be for you *generally*?

What do you believe His will is for you *specifically* (at this point in your life)?

#36 – Does He Know Us?

Matthew 7:21-23 *"Not everyone who says to Me, 'Lord, Lord' shall enter the kingdom of heaven, but he who does the will of My Father in heaven. Many will say to Me in that day, 'Lord, Lord, have we not prophesied in Your name, cast out demons in Your name, and done many wonders in Your name?' And then I will declare to them, 'I never knew you; depart from Me, you who practice lawlessness!'"*

Those who enter the kingdom of heaven are those who *do* the will of the Father. It is not enough to use God's name and power to do miracles; we must also have a personal relationship with Him that results in righteous living. We are judged according to the fruit of our lives (as we saw in the previous five verses), not according to the miracles we have worked.

The people Jesus referred to in verse 21 were instruments of God's healing and miraculous power. However, an instrument is not necessarily a servant. A servant is one who has given up his rights to his Lord. As we see in verse 23, these people still practiced lawlessness. They did not submit to the laws of God; they chose to be a law unto themselves. Refusing His Lordship, they were lord of their own lives.

God Can Use Anyone

God reserves the right to use whomever He pleases, and He displays His power as He chooses. Consider 1 Sam. 10:10-11. Before Saul was crowned king of Israel and was still virtually unknown, God anointed him to prophesy with the prophets.

In John 11:49-51, we see that God used the high priest, Caiphas, to prophesy Jesus' death. And in Luke 9:49, we read that a man who was not with Jesus and His disciples was casting out demons.

In Phil. 1:15-18, we are told that God honors His Word even when it is preached with wrong motives. He esteems and keeps His Word regardless of who preaches it.

Does He Know You?

In Matt. 7:23, Jesus said, *"I never knew you."* Commentator Arthur Pink believes that the people referred to in this verse were never truly born again. They were like some modern church-goers who have never repented and received salvation. The phrase "never knew you" implies that God did not approve or accept them. The same understanding is seen in Psalm 1:6 in the phrase, *"For the Lord knows the way of the righteous...."* implying that God approves of and accepts the way of the righteous.

Others suggest that Jesus was referring to disobedient believers. Even though they call Jesus "Lord," they do not do what He says. *"Those who practice lawlessness"* are those who go their own way and follow their own desires. They have developed a pattern of placing their agenda, pleasure, or plans before the commands of the Master.

Intimacy With The Lord

The Greek word for "knew" in Matt. 7:23 is **ginosko**, which refers to knowing through experience and perceiving through the senses. It means to know through an active relationship, through personal interaction, or through some level of intimacy. The Lord was saying, "I never had an active, intimate relationship with you. We did not personally interact. I did not see or hear you." According to Song of Songs 2:14, the Lord loves to look at us and hear our voices. He wants close fellowship with us.

Read Psalm 139:1-4 and Jeremiah 23:23-24. God knows each of us intimately! Nothing escapes His notice. Maybe the issue is not so much if God sees and knows us, but if we see and know Him in all that we do. Can we honestly say we *"acknowledge Him in all of our ways?"* **Proverbs 3:6** says, *"In all your ways acknowledge Him and He shall direct your paths."* The word "ways" in Hebrew is **derek**, which means "a road, a course, or a mode of action." In all of our actions, we are to acknowledge God, and He will direct our paths. The word, "acknowledge" in Hebrew is **yada**, which means to know by observation, investigation or firsthand experience. The highest level of **yada** is in "direct, intimate contact." This refers to life–giving intimacy, as in marriage. In a spiritual context, it suggests an intimacy with God in prayer that conceives and births His will and purposes. If in all our ways (our normal daily lives) we maintain **yada** with God, He promises to direct our paths toward fruitful endeavors.

Submissive Obedience

In Matt. 7:23, Jesus speaks to the lawless, the ones who lack a relationship with Him based on submissive obedience to His will. The relationship God wants with us is one of intimacy that is energized by obedience. What is the point of worshiping the Lord all day in song while living a life of compromise and deliberate sin? Read 1 Sam. 15:22-23. *"To obey is better than sacrifice"* (**1 Sam. 15:22b**). King Saul's rebellion cost him the kingdom! That is a warning to us—we must repent of all rebellion and choose to submissively obey God's Word to us, or we will forfeit the kingdom of God in our lives.

His confession of knowing us when we face Him on Judgment Day will be dependent on our obedience. As **2 Tim. 2:19** says, *"The Lord knows those who are His"* and *"Let everyone who names the name of Christ depart from iniquity."* We prove our relationship with Jesus by refusing evil. **1 John 1:6** says, *"If we say we have fellowship with Him, and walk in darkness, we lie and do not practice the truth."* The Lord is drawn to those who live in obedience to Him. In the same way, spirits of darkness are drawn to those who live in rebellion.

Read Isaiah 66:2. The one who trembles at God's Word will instantly obey Him. God is looking for people who delight to do His will. Our hearts' confession should be like that of King David as expressed in **Psalm 40:8**, *"I delight to do Your will, O my God, and Your law is within my heart."*

Cultivate a Love Relationship

Jesus said in **John 5:30**, *"...I do not seek My own will but the will of the Father who sent Me."* Our times of worship and fellowship with God will help us to obey His commands. When we avoid intimacy with Him, we find it easier to sin or compromise. As we go our own sinful ways, our love toward the Lord grows cold, and we often compromise further. It is our love for and fear of God that will keep us faithful to Him. Therefore, cultivating a love relationship with the Lord should be our highest priority.

Read Psalm 5. Verses 1-3 speak of seeking God each morning, looking up to Him, and speaking to Him. It implies childlike trust in and dependence on God. Verses 4-6 reveal God's rejection of those who do evil and choose iniquity. In verse 7 we see the heart of the psalmist again—he chose to embrace God's mercy, enter His presence, and worship the Lord in holy fear of Him. In verse 8, following his worship of God, he asks for guidance to walk in the Lord's righteous ways. This is a good pattern for us to follow: we should seek the Lord early each day and engage in prayer and worship. With a holy fear of God, we should pray for guidance to choose His righteous ways.

God Knows Us!

"But if anyone loves God, this one is known by Him" (**1 Cor. 8:3**). What a wonderful promise! As important as it is to do wonders in Jesus' name, to cast out demons and to prophesy, it is far more important that He knows us! We must set aside time regularly to interact with Jesus intimately and allow Him to see us and hear our voice. We need to depart from all iniquity, and choose to walk in His ways rather than in our own.

May the Lord never say to us, *"I never knew you; depart from Me, you who practice lawlessness"* (**Matt. 7:23**). Instead, let us live in such a way that He will say, *"Well done, good and faithful servant. Enter into the joy of your Lord"* (**Matt. 25:23**).

EXERCISE #37 – Matthew 7:24-27 ~ HEAR AND OBEY

1. Read Matt. 7:24-27. What is the difference between the wise man and the foolish man?

Has God given you any instruction recently that you have not yet obeyed? What is it? (Confess that to God, and write down how you plan to obey.)

2. After reading James 1:21-25, answer the following questions:

How are we to receive the Word of God?

What is the result if we hear the Word and do not obey it?

How do we continue in the "perfect law of liberty?"

3. What does Hebrews 4:12 say about the Word of God?

4. Read Psalm 19:7-11. How does the Psalmist describe the Scriptures?

5. In the passages below, what are some of the blessings that follow obedience to God?

Deut. 28:1-2 –

Isa. 1:19 –

Jer. 7:23 –

Heb. 5:9 –

Rev. 22:14 –

6. Devotional authors suggest that we read the Sermon on the Mount frequently to stay cognizant on what God expects of us as His children. Read all three chapters of Matthew 5–7 again, and write down any thoughts or instructions that you sense the Lord giving you.

#37 – HEAR AND OBEY!

Matthew 7:24-27 *"Therefore whoever hears these sayings of Mine, and does them, I will liken him to a wise man who built his house on the rock: and the rain descended, the floods came, and the winds blew and beat on that house; and it did not fall, for it was founded on the rock. Now everyone who hears these sayings of Mine, and does not do them will be like a foolish man who built his house on the sand: and the rain descended, the floods came, and the winds blew and beat on that house; and it fell. And great was its fall."*

At the close of Matthew 7, Jesus concluded His teaching to His disciples as earnestly as He began in chapter 5. He warned those who had heard His words not to be satisfied with just hearing them, but to be careful to practice all that He taught them. It is a false gospel that says we can be saved with no intention of obeying the Lord. The Sermon on the Mount describes the life that *can* and *must* be lived when someone abides in Jesus and lives by the power of His Holy Spirit.

A Hearing Ear

Although hearing the Word of God is important to build our faith, it is our *belief in* and *adherence to* the Scriptures that pleases the Lord. If we obey all that the Lord tells us, we will be secure in knowing that our lives are founded on the Rock, and we will not be shaken or overthrown by the storms of life. *"He only is my rock and my salvation; He is my defense; I shall not be moved. In God is my salvation and my glory; the rock of my strength and my refuge is in God."* (**Ps 62:6-7**).

Read James 1:22-25. If we hear the Word of God and do not obey it, we deceive ourselves and live in denial. Verse 24 says we tend to forget what we do not put into practice. Verse 25 says we are blessed in what we *do* (not merely in what we hear). An essential character trait of a believer is obedience. God wants us to have a hearing ear and an obedient heart.

The Lord *delights* in our obedience to His voice. Unfortunately, it is human nature to choose our own way and then to try to make up for our disobedience to the Lord through a sacrifice of time, a service rendered, or a financial gift. But according to 1 Sam. 15:22, God prefers obedience to sacrifices. We must obey what He says to us!

The Fellowship of Obedience

Read Amos 5:21-24 to see how God feels about offerings and worship that are given to Him in place of the justice and righteousness that He desires. According to Hebrews 2:11, Jesus calls those who embrace His righteousness "brothers." He enjoys fellowship with the ones who are becoming holy by yielding to His process of sanctification. He is not ashamed of them.

Sometimes we feel closer to our spiritual family than we are to our natural families. Jesus experienced this, too (Luke 8:19-21). Our deepest ties are with those who are like–minded in doing the Father's will. We usually have a special camaraderie with those who—like us—are preaching the gospel, strategically making disciples, caring for widows and orphans, and feeding the poor.

We find it harder to be with those who are disobedient to God's Word. It is doing God's will that bonds us with one another. According to John 15:14, the key to being Jesus' friend is to do whatever He commands. Our testimony should be like that of the Lord expressed in **John 4:34**, *"My food is to do the will of Him who sent Me..."* To do God's will should be the passion and nourishment of our lives!

Read 1 John 1:5-7. In order to have fellowship with God Who is Light, we must walk in light and truth. *Our level of fellowship with God and others depends on our level of obedience.* We cannot fellowship deeply in the Spirit when we are living hypocritically.

The reason for relationship is fellowship, yet it is possible to have relationship without fellowship. A disobedient child is still related to his parents, but their fellowship is broken until the child repents and is reconciled to the parents. A rebellious wife and an unloving husband are still married, but their fellowship is damaged. So it is with God and us. We are still His children when we sin, but our fellowship with Him is broken. By sinning, we forfeit His presence and peace; we find it difficult to hear His voice.

When we are estranged from God, we find it harder to relate with love and grace toward others. However, if we will daily apply the blood of Jesus to our hearts and lives and walk in truth with Him, we will have precious communion with Him and His people.

Read Psalm 1:1-2. There is a special blessing for the one who does not compromise in his spiritual walk, his stand for God, and the places where he rests and relaxes. He fears and obeys the Lord wherever he is and in whatever he does. He keeps his delight in and passion for the Lord strong by meditating in His Word day and night. That is a key for us. Meditating in the Word of God daily will keep us choosing the road that leads to life.

Consider the parable in Matthew 21:28-31. In the story of the two sons, one agreed to obey but did not. The other did not plan to, but later changed his mind. Who *did* the will of the father? Not the one who *said* what the father wanted to hear, but the one who *did* what was asked of him. Doing God's will is not saying, "I will do it." It is *doing* it!

The vineyard was the place of service to which the father called his sons; today it is the place where our heavenly Father calls us to serve. We are all to work in His vineyard, bringing others into a saving knowledge of Jesus and teaching them how to live in obedient fellowship with Him. Let us not verbally give our word that we will go; let's obey the Lord and GO!

Jesus' Strategy For Discipleship

The final words that Jesus spoke to His disciples in **Matt. 28:19-20** are: *"Go therefore, and make disciples of all the nations, baptizing them in the name of the Father and of the Son and of the Holy Spirit, teaching them to observe all I have commanded you, and lo, I am with you always, even to the end of the age."* His last command should be our first priority!

In verses 19-20, Jesus gave three commands and one promise:

1. Make disciples of all ethnic groups, everywhere! Introduce them to Jesus as the Messiah and coach them in their new faith in Him until they fully yield to His Lordship.

2. Baptize (fully immerse) them into the name (nature, character, Person, authority) of God as Father, the name/nature of His Son, and the name/nature of the Holy Spirit. Immerse them into a personal knowledge of (Greek: **ginosko**) and experience of each member of the Godhead. They will grow to know God through His Word and through personal encounters with Him.

So, introduce them to God as a loving, generous Father Who is holy and commands us to be holy. Teach them how Jesus functioned as God's Son and how *we* are to live humbly and faithfully as His children. Introduce them to the Person of the Holy Spirit so that they know His roles in their lives (Helper, Comforter, Counselor, Standby, Strengthener, Advocate, Intercessor) and His sustaining and explosive power.

3. Teach those you disciple to observe and obey all that Jesus taught. They should also be able to observe *your* obedience to His commands and be encouraged to follow your example.

If we are faithful to make disciples, Jesus *promised* that He will be with us always, even to the end of the age.

Jesus Taught with Authority

"And so it was, when Jesus had ended these sayings, that the people were astonished at His teaching, for He taught them as one having authority, and not as the scribes" (**Matt. 7:28-29**). Jesus taught with all the backing and authority of heaven. The same divine authority supports and stands behind His words today as we read them in the Sermon on the Mount. They are anointed Scriptures and must be obeyed now just as Jesus meant for them to be obeyed in the first century.

Reading Matthew 5-7 on a regular basis will keep us mindful of the culture of God's kingdom and of our responsibilities as His disciples. We are to welcome this teaching into our hearts and minds, and incorporate it into our daily lives. However, we are not to stop with our own personal obedience to the Lord. We are also to be faithful to teach others, as we read in **2 Tim. 2:2**, *"And the things that you have heard from me among many witnesses, commit these to faithful men who will be able to teach others also."*

Each of us who believe in Jesus as God's Messiah and have committed our lives to Him are commissioned to bring others into a knowledge of Jesus and a disciplined walk with Him. May the Lord grant us all the grace, strength, courage, and wisdom we need in order to obey this Great Commission and to walk out the Sermon on the Mount. May we be among those who do *all* of His will!

BIBLIOGRAPHY

American Heritage Dictionary (computer edition)

Amplified Bible (Grand Rapids, MI: Zondervan Publishing House, 1965)

Arthur, Kay, *How Can I Be Blessed* (Chattanooga, TN: Precept Ministries, 1985)

Auch, Ron, *Taught by the Spirit* (Green Forest, AR: New Leaf Press, Inc., 1991)

Auch, Ron, *The Seven Spirits of God* (Green Forest, AR: New Leaf Press, 1993)

Bickle, Mike, *Passion for Jesus* (Orlando, FL: Creation House, 1993)

Bridges, Jerry, *Trusting God* (Colorado, CO: NavPress Publications, 1988)

Broger, John C., *Biblical Counseling Foundation* (Racho Mirage, CA: Biblical Counseling Foundation, Inc., 1993)

Bruce, A.B., *The Training of the Twelve* (Grand Rapids, MI: Kregel Publications, 1988)

Bueno, Lee, *Fasting Your Way to Health* (Springdale, PA: Whitaker House, 1991)

Chambers, Oswald, *Studies in the Sermon on the Mount* (London, England: Oswald Chambers Publications Association, 1968)

Comfort, Ray, *The Ultimate Deception* (South Plainfield, NJ: Bridge Publishing Inc., 1993)

Duewel, Wesley L., *Mighty Prevailing Prayer* (Grand Rapids, MI: Zondervan Publishing House, 1990)

Foster, Richard J., *Celebration of Discipline* (New York, NY: Harper & Row Publisher, Inc., 1978)

Frangipane, Francis, *The Three Battlegrounds* (Cedar Rapids, IA: Advancing Church Publications, 1989)

Gothard, Bill, *Institute in Basic Youth Conflicts* (Institute in Basic Youth Conflicts, 1975)

Houston, James, *The Transforming Friendship - A guide to prayer* (Batavia, IL: Lion Publishing Corporation, 1989)

Joyner, Rick, *The Final Quest* (Charlotte, NC: Morning Star Publications, 1996)

Joyner, Rick, *The Harvest II* (Charlotte, NC: Morning Star Publications, 1996)

Kramer, Raymond, *The Psychology of Jesus* (Grand Rapids, MI: Zondervan Publishing House, 1977)

Lahaye, Tim and Phillips, Bob, *Anger is a Choice* (Grand Rapids, MI: Zondervan Publishing House, 1982)

Lewis, C.S., *The World's Last Night* (New York: Harcourt Brace Jovanovich, 1959)

Liardon, Roberts, *Smith Wigglesworth* (Tulsa, OK: Albury Publishing, 1996)

Life Application Bible (Carol Stream, IL: Tyndale House Publishers)

MacArthur, John Jr., *The Vanishing Conscience* (Dallas, Texas: Word Publishing, Inc.)

MacDonald, Gordon, *Rebuilding Your Broken World* (Nashville, TN: Oliver–Nelson Books, 1988)

Mayhall, Carole, *Words that Hurt, Words that Heal* (Colorado Springs, Colorado: NavPress, 1986)

Mumford, Bob, *The Purpose of Temptation* (New Jersey: Fleming H. Revell Company, 1973)

Murray, Andrew, *Humility* (Springdale, PA: Whitaker House, 1982)

Peterson, Eugene H., *The Message* (Colorado Springs, CO: NavPress Publishing Group, 1994)

Phillips, Bob, audio series on Christian character and the beatitudes

Pink, Arthur, *An Exposition of the Sermon on the Mount* (Grand Rapids, MI: Baker Book House, 1991)

Pippert, Rebecca Manley, *Out of the Salt Shaker & into the World* (Downers Grove, IL: Intervarsity Press, 1979)

Richards, Larry, *Remarriage: A Gift from God* (Waco, TX: Word Incorporated, 1990)

Robertson, Pat, *The CBN Counselor's Handbook* (Virginia Beach, VA: Christian Broadcasting Network, Inc., 1981)

Sanders, J. Oswald, *Every Life is a Plan of God* (Grand Rapids, MI: Discovery House Publishers, 1992)

Smoke, Jim, *Turning Your World Right Side Up* (Colorado Springs, CO: Focus on the Family, 1995)

Sorge, Bob, *Exploring Worship* (Canandaigua, NY: Oasis House, 1987)

Spirit Filled Life Bible (Nashville, TN: Thomas Nelson Publishers, 1991)

Swindoll, Charles, *Improving Your Serve* (Waco, TX: Word Publishing, 1981)

"The Christian Life" magazine (Sermon on the Mount article)

The Living Bible (Wheaton, IL: Tyndale House Publishers, 1971)

Thompson, Dr. Bruce and Barbara, *Walls of My Heart* (Euclid, MN: Crown Ministries International, 1989)

Urquhart, Colin, *Your Personal Bible* (Great Britain: Hodder and Stoughton, Ltd., 1994)

Warren, Neil Clark, PHD., *Make Anger Your Ally* (Colorado Springs, CO: Focus on the Family Publishing, 1990)

Watson, G.D., *Soul Food* (Shoals, IN: Old Paths Tract Society, Inc.)

Wilkerson, David, *Hungry for More of Jesus* (Grand Rapids, MI: Chosen Books, 1992)

Made in the USA
Columbia, SC
11 November 2021

4878640R00120